MAGAZINES AND THE MAKING
OF MASS CULTURE IN JAPAN

Magazines and the Making of Mass Culture in Japan

AMY BLISS MARSHALL

UNIVERSITY OF TORONTO PRESS
Toronto Buffalo London

ISBN 978-1-4875-0286-7

Studies in Book and Print Culture

Library and Archives Canada Cataloguing in Publication

Marshall, Amy Bliss, 1979–, author
Magazines and the making of mass culture in Japan / Amy Bliss Marshall.

(Studies in book and print culture)
Includes bibliographical references and index.
ISBN 978-1-4875-0286-7 (hardcover)

1. Kingu. 2. Ie no hikari. 3. Japanese periodicals – History – 20th century.
4. Periodicals – Social aspects – Japan – History – 20th century. 5. Popular
culture – Japan – History – 20th century. I. Title. II. Series: Studies in book and
print culture

PN5410.K55M37 2019   059′.95609042   C2018-905264-3

This book has been published with the assistance of the Steven J. Green School
of International and Public Affairs at Florida International University.

University of Toronto Press acknowledges the financial assistance to its
publishing program of the Canada Council for the Arts and the Ontario Arts
Council, an agency of the Government of Ontario.

 Canada Council **Conseil des Arts**
for the Arts **du Canada**

 ONTARIO ARTS COUNCIL
CONSEIL DES ARTS DE L'ONTARIO
an Ontario government agency
un organisme du gouvernement de l'Ontario

Funded by the   Financé par le
Government   gouvernement
of Canada   du Canada    Canadä

This book is dedicated to:

Catherine Wanslow
(a bodhisattva)

&

Lois Bliss
(a paragon)

Contents

Table and Chart ix

List of Illustrations xi

Acknowledgments xiii

Introduction: Why Japanese Family Magazines Matter 3
  Methodology 4
  Chapter Summaries 16

1. The Medium, the Message, and the Masses: Understanding
   Japanese Family Magazines 19
     Historical Background 20
     The Medium 23
     The Message 32
     The Masses 36
     Concluding Thoughts 42

2. The Splendid Power of Being in Perfect Harmony: How Two
   Publishers Made a Mass Japanese Audience 43
     Historical Background 43
     The Industrial Cooperative 49
     Kōdansha and Noma Seiji 58
     Top of the Bottom 64
     Getting the Magazines to the Audience 68
     Concluding Thoughts 74

3. "We Came, We Saw, We Astonished": How a Japanese
   Mass Was Won 77
     Historical Background 77
     Kingu 81

Ie no hikari 97
Editorial Content 110
The Children's Section 123
Concluding Thoughts 126

4. Reading Together: How the Audience Participated 129
    Contexts 130
    Readers 132
    The Participating Audience 143
    Media Interactions 153
    Concluding Thoughts 160

5. Learning to Consume: How Magazines
   Politicized Advertising 163
    Historical Background 164
    Advertising in Ie no hikari *and* Kingu 170
    Concluding Thoughts 182

Conclusion 187
    The Death of Kingu 190
    The Afterlife of Ie no hikari 193
    Why the Audience Remains 198

Bibliography 201

Index 215

Table and Chart

Table

5.1   *Ie no hikari* of the 1930s 175

Chart

5.1   Number of advertising pages in *Ie no hikari* 176

Illustrations

2.1 Inaugural cover image, *Ie no hikari*. 57

2.2 Advertisement, for *Kingu*'s January 1926 issue. 70

3.1 Inaugural cover image, *Kingu*. 83

3.2 Inaugural cover image, *Fuji*. 87

3.3 Comic, *Kingu*, December 1938. 95

3.4 Elementary syllabary with military theme, *Ie no hikari*, January 1938. 119

3.5 "Finally towards the Conflict in China!" *Ie no hikari*, November 1937. 121

3.6 "The Goals of Our Inspiring Imperial Army," *Ie no hikari*, November 1937. 122

3.7 "Various Weapons," *Ie no hikari*, February 1938. 124

3.8 "City Air Defences," *Ie no hikari*, February 1938. 125

4.1 Photographs of rallies, *Ie no hikari*, September 1928. 151

4.2 "Events of 1911," *The Illustrated Meiji Taishō Shōwa*, January 1931. 158

4.3 "Annexation of Korea," *The Illustrated Meiji Taishō Shōwa*, January 1931. 159

5.1 Niigata Volunteer Labour Group photo/Club toothpaste ad, *Ie no hikari*, December 1937. 172

5.2 Gatefold table of contents, *Ie no hikari*, September 1933. 173

5.3 Hakubieki advertisement, *Kingu*, May 1931. 178

5.4 Hakubieki advertisement, *Ie no hikari*, January 1938. 180

6.1 Cover, *Ie no hikari*, January 2010. 195

6.2 "An Onion Dressing Born from the Inspiration of Shimonita," *Ie no hikari*, January 2010. 196

Acknowledgments

All translations provided here are mine unless otherwise noted. Japanese names are in the Family Given fashion, except in the cases where the author has published in English and listed their name in the anglicized fashion.

I wish to thank the many people and organizations who have supported me in the task of bringing this research to print. The generous funding of the J. William Fulbright Commission and Fulbright Japan as well as the Japan Foundation supported me on essential research trips to archives in Japan, without which I would not have been able to complete this work.

I thank my contacts and friends in Japan: Yamada Shunji at Yokohama City University, and the *sensei* and staff at the Interuniversity Centre, Ōtake Hiroko, Akizawa Tomotarō, Ōhashi Makiko, and Tanaka Junko, who have my utmost respect and affection. I also thank the Printing Museum in Tokyo, the National Diet Library and the libraries of Waseda and Tokyo Universities.

Fellow historians and Japanists Cynthia Brokaw, Deborah Cohen, James Dorsey, Steve Ericson, Sarah Frederick, Carol Gluck, Mary Gluck, Andy Gordon, Karl Jacoby, Aurora Morcillo, Nagamine Shigetoshi, Amy Remensnyder, Ken Ruoff, Robert Scholes, Franziska Seraphim, Kerry Smith, Susan Smulyan, Mark Swiclocki, Sandra Wilson, and Louise Young have all aided me at various stages in the process of researching and writing this book. They have my deep gratitude and respect.

My family and close friends have been indispensable: Captain Matt Buckley and Steve Dixon for our weekly group diversions with Matt Diel, who also shared his beloved red pen; Trudy, Big Gene, and

Kathleen, who have given much love and acceptance. Lois is ever a light to me, and because he never fails to be supportive when I most need him, Dad. The Donna, not enough space here for my thanks. Kate and Whitney make me proud constantly. Eli and Max are the most brilliant energetic monsters stuck with me as a mother but give me hope. And lucky advantage Eugene, for everything.

MAGAZINES AND THE MAKING
OF MASS CULTURE IN JAPAN

Introduction: Why Japanese Family Magazines Matter

Mass culture is a rope. Braided from myriad human threads and pulled by various figures of status, it is damnably long and tangled, but, ultimately, it is a contingent human construct over which we have some degree of collective power. We may fashion it into a noose, with which we hang ourselves; or else a ladder, a means to escape our modern predicament. While certainly not the first to see mass culture as our deliverance or doom, I am interested in tracking the situated historical process of the development of mass culture in Japan over the course of the twentieth century.

This work is concerned with two periodical print publications central to that mass culture's development: *Kingu* (King), published by the profit-driven company Kōdansha, and *Ie no hikari* (Light of the Home), published by the farming cooperative Sangyō Kumiai. The motivation for this focus is to highlight underappreciated continuities that were present in the lived experiences of millions of Japanese during the decades before, during, and after the Second World War.

Hegemonic forms of culture in Japan embodied the most significant continuity of the transwar years. From the early decades of the twentieth century of so-called Taishō democracy, through wartime fascism of the 1930s and 1940s, and into the postwar reconstruction years from 1945 roughly until the mid-1960s, there was a decisive restriction of behaviour and expression for most Japanese citizens. These restrictions emerged amidst a growing mass culture that appeared to offer greater participation, choice, and agency to its members. Investigating this historical progression helps to explain certain inequities that existed in twentieth-century Japanese society and have reverberations still felt today. Moreover, this constrained reality arose from the disproportionate ability of some individuals to concretely articulate, distribute, manage, and revise culture itself.

These restraints on daily life were sometimes subtle and sometimes blatant, but the kinds of life most Japanese could imagine for themselves – the ones they believed to be possible – and the actual lives they led unfolded within the confines of transwar culture. Mass magazines were the first cultural products that should be called mass media, and they were essential to the mechanisms behind the spread and naturalization of mass culture in Japan and thus centrally articulated the boundaries of that culture. Let us here untangle the rope of mass culture, to hold it under a magnifying glass and investigate: Who chose the threads? What material comprised it? How were the threads spun? What did they secure and what did they fence out?

This research presents an empirically embedded cultural history that provides a framework for understanding processes that happened not just in Japan but also elsewhere in the world.[1] The mosaic created by the various aspects of transwar media culture provides a composite picture of the mechanisms behind the birth of a Japanese mass audience, though more specific and detailed, to mix artistic metaphors, than impressionistic.

This project investigates different facets of Japanese media. Mass magazines in Japan developed and expanded such that the new, and yet simultaneously recognizable, features of these publications obscured their naturalization. To many readers, magazines must have seemed quite similar to other kinds of print media, and to some extent they were. The consequences of the spread of such media, however, and the assimilation of the cultural practices surrounding their consumption warrant deeper analysis.

Methodology

In the mid-1960s Marshall McLuhan contended, "Just as we now try to control atom-bomb fallout, so we will one day try to control media fallout." With this prediction, intensely pertinent to the Japanese context,

---

1 It is largely out of my respect for Carol Gluck and her call for historians (especially those of Japan) to strive for such scholarship that I have made an attempt to approach what she describes; see Gluck, *Two Lectures by Carol Gluck* and "After the Shipwreck."

I embrace McLuhan's concern with the media in and of itself as worthiest of our attention. His disquiet with media fallout was prompted by his conviction that "the medium is the message."[2] This observation seems simple enough as stated, but the tangible application of this revelation or its translation into a scholarly method deserves explicit articulation.

Despite scholarly and popular emphasis on the medium being the message, what comes across after repeated exposure and inquiry is that the medium exists as *the combination* of content and form. McLuhan saw media as "extensions of ourselves," meaning human cultural arte-facts.[3] Understanding medium as mechanism, motor, and meaning requires that we look at what it is and how it functions socially, while also remaining attentive to what it contains. To understand better the mechanism of the medium, McLuhan habitually took note of and inter-preted content as well. His work methodically analyses concrete exam-ples of what was in books, broadcasts, and billboards ranging from the Bible to Budweiser, *Finnegans Wake* to Ford.

The interplay between these two facets is integral to media; in order to understand one, you need to understand the other. McLuhan cared about the medium *and* the message alike; otherwise he would have ignored one or the other. And he did not, since he paid deft attention to both. The *medium* (the set of mechanisms created to reach a mass audience) mutually conditions and is conditioned by the *message* (mass political identity, consumerism, etc.). When it seemed most relevant to discuss one aspect, that became the focus; the reverse was also the case. This tactic is neither inconsistent nor uneven.

The cultural mechanism under examination here is a structural phe-nomenon. Thus, this project principally tracks magazines as a *medium* for culture creation rather than the cultural products – specific content or ideas or images – that they distribute. However, without having the concrete specifics of the content within that media, the picture would be flat, lifeless, and hollow. My interpretative balance accordingly attempts to do justice to the Janus-faced nature of such human cultural extensions.

The editors of *Ie no hikari* and *Kingu* discerned that how they created, promoted, and distributed their publications was just as important as what they put between the covers. The content was painstakingly

---

2 McLuhan, *Understanding Media*, 305, 7.
3 Ibid., 7, passim.

chosen to be accessible, entertaining, and beneficial to the readers, but the methods by which these magazines were pushed into the households of millions of Japanese readers were even more scrupulously selected. Both the content and the mechanisms, moreover, fitted neatly with state designs and nationalistic rhetoric, providing mass culture with a false homogeneity heralding the rise of the middle-mass, blending outward class distinctions, and feeding the myth of meritocracy.

Since the purpose of this study does not lie in explaining why there was mass support for the Pacific War, for example, this is not a study of propaganda, ideology, or fascism per se. Accordingly, moving away from conceptions of popular culture in Japan in the first half of the twentieth century (which focus on the buildup to war with its impact and aftermath) allows us to illuminate the continuities in daily life that existed across the transwar years. We can also more accurately track shifts in social and cultural practices in the everyday lives of Japanese who lived in these years.

The concepts of *culture, mass, massification,* and *naturalization* reverberate throughout this project, so it seems best here to explain them explicitly in the hopes of achieving some conceptual and interpretative clarity. The conception of mass culture deployed is one that is based, very simply, on both halves of the phrase: *mass,* meaning as wide a swathe of the population as one can achieve, demographically and numerically speaking; and *culture,* meaning the habits and practices of people in their everyday lives.

Culture is most convincingly understood as a symbolic system, as articulated famously by Clifford Geertz.[4] John B. Thompson has also explained how "structured contexts," circumstances embedded within certain contingently created places and times, allow us to meaningfully decipher culture via symbolic forms in such contexts – namely, those that also create and reproduce particular, often inequitable, power structures.[5] I combine these understandings of culture more generally with James Carey's notion of communication specifically as culture, defined as "a symbolic process whereby reality is produced,

---

4 Geertz, *The Interpretation of Cultures,* 5, 10, 12, 17, passim.
5 His exact words are "The analysis of cultural phenomena involves the elucidation of these socially structured contexts and processes as well as the interpretation of symbolic forms; or ... the interpretation of symbolic forms *by means of* the analysis of socially structured contexts and processes" (Thompson, *Ideology and Modern Culture,* 12).

maintained, repaired, and transformed" that is best understood as a "form of action – or, better, interaction – that not merely represents or describes but actually molds or constitutes the world."[6] These magazines helped create mass Japanese culture and involved these communal meanings, individual practices, and connections to society at large as sites of interaction and markers of power. This project explains the meaning of the magazines *qua* magazine, providing the context of their production so that their meaning within Japanese mass culture can be more clearly understood.

This research highlights the importance of the seemingly innocuous acts of mass leisure consumption of magazines and the goods advertised therein. Through understanding how these magazines created and conditioned both *mass* and consumer culture, we thus begin to understand the creation and direction of a new form of social participation and understanding. As such, looking at mass magazines is an essential part of understanding not only the culture but also the *politics* of the massification of Japan.

Unravelling structured contexts suggests a precise use of the term *mass*. In agreement with my own usage, Richard Ohmann argues for a particular definition of mass culture and claims that it is essential for understanding modern society in general. His definition states that "mass culture … includes voluntary experiences, produced by a relatively small number of specialists, for millions across the nation to share, in similar or identical form, either simultaneously or nearly so, with dependable frequency; mass culture shapes habitual audiences, around common needs or interests, and it is made for profit."[7] Each aspect of this well-crafted characterization applies to the Japanese case, so let us unpack it more fully.

The culture embodied by the mass audience in transwar Japan was intimately connected with print media and thereby to more conventional institutional forms. The audience for mass magazines included millions of people from every sector of the populace, including those in the Japanese colonies while they existed. Japan gained its first formal colony of Taiwan in 1895, Sakhalin (Karufuto) and the Liaotung Peninsula in 1905, Korea in 1910, and the South Sea Islands in 1914; and these all remained part of the Japanese empire until the end of the Second

---

6 Carey, *Communication as Culture*, 19, 64.
7 Ohmann, *Selling Culture*, 14.

World War in 1945. Magazines like *Kingu* and *Ie no hikari* were distributed throughout the four Japanese home islands and the imperium as a whole. Increasingly after the mid-1920s, moreover, the ready availability of mass media caused a *naturalization* of the practice of interacting with magazines as a major portion of one's leisure activities. The saturation of magazines in everyday life in Japan went hand in hand with the growth of a unifying mass culture and is, therefore, why these periodical publications are a useful window on culture at large.

Mass is often placed in tension/opposition with *popular*, especially in discussions concerning literary production. In part, my interpretation of the category of *mass* is an attempt to circumvent the semantic (rather than conceptual) debates that exist in some previous scholarship concerning this topic. Consequently, this work assumes that the concept of *mass* itself is socially constructed. By this I mean that our conception of what the masses *are* does not refer to some objective category or entity in the world, but rather reflects our understanding of definitions, populations, and historical trends as results of the structured contexts in which they are produced.[8]

In addition, this deployment of the term *mass* seeks to designate a difference from what came before. Consumers of manufactured and directed mass culture did not require any demographic similarity, such as level of education, residential location, gender, occupation, or age.[9] As Marilyn Ivy describes it, "'Mass culture' would thus indicate culture as commodified and administered, pretargeted and produced for large numbers of consumers: the masses."[10] This use of *mass* combines a gargantuan and extremely diverse audience with the commodified nature of their social participation. At the heart of useful scholarly applications of *mass* exists the desire to mark a distinct cultural phenomenon: a cultural experience that breaks significantly from previous practices for the reasons just mentioned.

And while *millions* is an admittedly arbitrary figure by which to define mass, the simple fact is that, in Japan, before mass magazines such as

---

8 This is not a novel understanding of the concept of mass; for example, see Adorno, *The Culture Industry*; Thompson, *Ideology and Modern Culture*; Kammen, *American Culture, American Tastes*; and Lipsitz, *Time Passages*. The idea is also present in certain Japanese theoretical interpretations of Leopold von Wiese; see Schäfer, *Public Opinion, Propaganda, Ideology*, 91.

9 Thompson, *Ideology and Modern Culture*, 19–20.

10 Ivy, *Discourses of the Vanishing*, 195.

Kingu and *Ie no hikari*, there were only localized regional consumption-related phenomena, which failed to achieve the kind of cultural resonance of a shared national mass audience. The synchronicity of the audience is important, as in McLuhan's labelling the advent of mass production and automation as "an instant inclusive embrace"; thus these phenomena behave like an asymptote that approaches but never achieves perfection either in total number of participants or exact simultaneity.[11] It is, however, one of the threads that ties the *mass* together.

I also use the term *massification*. This might be a somewhat inelegant expression, but it is an intentional one.[12] In part, it attempts to capture the usage of the original Japanese that appeared intermittently in the writings and statements of the magazine producers under study here. The term *taishūka* is often translated in the present day as "popularization" or even "democratization." At the end of the nineteenth century and the beginning of the twentieth in Japan, debates over *taishū* (the masses; public) and its linguistic predecessor *minshū* (the people; public) erupted when these terms came to be used extensively and widely in Meiji-era conversations about nation building and education of the citizenry in public discourse.[13] More specifically, contemporary scholarly conversations about *taishū* have centred on the exact intellectual implications of their transformation and use in the early decades of the twentieth century. However, it is sufficient here simply to know that the component parts – *taishū* and -*ka* – literally translate to "the masses" (or "the general public") and "-ification" respectively; thus, in putting them together to create "massification" is not inappropriate.[14]

---

11 McLuhan, *Understanding Media*, 349.

12 I am not the first person to have used this word, but since the term seems to largely be the domain of those concerned with media technology and higher education, it is uncommon to Japanese studies. See Cohen, *Self Consciousness*; Rogers, *Communication Technology*; Gibbons, *The New Production of Knowledge*; Suarez-Villa, *Invention and the Rise of Technocapitalism*; Curaj et al., *European Higher Education at the Crossroads between the Bologna Process and National Reforms*; Cook, Glickman, and O'Malley, *The Cultural Turn in U. S. History*, 298.

13 In relation to the use of these terms in relation to media see Ariyama, "「民衆」の時代 から「大衆」の時代へ (From the Era of 'the People' to the Age of 'the Masses')."

14 大衆化- Indeed, two other Japanists have recently seen fit to do the same. See Ruoff, *Imperial Japan at Its Zenith*, 33; Sato, *The New Japanese Woman*, 42. For more on the *taishū-minshū* (aka "mass-popular" in the Japanese context) discussion, see Kogawa, "New Trends in Japanese Popular Culture"; Ivy, *Discourses of the Vanishing*, 195; Robertson, *Takarazuka*, 32–5.

Another distinction is captured by choosing *massification*. *Popularization* might apply to a product or practice; a book or song can become popular. *Massification*, on the other hand, is something that happens to a demographic or a group of people as they become collected into an abstract mass. The contemporary use of the term *taishūka* has two dimensions: one, the popularization of print media (i.e., *katsuji media no taishūka*); and the other, the massification of the society brought on by print media, or, the making of something into the masses (i.e., *katsuji media ni yoru shakai no taishūka*).[15] It is the second connotation of the word, implying an active change to society, that is invoked in this work. Further, since similar patterns and generalities happened elsewhere in the world, I have chosen *massification* to describe the mission of these publications so that we might better articulate the ways in which Japan does and does not resemble other places where mass culture developed along different lines, and the political implications of those differences.[16]

Some might cry, "Anachronism!" but in this case, that is not as damning as one might think. These Japanese publishers *were* ahead of their times, and it was because they saw something different in *mass* (and spoke of it thus) that they could accomplish what they did. Because the president of Kōdansha, Noma Seiji, and those at the Industrial Cooperative envisioned *taishū* in unique ways, they prefigured what it could become. Let me here preview one example of the way in which Shimura Gentarō (second president of the Cooperative) used the term. *Ie no hikari* published an editorial explicitly stating that the "massification of the Cooperative" meant giving women and children – those previously not interested or invested in the organization, in most estimations – direct access to the ideas behind the organization's activities as well as to the means to participate communally in them through the Co-op's magazine.[17] This particular conception of *massification* is at the very heart of my argument.

Massification of the Japanese audience combined various demographics and gathered across age, class, gender, educational, geographic, and political lines. These publishers understood that, while

---

15 Here I am indebted to Atsuko Aoki for helping clarify my thoughts on the articulation of these usages.
16 For a discussion on the various twentieth-century conceptions of the political import of massification, see Schäfer, *Public Opinion, Propaganda, Ideology*, 106–7, passim.
17 志村源, "産業組合の大衆化 (The Massification of the Industrial Cooperative)," 17.

Meiji-era attempts to inspire the population along national lines had succeeded in creating self-cognizant *citizens* of Japan, there was room for further and more intimate infiltration into the hearts, minds, and homes of the population. Crafting "common sense" and normalizing new cultural practices was one motor for this process that involved the audience's voluntary participation and active engagement.

Naturalization and *normalization* are terms that might be too heterogeneous in meaning to go without further explanation. *Normalization* is the process by which some activity or product, which was previously not common among large sectors of the population, becomes part of the commonly understood communal culture of a place. For example, magazines were not read by the vast majority of the population in Japan in, say, 1910, but by 1940, hardly a citizen in the empire would have thought of magazines as rare, strange, or somehow not perfectly "normal." This concept is largely used interchangeably with *naturalization* in this study, because the latter does not mean naturalization in the sense associated with the gaining of citizenship – though a certain nuance of being a Japanese citizen in a new community of mass magazine readers does have some resonance. Family magazines were the means by which participating in the Japanese mass national audience became normalized and naturalized.

Family magazines, especially *Ie no hikari* and *Kingu*, created a mass, national, consumer audience. In creating this audience, these magazines influenced and conditioned the national culture of Japan. Mass culture helped to constitute and constrain lived experiences.[18] Binding with the discursive ropes of culture, these magazines restricted options in the social realm – for what it meant to be Japanese, to be a man or woman, to be a good citizen, a dutiful child, etc. – and the more people interacted with these discourses, the more this trend held true.

---

18 As McLuhan affirms, "That our human senses, of which all media are extensions, are also fixed charges on our personal energies, and that they also configure the awareness and experience of each one of us, may be perceived in another connection mentioned by the psychologist C.G. Jung: 'Every Roman was surrounded by slaves. The slave and his psychology flooded ancient Italy, and every Roman became inwardly, and of course unwittingly, a slave. Because living constantly in the atmosphere of slaves, he became infected through the unconscious with their psychology. No one can shield himself from such an influence'" (*Understanding Media*, 21, quoting from Jung, Baynes, and Baynes, *Contributions to Analytical Psychology*).

Even so, the mass culture these magazines created could not *completely* control and homogenize, nor did it need to. There are ways in which some of the audience could have read against the grain of this culture – the point is not that the culture was all-consuming or wholly unbeneficial. Massification does not require complete compliance, homogenization, or even belief; its elasticity and interpretability create an atmosphere of belonging, acknowledgment, and resonance that nationalism, especially in less flexible state-sponsored senses, had failed to achieve on its own.[19] Participating in or being influenced by mass culture was, however, increasingly difficult to avoid.

People over the first half of the twentieth century increasingly sought information and advice from magazines, in part because the experiences of their parents and grandparents – historically the main source of common sense and social wisdom (read: cultural meanings) within communities – were less relevant to the modern life that presented itself to many younger Japanese in the middle-twentieth century. In this way, mass magazines served to speed the breakdown of the "traditional" family even as they sought to reinforce that very institution. This disjuncture between the espoused goals and actual results of the publications like *Ie no hikari* and *Kingu* is another feature central to mass media.

Histories of Japan, whether concerned with intellectual elites, politicians, or military figures, generally focus on specific dates in the Japanese landscape (e.g., 1868, 1912, 1926, 1937, 1941, and 1945). We need to collectively acknowledge that dates central to elites and scholars (in Japan during the years in question and to us today) may not have been nearly so significant to people, say, living on a farm in Akita Prefecture in 1930. Rural Japanese in the transwar era were on a calendar of significance distinct from, but perhaps parallel to, that of important people in Tokyo. The progression of Japanese mass society was nothing if not contingent,

---

19 Miriam Silverberg, for example, has argued against Sheldon Garon's constrictive reading of reforms and highlights this very dichotomy: "For example, although Garon rightfully points to the influence of *Ie no Hikari*, as a source circulating tips on household management sanctioned by the state to one million households, a close reading of the magazine of the rural cooperative movement reveals another side of its treatment of modernity ... articles in *Ie no Hikari* also directly and indirectly point to the draw of modern culture in the countryside. As late as 1939 ... not all rural women were accepting the state-sanctioned version of modern life as the ideal existence" (*Erotic Grotesque Nonsense*, 35). The relevant section of Garon is *Molding Japanese Minds*, 126–7.

and to understand what was going on in the lived experiences of everyday Japanese, we need a different timeline from the one historians have, because of habit or theoretical commitments, consistently drawn. Perhaps even numerous timelines are required, much as Gail Hershatter suggested with rural Chinese women, foregrounding how women's labour was "acknowledged and invisible" through the irreversible reordering of space and time after the Chinese Revolution.[20] Conceptions of multiple temporalities, wherein shifts or similarities in everyday practices were more significant for these people than government policies, expansionist wars, or foreign occupations, constructs a much richer understanding of the embodied experience of Japanese people.

The ways in which everyday Japanese life witnessed much continuity in the transwar years is evident in the study of mass culture. Contemporary media built on the success of television and radio, which capitalized directly on structures and practices that arose from print media like *Kingu* and *Ie no hikari*.[21] Identification of the intricacies of how magazines were made and spread illuminates our understanding of features central to the twentieth century in Japan. The impact of these products on culture cannot be overstated. Combining the mechanism and naturalization of reading magazines with newspapers and other forms of consumer entertainment (e.g., department stores, expositions, sporting events, etc.), the explosion of commodities aimed at "the masses" in the postwar years is hardly surprising, nor is the rampant consumerism that accompanied them.

Studies using a "transwar" perspective to track those phenomena have effectively traced the development of the middle class in Japan through habits of consumption and leisure. Similarly, the persistence of consumerism and consumption against the backdrop of empire (or in a more gestalt conception of Japan's situation, within the imperialistic world order of the early twentieth century) is a major assumption of my research as well. Along these lines, the proud Japanese consumer (presented in the work of Gordon, Partner, Ivy, and others) who supported Japan's progress in the international market throughout the post-Occupation decades is unsurprising, considering the ideological motivations and nationalistic core of these magazines as major sources

---

20 See Hershatter, *The Gender of Memory*.
21 The work of Ivy ("Formations of Mass Culture") and Partner (*Assembled in Japan*), to name two examples, supports this connection.

of Japanese consumer habits from the prewar and wartime years.[22] These studies show that, even during depression, war, and occupation, there were major continuities between lifestyles and consumption habits of the Japanese populace.

Likewise, transwar gender norms in Japan also make sense in light of the nature of the mass audience created in the interwar years. The notion of housewife as household manager in Japan was already in place by the 1930s, even if her real-life counterpart had not yet begun to identify as such or consume to the full extent of her (postwar) capacities, and even if, instead of an absent corporate solider and "salaryman," her husband was away fighting an actual war abroad. Japan's growing mass media is an underutilized source for tracking the origins of these transwar continuities and is, thus, the bedrock of this project.

The Japanese everyday life experiences in the twentieth century reflect an essential continuity of culture with somewhat varied, though still hegemonic, façades. In other geographic and temporal contexts, Jason Stanley has defined and deconstructed ideology and how it works through vehicles of propaganda, defined as "an institution that represents itself as defined by a certain political ideal, yet whose practice tends to undermine the realization of that ideal." While my work is not a study of propaganda per se, this work is in fundamental agreement with and provides further evidence in support of Stanley's conception of propaganda and its complex and intimate relationship to ideology. Understanding propaganda and ideology in this way also warrants a transwar perspective because underlying the system – whether the ostensibly democratic prewar, the fascist colonial regime of the war years, or the American-style "democracy" (in fact, military occupation) of the postwar – there persisted "an illiberal, undemocratic reality."[23]

By participating in the consumption of these magazines, Japanese experienced the naturalization of certain ideas, such as the supposedly beneficent and justified mission of Japanese imperialism, or the purportedly advantageous global rise of the nation-state. This meant

---

22 See Garon and Maclachlan, *The Ambivalent Consumer*; Gordon, "Consumption, Leisure and the Middle Class in Transwar Japan" and "From Singer to Shinpan"; Kushner, *The Thought War*; Minichiello, *Japan's Competing Modernities*; Ruoff, *Imperial Japan at Its Zenith*; Partner, *Assembled in Japan*; Ivy, *Discourses of the Vanishing*.

23 If one wants to understand propaganda, Stanley's work is well worth the read, and though I do not attempt to duplicate such work here, I fully support his assessment and explanation of the processes and results (*How Propaganda Works*, 59, 11).

that Japanese people were also implicitly supporting nationalism and empire – economically at the very least, since the profits from these magazines strengthened organizations that actively buttressed Japanese militarism and imperialism domestically during the Second World War and the American military-industrial complex after it. Acknowledging the complicity of capitalist institutions within state structures for reinforcing hegemonic discourses is essential to my critique. Hegemony, ideology, and their attendant concepts are not new discussions by any stretch of the imagination, but I do conceive of media as a means of supporting state and elite power.[24] Mass media is clearly a realm of political discourse in which a seemingly unbiased medium provides a powerful avenue for reinforcing and maintaining hegemonic power among the populace.

What is most interesting about the family magazines of Japan is not how they managed to engineer model Japanese citizens, as the editors had hoped, but rather how they embodied *conduits* for particular kinds of social and cultural practices centred on consumption – the very mechanisms for the upkeep of that culture. Likewise, seeking to exhume and exhibit this conscious, creative process is an attempt to counteract the tendency of commodities, advertising, and media to obscure their own normalization and infiltration into common-sense attitudes about society. As Adorno would suggest, "to take the culture industry as seriously as its unquestioned role demands, means to take it serious critically, and not to cower in the face of its monopolistic character."[25] As such, an examination of the mechanisms by which a particular kind of Japanese consumer was fashioned from magazines and of the naturalization of the cultural practice of reading mass magazines in the late 1920s and early 1930s is what follows in the chapters here.

Several important caveats: I don't say that fascism, militarism, nationalism, and patriotism were straightforwardly *caused* by these magazines. Nor am I saying that the magazines are the *only* important cultural phenomenon with regard to the creation of a mass culture in Japan. It may be, nevertheless, that the mass audience in 1920s (or 1950s) Japan was particularly primed for certain values (e.g., fascist/nationalist/militarist/democratic/pacifist, depending on the decade).

---

24 Foucault, *Discipline and Punish*; Geertz, *The Interpretation of Cultures*; Gramsci, *Prison Notebooks*; Herman and Chomsky, *Manufacturing Consent*.
25 Adorno, *The Culture Industry*, 102.

It is also an open question whether other national mass cultures had so explicitly ideological an origin as Japanese mass culture, via these magazines, seems to have had.

Neither is there a significant engagement in this study with these publications in the Japanese colonial context. This is certainly *not* to suggest that the colonies or empire are not important – they undoubtedly are – but my interest is with the metropole of the homeland. The reality that was constructed, continued, contested, and changed within the empire by the media (in Japan and elsewhere) was the very atmosphere of culture and society: a society that was engaged in becoming modern, waging wars, losing them, recovering, and blending into the global environment once again. This absence is also conscientious because Japan's colonies were lost in the postwar years, but the social and cultural continuities were not. The persistent trends being tracked here existed alongside different kinds of imperialism, but not always *colonialism* in the strict sense.

These magazines were central originators of a Japanese mass culture; unravelling the weave (or unpacking the meanings and methods) of these omnipresent artefacts is the task at hand. This culture and its processes were contingent, as well. There is no true end detailed here because the process is ongoing. As such, perhaps it can allow us to think of alternatives to mass consumer culture. Even if we cannot escape our modern predicament, we can at the very least climb the rope and improve our vantage point over it.

Chapter Summaries

Chapter 1 explains some traits of the medium of magazines: what they were, what was in them, and who consumed them. It was their distinctive format and all-inclusive audience that allowed magazines to be as significant a player in the growth of mass culture as they were. But more than merely being the vector of certain viral ideologies, these magazines created the very infrastructure by which shared attitudes – be they everyday life activities, political views, or product preferences – could be transmitted. This chapter discusses both some of the formal properties of the medium and the ideological premises on which they were built in order to contextualize the creation of Japanese family magazines.

Chapter 2 argues that the publishers of *Kingu* and *Ie no hikari* had specific visions for creating and engaging a Japanese mass even before the appearance of their magazines. These visions (or goals or missions) were to create as broad and diverse an audience as possible, so that the publishers could use the magazines to transmit their own ideals. The specific target for both publications from the beginning was the "family." The chapter provides a brief historical survey of what came before mass magazines, then tracks the planning of those at the Industrial Cooperative, and of Noma Seiji and his staff at Kōdansha, who imagined these magazines and made their ideas into reality printed on pages and distributed throughout Japan. They used *Ie no hikari* and *Kingu* to bring their messages to the people and to naturalize the practice of buying, reading, and discussing magazines. This is an examination of the means of transmission, the mechanism for the spread of mass culture itself.

Chapter 3 provides a close reading of the first several issues of each of these magazines, from which one can deduce that the magazines, in fact, adhered to their editors' visions. These magazines were explicitly aimed at creating the broadest possible audience for their products, but with the express intent of transmitting and instilling beliefs (particular meanings and understandings of the world) in that audience. Social transformations, which intensified after the worldwide Depression and the Manchurian Incident, also helped to foster a sense of common interest in powerfully persuasive ways, and commercial publishers managed to profit financially by eagerly encouraging these processes. The central ideas and discourses present in the magazines that grew directly from the producers' convictions and commitments, discussed in the second chapter, are detailed more fully in this third chapter. As such, it is a study of the content of the media contained in the articles and images of these vital publications during their early years and through the 1930s. Chapter 3 additionally displays the magazines' children's sections, which express, from a slightly different angle, the values being transmitted to the most impressionable members of the audience.

Chapter 4 tracks the creation of the Japanese mass audience of the magazines, in terms of their circulation numbers (which represent only a small fraction of the actual number of people exposed to these publications), and also in terms of their becoming a central feature in the everyday lives and workplaces of Japanese across an astonishing range of demographics. Other media and leisure activities were present in this era, and there was a time in Japan when reading magazines was *not* an option. So the very fact that these magazines managed to penetrate the culture so widely and so deeply is evidence for success at building the audience that their creators sought. The spread of these periodicals, moreover, happened through concrete actions and methods conjured by those at Kōdansha and the Cooperative. *Ie no hikari* and *Kingu* became the focus of reading groups, rallies, and educational programs that placed them in a special cultural role – that of conveying what their creators took to be a shared Japanese experience.

Chapter 5 turns to explicit conversations about advertising and the role it played in selling not only the magazines themselves but also the products advertised within them, which began before a single issue of *Kingu* or *Ie no hikari* had been drafted or sent to press. The self-conscious nature of the birth and development of magazines – advertising included – is thus particularly revealing about the process of naturalizing new consumption habits and the attendant shifts in cultural practices. The advertising within these periodicals would have been viewed by many millions of people in Japan. Though a complete survey of the over seventy thousand pages published between their founding in 1925 and 1940, for example, is impossible here, a representative selection of advertising that illustrates the consistent relationship between advertising's promotion of consumerism and the magazines as mass entertainment is provided. This relationship further supports the notion that consumerism itself is an important conduit of meaning making within mass culture. The chapter investigates the advertising and formal design properties present in *Kingu* and *Ie no hikari* and tracks their trends in order to suggest how the commercialized nature of magazines provided a complementary layer of socialization. Put more simply, these magazines provided lessons for their readers on how to participate in the Japanese *mass* not just as citizens but also as consumers.

The concluding chapter summarizes how these magazines were ideologically charged and incredibly successful as products and commodities that also produced a mass culture. By providing an avenue for the creation of so broad a consumer group, these magazines laid the foundations for a Japanese mass culture and had significant subsequent ramifications for the postwar transformations of mass culture and social practices surrounding mass media.

Chapter One

The Medium, the Message, and the Masses: Understanding Japanese Family Magazines

In general, magazines have a reputation for going bankrupt after about three issues. Were someone to manage to sell twenty thousand issues of a magazine like this, flowers will bloom on telephone poles.[1]

Mr Yamada, Tokyo, 1923

In the early decades of the twentieth century Japan, there were not many who considered magazines to be a lucrative enterprise, much less an important cultural product. Nevertheless, by the late 1920s it would have been unthinkable to find a person in Japan who could not at least name a popular magazine title, even if they did not themselves regularly purchase one. It was in the interwar era (1918–37) that this practice and the meanings associated with it became naturalized. By looking at them askance – making the familiar strange – we can learn from magazines how certain things become "normal" and "everyday," even when the original processes by which they happened are opaque.[2] Though

---

1   This sceptical statement came from a Mr Yamada, a member of the Industrial Cooperative who hailed from Toyama. 北村, 家の光の四十年 (*Forty Years of "Light of the Home"*), 9.
2   My perspective has partially grown from exposure to everyday life studies, which caused me to consider the importance of commodity culture and social norms in relation to the daily, lived experiences of Japanese people. One particularly effective thesis among those self-proclaimed everyday life theorists is Ross, *Fast Cars, Clean Bodies*. See also Michel de Certeau, *The Practice of Everyday Life* (Berkeley: University of California Press, 1984); Ben Highmore, *Everyday Life and Cultural Theory* (London and New York: Routledge, 2002).

blossoms did not in fact sprout from the telephone poles, Mr Yamada was utterly wrong about his assessment of the significance and profitability of magazines. This is a story about why it was that so many magazines had failed in the past and why some came to be centrally significant to new and lasting practices that became ubiquitous features of Japanese society. But more broadly, it is an explanation of the birth of mass culture in Japan.

Historical Background

Japanese leaders boldly and creatively envisioned what Japan could become in the transition from the shogunal regime that ended in 1868 and the constitutional monarchy that was established with the Meiji Restoration thereafter. Transformations manifesting in Japanese society were thoroughgoing in the Meiji years, despite some lasting continuities from the preceding Tokugawa era that had provided the foundation for roughly 250 years of peace and relative stability. Some of the changes are easy to track: economic, physical, and social transformations were dramatic and rampant.

Technologies flourished thanks in part to newly gained and nearly unrestrained access to objects, practices, and knowledge from outside of Japan. Telegraph machines and lines were installed, though not entirely welcomed by all, increasing the speed and precision of communications. The national mail service began in 1872, building on a previous infrastructure created by the Shogun and maintained by *Daimyō* who were the leaders of domains that were replaced with prefectural governors after the establishment of the Meiji government. The metric system was adopted in 1886, allowing for easier participation in the global scientific community. In addition, printed money with a national currency replaced the various regional currencies present in each domain during the Tokugawa years. These were just a few of the conspicuous innovations of post-Restoration Japan.

In terms of changes to the physical scenery, transportation drastically altered the very landscape of Japan as tracks and locomotives snaked between cities and towns across the country, beginning with the first line established from Yokohama to Tokyo. Numerous political arguments about where stations should be and where lines should go preceded their construction, as it was clear to politicians and business leaders at the time how impactful the presence of stations would be. Later, street cars and gas lights in the cities became increasingly common as well. These new ways of viewing and things to view shifted how Japan physically looked over these decades in irreversible ways.

Western advisors visited at the behest of the Meiji leaders to provide commentary on education as well. The new compulsory coeducational educational system expanded, contributing to greater gender equality, advanced literacy through standardized language learning, and integration of a national curriculum. Such reforms established the foundation of the coeducational system, with primary, secondary, and higher educational facilities, that continues in a revised form today. Standardization of education across the country helped to create a more articulate and aware public and was also designed to inculcate certain ideas about being Japanese. Higher education was a new channel to success and access to power, as colleges produced government bureaucrats. Being a civil servant had a high social status, and even though such positions did not offer particularly high pay, civil service came with a prestige not easily obtained by the lower classes in the previous era. These changes allowed the educational system to broadly impact Japanese society in ways that were largely viewed as positive.

As the Meiji reign progressed, the effect of these restructurings shifted daily life for those in Japan, just as such changes were transforming many cities around the globe after the turn of the twentieth century. Introducing the Gregorian calendar marked a major shift in the conception of time. Notions of objective uniformity and precision were valued over the seasonal, lunar measures of time which had prevailed for centuries. This also spurred the creation of new school calendars, salary payments, and other such markers of collectively dividing one's time in days, weeks, months, and years, which tied the various regions of Japan together domestically in addition to connecting the nation to the increasingly entrenched global standard.

Another worldwide standard by which Japanese leaders found themselves being measured related to imperialism. A new kind of imperialism developed in the late 1800s and early 1900s whereby one-quarter of land on earth was newly acquired by the various powers. The United Kingdom gained roughly four million million new square miles of territory, while France, Germany, and the United States also gained new property. The rapid increase in land grabs marked the international environment in which Japan entered the scrimmage. Few places in the world were left unmolested in the process, places like Morocco, Libya, Arabia, Persia, Tibet, Afghanistan, and Japan among them. Not many countries, especially in East and Southeast Asia, managed to avoid coming under the sway of the colonial and imperial powers as Africa, South America, and South Asia were all devoured.

Japan gained its formal empire territories rapidly and only a few years after opening to the world after its semi-seclusion of the 250 Tokugawa years. The formal colonies of the Japanese empire came in turn: Taiwan (1895), Sakhalin/Karafuto (1905), the Liaotung Peninsula (1905), Korea (1910), and the South Sea Islands (1914). The Japanese public was truly interested in the empire and the colonies; Japan became a colonial power at almost the same moment that it became integrated into new global politics under unequal treaties, thus confronting the West economically and politically just as it was simultaneously becoming a colonial power.

The context of Japanese imperialism is one of mass participation by enthusiastic powers. Japan was simply joining a feast already in progress. The Japanese colonial rhetoric from leaders, however, was different from that of the rest of the Western powers: Japan was an *Asian* power and civilizing force for Asia. Even if the rhetoric of civilization and benevolence failed to acknowledge the eventual brutal reality, very much like colonial rule by the Euro-American powers in most places, Japan was geographically and culturally proximate to its colonies (excepting perhaps the South Seas). The distances were quite different for Japan than for the UK, US, or most other European empires, and this impacted, for example, who could travel to the colonies. Moreover, Korea and Taiwan were culturally proximate, with Confucian and Buddhist influences creating a supposed affinity that the UK and others in the West could not claim to share with their colonies. The colonial models and structures of rule were similar, but the Japanese leaders' goals and outlook in rhetoric were different.

Apart from Taiwan, where military and strategic concerns were at the forefront of discussion about the acquisition of that colony, these claimed cultural similarities created the impression that Japan's relationships with its colonies were different from those of the Western powers. Popular attitudes were correspondingly affected by this impression as well. After the Second World War, the West was increasingly seen as selfish and extractive, especially the British in India, whereas Japanese politicians viewed themselves as self-sacrificing, giving something up by becoming a colonial power to help Asia rise in the world. Further, this martyr role was largely embraced by the domestic media and population at large.

Japan's spectacular international success was one of the major reasons that it managed to distinguish itself from the other countries in

Asia during this time of exploding imperialism. How was it that Japan could go from a low-tech, agriculturally based society in the late 1880s to one of the world's most high-tech global competitors just fifty to seventy-five years later? Part of this narrative that deserves more attention is the role of media in creating a Japanese mass, a mass moreover that participated and was invested in their collective global fate.

In the dawning days of print media in Japan, early modern publications were the first to expand into what could be called a popular medium.[3] But it would not be until the 1930s that Japanese print media could be truly called *mass media*. This distinction is key. Once the vast majority of *all* Japan's citizens were engaging with print media – not just some subset of the population, but women as well as men, educated elites as well as those with only basic schooling, the poor as well as the wealthy, and, most compellingly, farmers in the far-flung prefectures as well as residents in the heart of Tokyo – mass media became a social institution that powerfully shaped public discourse while simultaneously participating in the creation of the very culture of which it was a part. Specifically, Japanese family magazines help to trace the circulation of cultural memes and social practices in and around cities and out in villages and hamlets, and the multidirectional flows among them. More importantly, they bestow the very structure for this interaction to happen.

The Medium

Magazines were the first form of media to capture mass audiences in Japan, and once they had taken hold they quickly enveloped the empire. Though magazines had existed alongside newspapers before the late 1920s, the nature of those earlier publications, in terms of content and price, prevented them from expanding to reach more than demographically narrow segments of the national audience, even if they were increasingly influential within the cities. There were several magazines by the late 1930s, however, that could boast circulation figures of over a million, pulling readers from all walks of life. Furthermore, it was far from uncommon for people to come together and listen as one person read aloud to a group; in this way, these media reached far greater numbers than their circulation statistics alone suggest.

---

3 More on this discussion below, but see also Berry, *Japan in Print*; Rubinger, *Popular Literacy in Early Modern Japan*.

It is relatively uncontroversial to observe that by the 1960s there was a mass Japanese national *consumer*. More controversially, I suggest that this consumer figure can be explained by the mass national *audience* that family magazines of the interwar era had created, embodying all three of these elements (mass, Japanese, consumerism) from their inauguration. This chapter analytically narrates the creation and development of such publications, one explicitly capitalist and one outwardly agrarian, based on missions with an overarching desire to create a mass Japanese magazine audience. What follows will explore the differences in method and tone of the two most successful family magazines in Japan while showing how their mass audience became unavoidably naturalized to consumer culture and prefigured the postwar Japanese consumer in ways that provided substantial transwar cultural and social continuities.

Through tactics that simultaneously borrowed and deviated from the advancement of periodicals like the *Saturday Evening Post* and the *Ladies' Home Journal* in the development of mass culture in the United States, the creation of the family magazines *Kingu* (King) and *Ie no hikari* (Light of the Home) specifically served to embed mechanisms of mass communication and socialization within Japanese society. These mechanisms, furthermore, had not previously existed and worked to facilitate a dissemination of hegemonic forms of discourse in Japan in the first half of the twentieth century. Rather than having been instigated by the inexorable march of capitalist progress, I argue, the evolution of media, advertising, and consumer culture in Japan could not have developed in the particular way it did without the ideological objectives of these dominant periodicals as a crucial driving force.

Magazines are worlds unto themselves; opening the pages of *Kingu*, for example, allowed Japanese in the 1920s and 1930s not only to enter the world that the magazine created but also to participate in the community of *Kingu* readers. *Ie no hikari*, as well, afforded the basis for a special membership for Japanese. This collective (transcending age, religion, education, location, and class) signified the birth of a new grouping altogether, different from simply being subjects of the Japanese empire; they were a modern Japanese mass: produced, managed, and commodified.

The creators of these magazines, Noma Seiji (with his subordinates at Kōdansha Publishing) for *Kingu* and key members at the Sangyō Kumiai (the Industrial Cooperative) for *Ie no hikari*, each aimed to instil their own beloved principles in the Japanese nation. This desire led to their independently creating a new category of cultural artefact for their conceptions of a mass audience, the "family magazine." Family magazines formed a novel category of consumption, moreover, one that transformed social practices around reading. The seeds of Japan's postwar love affair with consumption, the middle class, and Japanese exceptionalism grew from the soil of magazines where discourses about how and what Japanese should do, acquire, and think were omnipresent. Though the mission of these publishers was to unite an audience around a shared set of values, the unanticipated result was the creation of mechanisms for sustaining that audience (viz., the Japanese masses) and to induce them to be consumers. The content they were consuming may have shifted over the years, but the core identity of the audience did not.

These two magazines started from thoroughly dissimilar backgrounds and financial and distribution structures, but they overlapped in their ultimate goals and had since their inception. The magazines' editors hoped to help create an ideal Japan by providing a nationally unifying leisure and educational resource. Because the producers of these publications each had a particular vision, one in which all people in Greater Japan were participants, they each created mass magazines unified around their principles and ideals. One remarkable thing about this is that the production and circulation of meaning that these magazines embodied was also a defining feature of Japanese culture in these years.

So, what does one do, exactly, when reading magazines? It is in some ways a very bodily activity for those leafing through the bound paper pages, as reading magazines requires a certain amount of free time to sit, or stand, or lounge while resting the body and allowing the mind to engage in thoughts prompted by what is seen. Though the reader may not always be conscious of it, the content conveyed in the text of a magazine cannot be separated from the accompanying visual material – the pictures, comics, art, advertising, and graphic design – because, when he or she turns the pages of a magazine, all the elements are there together, to be perceived with the eye as smaller parts of an integrated whole.

As a leisure activity, magazines can also provide a group social activity with one person reading aloud while others around listen, comment, and discuss. We can easily imagine someone reading an article, or a portion of one, to those in the room, occasionally passing it around to share the illustrations or photos, while all chat about the topic at hand and how their individual ideas compare or contrast with those presented in their favourite monthly reading. Such behaviour was not imaginary, however, because this practice actually occurred throughout Japan in the mid-twentieth century through fan clubs, rallies, and workplace discussions in addition to the less documented social habits of communal reading in individual households or gatherings.

Thanks largely to the educational improvements of the Meiji government, most of the Japanese population was literate by the 1920s, but even those who couldn't read magazines like *Kingu* and *Ie no hikari* (elderly rural women, for example) would have been able to understand the content were someone to read the magazines aloud. Indeed, these magazines were written to be understood by everyone, and the practice of reading aloud (*ondoku*) persisted well beyond the maturation of the national educational system established by Meiji reforms. Even in a highly literate and textually rich society like Japan, reading aloud and the use of voice and oral communication in social reading practices impressively helped, rather than hindered, the spread of individual non-communal forms of reading as larger and larger portions of the Japanese population became fully literate.[4]

Mass media took its place within this established cultural practice of reading together, but also thereby altered the nature of those social interactions for the average Japanese. Investigating transformations in social practices surrounding reading shows that certain individual and family activities, although seemingly disconnected from centres of power and performed in locations scattered throughout the empire, actually served to reinforce participation in the nation. They, moreover, helped to foster a sense of belonging and inclusion within the

---

4 The work of Yamada Shunji is both under-referenced and highly illuminating on the topic on the topic of *ondoku*; see 山田, "文字文化としての音読と黙読 – 歴史の重層的な把握をめざして (Print Culture for Reading Aloud and Silent Reading – Towards a Multi-Layered Understanding of History)," 236–40. Yamada has, moreover, also done excellent work towards improving our understanding of the creation of modern newspapers in Japan in the late 1800s and early 1900s, as well as creating a framework for analysing letters to the editor and unravelling the intriguing relationship between readers and their favourite media and how newspapers were shared socially. 山田, 大衆新聞がつくる明治の〈日本〉 (*The Creation of "Japan" by Popular Meiji Newspapers*). On the topic of *ondoku*, many also cite the heavy influence of Ai, for one: Smith, "The History of the Book in Edo and Paris," 348–9; 前田, "音読から黙読へ (From Reading Aloud to Silent Reading)."

whole in a way that such practices had failed to do in any previous iteration.[5]

As a medium, magazines have the power to entertain, but also to model new ideas and attitudes about the world around the reader – one understands what is "normal" or "natural" both in ways that are immediately obvious and in others that are far more subtle.[6] When, with fellow readers, a person looks through the lens of magazines to view the world, they can see the same products, applaud characteristics, envision solutions to common problems, imagine possibilities for their world, and habituate themselves to daily activities and interactions. They are, in short, participating in a certain collective culture and meaning making that are partially created by their choice of leisure activities.

Increasingly over the first half of the twentieth century, whether they were farmers turning pages with hands rough and dry from planting and backs sore from the burden of carrying children or crops, or workers fatigued from labouring at a factory or in an office in a bustling urban centre, Japanese people were spending a greater portion of their leisure time engaging with magazines. By the late 1920s, *Kingu* and *Ie no hikari* had moved to the top of the popularity list.

It might be helpful to think about what a magazine is in greater detail and how it differs from other media. The English word derives from the French *magasin*, which originally had the meaning of a place to store goods (usually ammunition), but in the mid-1600s came to denote a place where collected information was stored, namely a serial publication. The first usage in English was the 1731 British publication named the *Gentleman's Magazine*. "Magazine" was translated into Japanese (雑誌 or *zasshi*, which literally means "miscellaneous records," pronounced roughly *zäh-shē*) in 1867 in the publication *Seiyō zasshi* from the francophone derivatives and thus refers to the same kind of serial periodic publications for leisure reading. *Zasshi* can also denote certain

---

5 And while further work could be done to investigate the exact nature of the dissemination of these publications into the furthest reaches of the Japanese imperium, my configuration supports discussions about supplemental forms of education where commercial products reinforced notions present in official forms of citizen/subject creation like textbooks, Imperial Rescripts, and the like. See Ruoff, *Imperial Japan at Its Zenith*; Young, *Japan's Total Empire*.

6 The ways in which this happened specifically for women is central to the work done by Sato (*Turning Pages*) and Frederick (*The New Japanese Woman*).

kinds of governmental bulletins and academic journals, but was and is generally used to mean periodicals for entertainment and general readership just as with the French and English terms.

This is not to say that Japanese magazines were based solely on Western models, though. Noma Seiji at Kōdansha, at least, was interested in the practices and profits of contemporaneous American publications and certainly was aware to some extent of how the magazine industry there progressed. Regardless, by the 1920s, the term was commonplace in Japan, and there were even different categories of magazines for readers to peruse: *sōgō zasshi* (general interest or cultural review magazines); *fujin zasshi* (women's magazines – a burgeoning category taking up an ever greater share of the market); *shōnen zasshi* (youth magazines); and so forth.[7]

In the case of newspapers (and prior early modern publications) that were so popular in the cities, the mass culture of these new family magazines is different from the sense of *Japaneseness* found in earlier years. In the years between the two world wars, for example, newspapers were regionally focused and decentralized in their content production, as opposed to magazines, which had a unitary (and thus unifying) content production team for the entire nation. Similarly, newspapers were simply not marketed in the way magazines were and failed to enter the same niche of "useful entertainment." This is not to say that newspapers were not read widely; they were, but the market was able to sustain both types of periodicals.

The creators of both *Kingu* and *Ie no hikari* had conversations about these very categories for magazines and sought to mould one, the category of *katei zasshi* (family magazine), to their ends. Their aims were grand. While there had been magazines that could be categorized as family magazines before the 1920s, the targets of such publications were elite families in mainly urban settings. Those at the Sangyō Kumiai and in Noma's employ each drafted a magazine that was explicitly *not* a women's magazine, nor a children's magazine, nor even a general interest magazine, but one that incorporated aspects of all of those and offered a new formulation with things for the entire family (as they envisioned it) within its pages. This was the innovative *family magazine*.

---

7 Early modern counterparts – journals for elite readers, for example – did exist. For details on some of these publications, see Berry, *Japan in Print*.

The reason these magazine editors were so obsessed with creating a successful formula with broad interest for the style and content of their magazines was understandable. Wider appeal equalled greater circulation numbers; with greater circulation comes greater influence and revenue. They therefore sought to attract readers of all ages, educational backgrounds, and social standings.

At the Kumiai, for example, the argument was made that other general interest magazines available in the early 1920s had no articles on the home or agriculture. Women's magazines had articles on the home, but it was an upper-class urban home they had in mind. Much of the Japanese population was still rural in the middle of the twentieth century and only a relative few could have been considered middle class, despite growing perceptions that that demographic was expanding. Publications for male farmers had no content about the home or leisure, even though farmers were increasingly curious about and enticed by urban entertainments. Further, youth publications were so specifically aimed at children that adults would not find much to stimulate their interest.

Each of those individual types of magazine was selling for an average of fifty sen an issue. One hundred sen is equal to one yen, and in 1925 you could get a bottle of beer for about forty sen, a bowl of *udon* for ten, a coffee for five, and a pack of cigarettes for about twelve.[8] Since far less than half the population at that time could afford more expensive newspaper subscriptions either, no average family could manage to purchase multiple magazines, one for each member of the household, because the total cost was prohibitive: more than one yen per month for just two publications.

"Markets are shaped, not discovered," after all, and this is exactly what happened in Japan.[9] Noma himself stated,

Once I heard the story of an American publisher … who was getting out a million copies of one magazine, and I said to myself that there was no reason why we could not do the same in Japan. It was my starting point, and was with me a strong faith, a conviction, and now I have the satisfaction of knowing that the Japanese have an inexhaustible capacity for reading magazines, a capacity which can yet be exploited. Once upon a time,

8 奥原, 家の光の二十五年 (*Twenty-Five Years of "Light of the Home"*), 28, 30.
9 Ohmann, *Selling Culture*, 91.

reading was a task, a study, the pastime of the highly educated; that they should read for amusement, or as a means to make up for lack of a regular education, did not occur to the general public. One reason was that there were no popular magazines edited for those purposes, and if there were, they were not advertised enough. In a country like Japan, where, thanks to our kana, even coolies and other uneducated folk can read to some extent, it was obvious that we could make them read magazines, if only they were interesting enough, and were advertised enough.[10]

Several of the points Noma makes here are worth highlighting. First is the argument that Japanese could be persuaded to consume magazines in greater numbers than in the past, but needed to be convinced to do so. Second, both *Kingu* and *Ie no hikari* included pronunciation guides (also known as *rubi* or *furigana*) on all *kanji* (Chinese characters used to write Japanese) to help those who were only partially literate. This meant that these producers greatly expanded the number of people who could access and understand their magazines by including *kana* (phonemes in the Japanese syllabary serving as glosses for vernacular pronunciation) that even the most uneducated Japanese would have known.[11] And finally, the content of the magazines mattered both because it could attract a new audience and because it could be entertaining *and* educational. Consequently, the Kumiai and Kōdansha editors deliberately *created* a mass market for their magazines and in so doing, arguably, helped to create mass Japanese culture.

With this kind of ambition in mind, *Kingu* had a massive ad campaign in late 1924 (in anticipation of the release of the first issue) that touted that "one issue per household" was all the family needed for their entertainment.[12] This slogan was based on Noma's profound confidence that he could provide everyone with something interesting and beneficial.[13]

---

10 Akimoto, *Seiji Noma "Magazine King" of Japan*, 9–10. For a definition of *kana*, see below.

11 For a more thorough discussion of the history of *rubi* and their use in Japanese literature, see Ariga, "The Playful Gloss." For a discussion of *kana* glosses in early modern publications, see Rubinger, *Popular Literacy in Early Modern Japan*, 89.

12 永嶺, 雑誌と読者の近代 (*Modern Magazines and Readers*), 223.

13 This is also apparently still the line of thought at Kōdansha, as their homepages (both English and Japanese) make mention of Noma and this philosophy. See "講談社「おもしろくて･ためになる」出版を"; 講談社 (Kodansha Ltd), "Home Page."

Further, those at *Ie no hikari* heatedly debated how much to charge for their magazine before settling on twenty sen an issue, which was less than every other general interest magazine on the market at the time, including *Kingu*, which sold for fifty sen like most other monthlies. Reading through scores of issues of *Kingu* and *Ie no hikari* makes it clear that there was indeed entertainment for everyone, with sections for children, on the home, various kinds of fiction, and *manga* (comics). But the content was tailored for each target demographic in a subtler version of the way Henry Ford could make a person buy a car in any colour – so long as it was black.

The values and ideals that were dear to the publishers heavily coloured the content offered in the decades that these two magazines were published. A certain vision of Japan was created serially in the pages of every issue, just as stories unfolded in the episodic fiction. This vision helped to foster a cultural environment, for example in wartime Japan, that dovetailed easily with state-sponsored shifts towards insularity and national jingoism.

While mother could find something to hold her interest in *Kingu*, she was being guided into viewing her world as one that conformed, for instance, to notions of gender roles that increasingly limited her options. Sons and daughters could find entertainment in *Ie no hikari*, but in ways that, say, encouraged obedience to ideals that restricted what was possible. Father would enjoy each month's issue, while, to give one example, he became normalized to discussions about ideologically charged political issues that concluded in unswerving support of the state, in part through his labour. Similar to Adorno's description, "something is provided for all so that none may escape," Japanese family magazines tied the family together collectively and all-inclusively.[14]

The creators of these publications understood that with such wide exposure came profound influence. Particularly, even with the first cover of *Ie no hikari*, the Sangyō Kumiai explicitly discussed the appropriateness of the proposed articles and accompanying cover image because they were aware of the influence they could have over their audience in terms of ideals and desires, not just in the content but also in the imagery. Similar discussions occurred with the editors at *Kingu* about the look and style the magazine wanted to project. This means that they both, though independently, were aware of their power to

---

14 Horkheimer and Adorno, "The Culture Industry," 5.

communicate, through images and text, with the audience they had cultivated.

No matter how successful these magazine producers were at achieving their respective objectives, however, this study hopes to highlight the *unanticipated* results of their missions. In the Japanese context, the work of scholars like John Dower and Alan Tansman does much to show how ideology, no matter how all-encompassing or homogenizing it seems, is, in actuality, extremely malleable. Put another way, "the ideological underpinnings of inculcation were kept abstract enough to be flexible,"[15] and because of this, the most important legacy of these magazines is expressly *not* any particular ideology contained in their pages but, rather, the *mechanisms* for creating a mass consumer audience and communicating with that audience instead.

That being said, while the medium is the focus of this study, the message does have captivating examples for us as well. What was it exactly these publishers were trying to convey? What were the meanings circulating in interwar Japan?

The Message

Sangyō Kumiai Central Committee members, like Shimura Gentarō and Arimoto Hideo, who spearheaded the drafting of *Ie no hikari* hoped to bolster the self-esteem and productivity of farming communities, and to see the reinvigoration of rural homes and the self-actualization of farmers, by promoting self-help, cooperation, revitalization, and rationalization of everyday life. They sought to improve the quality of life for all Japanese by starting with those they viewed as the backbone of society – farming villages and homes. The editors of the magazine imagined a Japan that had the capacity to transform itself through changes in social practices.

Noma Seiji and those at Kōdansha wanted to assist in the development of their Japanese compatriots, but instead of focusing on the farms they focused on individual subjects anywhere in the empire as an essential part of the whole. They did this by promoting filial piety, sincerity, perseverance, and personal success through ambition and initiative, in line with the *risshin shusse* ("rising in the world," or more

---

15 In this passage Tansman is referring to fascist Japanese ideologues ("Introduction," 11); Dower, *War without Mercy*.

loosely "social mobility") ideas that were circulating at the time. *Kingu* offered a dream of a Japan comprised distinctively of confident, competent citizen-subjects who could be proud of their heritage in the world community.

Both magazines sought to provide entertaining, enriching, educational material for the readers in an appealing format perfect for leisure-time consumption. All this would be intriguing enough, but their underlying values also remarkably and unambiguously supported the nation-state.

In an article in the first issue of *Kingu*, the reader was told that the result of the editors' work "is not just the production of a mere commodity, allowing benefits to the consumer, but it is a relief, an encouragement, and a cultural development, which carries out its mission based on an intense consciousness of the nation"; it was "not like soap or face powder and other such products," it was "food for the soul."[16] This is a profoundly charged statement that draws our attention to the complicated relationship between the producers of a mass cultural product, with particular conceptions of their goals and beliefs, and those who consume it. The statement reinforces the idea that magazines are not like other commodities on the market, but can hold a special place within society as cultural conduits.

Noma himself, when pressed in an interview in the late 1920s to articulate his mission, said:

> In one word, it is to make Japan great ... Without being able to say why, I believe in the doctrine of Greater Japan. It is the first duty of every Japanese, I think, to become a great man in whatsoever his calling lies, and thereby contribute to the greatness of his country ... A great Japanese is he who burns with ambition – the ambition to serve the Emperor and his country; is perfect in morals, that is, filial to parents, loyal to the Emperor, faithful to friends, honest in work, strong in will, and valorous in fighting. You see nothing new in all this! But that is the dominating principle of my heart in regard to my magazines. Take any of my nine magazines, and scan the thousands of their pages, and you will not find a page given over to mean stories which contradict this principle.[17]

16 「キング」編輯局同人, "『キング』が世に出るまでの苦心 (The Agony Until *King* Appeared)," 280.
17 Akimoto, *Seiji Noma "Magazine King" of Japan*, 11–12.

Even if we admit that this statement must be viewed with a certain degree of scepticism due to its self-aggrandizing nature, such a public statement about the overtly idealized and value-laden focus of the magazines cannot simply be ignored either. Noma thought he was providing a moral service for the benefit of Japan, promoting filial piety, honesty, faithfulness, loyalty, strength, and valour. This was a momentous mission and one that was pursued with dedication and vigour.

Similarly, in the first issue of *Light of the Home*, an article titled "Light of the Home, Light of the Nation" unequivocally voices analogous themes:

> ... soon *Light of the Home* will be the light of the village and also the light of the nation. Thus, in politics and the economy we also shoulder the responsibility of our seventy million compatriots along with that of the destiny of Greater Japan, in order to be able to stand competitive in the world arena.[18]

The editors' conceptions of what it meant to create and distribute magazines involved a desire to shape the population to help realize a new, improved, modern Japan. Moreover, they saw this as a possibility specifically because an ideal Japan originated in *cultural* development.

The magazines resulting from these aspirations made it possible to reach hitherto unheard-of numbers of people within the Japanese empire and exert a profound influence over the discourse present in mainstream society.[19] The naturalization and internalization of the images and values present in the media are part and parcel of mass

---

18 Here the figure given for the population of Japan is inaccurate; since the statistics for the Japanese islands proper are estimated at around sixty million in 1925, with the colonies included the total would be more like eighty-four million. 岡, "家の光、国の光 (Light of the Home, Light of the Nation)," 25.

19 Though it is not central to my argument here, let me explain briefly what I mean by discourse. Timothy Burke's discussion of discourse has influenced my understanding, specifically where he says: "The concept of 'discourse' as derived from Foucault and similar theorists is powerful only as long as scholars insist that it means more than a particular form of talk or a particular assemblage of tropes, narratives, and texts. A discourse is talk that works through particular institutional arrangements of power and knowledge, that circulates and organizes conversations between specific producers and audiences, that relies on specific conventions for establishing authority. And in so doing, a discourse produces the effects of power within the self, as a form of discipline" (*Lifebuoy Men, Lux Women*, 31).

culture, especially in the transwar era of Japan. Actual lives, individual selves, were changed and re-habituated by the content of these magazines and largely regardless of the audience members' individual wills. Unravelling the ideological content of the magazines, therefore, is essential to understanding popular discourses about society and the individual's place within it.

One issue that concerns me, as should by now be clear, is how culture was produced and consumed in the transwar years, but I also want to make the point that, for the audience, consumption was about content. Readers didn't buy magazines because it was the modern thing to do, for example. They bought magazines, issue after issue, month after month, because of what was in them and, as the years progressed, for the cultural capital they could provide. Readers cared about the content of those magazines; and to some extent, so should we.

The content of magazines – in the Japanese case primarily through the messages of *Ie no hikari* and *Kingu* – when consumed by most of the populace can shift the norms of society, especially on issues that are new or developing. This is in part how we can explain the popular support of the growing militarization of Japan over the course of the 1930s and 1940s that has been discussed on a political and ideological level by scholars like Louise Young, John Dower, and others.[20] What magazines helped to provide was a layer in a system which, at the institutional level, was working towards mass mobilization by the state and military, but that nonetheless was working in complete harmony with the parallel expansions of new forms of consumerism signified by publications like *Kingu* and *Ie no hikari*. But at a more fundamental level, magazines made it possible to make and then sell culture itself.[21]

---

20 See Young, *Japan's Total Empire*; Silberman, Harootunian, and Bernstein, *Japan in Crisis*; Dower and Harvard University Council on East Asian Studies, *Empire and Aftermath*; Davidann, *Cultural Diplomacy in U.S.–Japanese Relations, 1919–1941*.

21 Richard Ohmann has something useful to say along these lines: "I suggest that ideology in the narrower sense, as spun out in the pages of the magazines, was of less moment than ideology in the expanded sense, as embedded in the production and consumption of magazines ... in reestablishing the social order on a somewhat different basis, ideology at other levels seems to me to have done more decisive political work. One example is the incorporation of culture ... More important, I think, is that the change *naturalized* cultural production as itself big business" (*Selling Culture*, 347).

The everyday practices of Japanese people were altered irreversibly because of the development of mass culture. At the simplest level, this is evidenced by the fact that suddenly millions of Japanese were collectively consuming magazines when they had not done so before. The massification of Japan began during the interwar years and it started with the magazines under analysis here. While the culture industry that exists today – with television, film, marketing firms, social media, etc. – has taken the humble beginnings of mass culture to new heights (or depths, depending on one's ideological leanings), one cannot understand the progression of something until we understand its origins. Not, obviously, because the birth of a thing sufficiently explains what it grows into, but rather because, without the particular origins of magazines, mass culture in Japan would likely look quite different today.

The Masses

These publishers had seen universal male suffrage granted in 1924 as one example of how the "public" could be expanded, and they raised the stakes yet higher. *Ie no hikari* and *Kingu* were not *popularizing*, in the sense of making something elite or uncommon palatable for a larger population, as had been the case for publishers of the early modern period (generally construed as ranging from 1603 to 1868). They were interested in *massifying* their audience, i.e., making the whole empire their audience, and the conduits they employed were their magazines. It was unambiguously the vast multitude of the population, all demographics included, as consumers, on which their aspirations focused. These magazines created a shared experience for the overwhelming majority of Japan's people in a way that is expressly conducive to the fantasy of unity and harmony in the face of a frightening modernity.[22]

The massification of Japan provided powerful and comforting commonalities that allowed the audience to persist through the transwar years, though many likely did not remember how it had happened if they had ever been aware of it to begin with. In some ways, this configuration of mass serves to cannibalize class (i.e., in the Marxist sense of class) in

---

22 As Alan Tansman parses it, "the 'core myth' of fascism provides the possibility for an experience of immediacy and unity that counters the alienation and fragmentation of the modern individual" ("Introduction," 6). See also Harootunian, *Overcome by Modernity*.

that it promotes harmony and unanimity for the sake of the nation that minimize or erase difference and thus – in theory, if not in actuality – eradicate class antagonism. A mass audience conceals inequity, dissent, and radical possibilities for alternatives. In addition, *mass* highlights this exact kind of obliviousness. When the world is smoothed over and made artificially whole, in the way these publications construed it, difference, discontent, and disparity are flattened as well.

Defining the family as these magazines did meant that a great number of people were obscured or forgotten. And while ethnic minorities like Okinawans (from the southern Japanese islands once part of the Ryūkyū Kingdom) and Ainu (indigenous peoples from Hokkaidō and northward) were occasionally represented or discussed in blandly unobjectionable ways in these publications, homosexuals and lesbians, for example, most certainly were not. Likewise, *burakumin* (those historically considered to be Japanese outcasts), orphans, the mentally ill, and other disenfranchised groups continued to be marginalized by the attempts to create a socially acceptable audience of "everyone" in the heteronormative family to which these "family magazines" could be sold. Thus, the desire of these publishers to create an audience that helped alleviate the perceived traumas of the modern age through cultural development certainly fitted within the political moves to mobilize Japanese behind the unquestioning collective support of Japan, as either empire or nation.

These magazines were situated centrally in a cumulative shift that affected everyone in Japanese society. The fact that so many people from all over Japan and its colonies and Japanese enclaves of any appreciable size abroad were participating in the reading of these magazines makes them undeniably important products for understanding these years. This is also not to suggest that there was no sense of *nation* before the 1920s, but it is really the newness of *mass* that is significant. The sense of being Japanese due to increasing domestic travel and a growing sense of a shared "Japaneseness" that may have existed as early as the latter years of the Tokugawa era was something different from the mass national culture that developed during the years preceding the Pacific War and that thrived over the transwar span.

Each month consumers of *Kingu* or *Ie no hikari* perused the newest issue of the identical magazine – in Sapporo, Tokyo, Okinawa, Los Angeles, Taipei, and Seoul. The process of creating citizens within the modern nation-state, whereby members came to see themselves as being a part of a larger, explicitly national, culture specifically through a sense of time that is shared, a common language standardized for understandability, an interconnection of all regions of the empire physically and culturally, and a conceptualization of the self in terms of one's relationship to the nation all were facilitated in Japan by the practice of consuming magazines.[23] *Ie no hikari* and *Kingu* participated in the creation of this simultaneity by authoring "a sequence of intense present moments, each filled with a number of noteworthy persons and events about which 'everyone' knows," thereby drawing their audiences into a world of and by the magazines.[24]

Those like Noma Seiji at Kōdansha and the Central Committee members of the Sangyō Kumiai associated with *Ie no hikari*, like Shimura Gentarō, Arimoto Hideo, and Hirada Tōsuke, were educated individuals who saw themselves as distinct from their audience and who worked to produce magazines to vend to the people "out there" in Greater Japan. While intriguing complications to this picture arose (in cases like that of reader-submitted content, to name an example addressed more fully in a subsequent chapter), for the most part *Kingu* and *Ie no hikari* were produced by people personally unacquainted with and removed from their audiences.

These producers independently realized that the old target of the publishing world in the late nineteenth century was no longer the most relevant audience. Those at Kōdansha comprehended this and were truthfully able to claim that they could "make subscribers out of those who were not previously reading magazines."[25] Far more of the population was aware of and engaging with these magazines by the end of the 1930s than was not; and Japanese were participating in the community those periodicals had helped to create, the masses. Combining the audience of *Kingu* with that of *Ie no hikari* equals the masses of Japan.

The consumption of these magazines and the cultural interactions that occurred around them also happened in a *social* context, an environment that was frequently reinforced through non-official support by governmental and private institutions (in barracks, schools, hospitals, and large companies). Group activities, like the reader rallies, fan

---

23 The processes of citizen building has received a good deal of attention. See Anderson, *Imagined Communities*; Fujitani, *Splendid Monarchy*; Gluck, *Japan's Modern Myths*; Schivelbusch, *The Railway Journey*; Weber, *Peasants into Frenchmen*.
24 Ohmann, *Selling Culture*, 15.
25 社史編纂委員会 (Committee for the Compilation of the Company History), 講談社の歩んだ五十年 (*The Path of Kōdansha's First Fifty Years*), 666.

clubs, and reading aloud that focused on *Kingu* and *Ie no hikari*, fuelled the creation of a shared culture specifically linked to the consumption of these media. The audience for these publications was comprised of consumers who also fitted neatly into the Japanese empire, as Miriam Silverberg's concept of the consumer-subject so compactly evokes, and as Nagamine Shigetoshi reiterates:

> it cannot be said that each of one million readers of *Kingu* among the read-ing "multitude" for mass magazines was reading by themselves alone as an atomized audience. Rather, *Kingu* had a strong current of collective recep-tion that featured a sense of community. Among the young, the military, in schools and at the office it bound cohorts together; *Kingu* was read collec-tively. *Kingu* was not only for the isolated urban worker reading alone into the night. At times it was the family reading together for entertainment, at times the text used by fan clubs of youths, then again it was the only magazine widely accepted in the military; *Kingu* was a medium that also served the role of binding the office together. It was widely used and read as a collective, communal influence. This was an important factor in the construction of *Kingu*.[26]

These magazines brought people together and changed how they spent that time together. The collective nature of the reception of these periodicals is central to the making of the masses; the audience included those from all points of the empire of any age. *Kingu* and *Ie no hikari* became successful enough, moreover, to provide models for other mass media that followed.

The audience that these magazines created was new. Prior to the 1920s and 1930s, it would be difficult if not impossible to find such a demographic or the attendant social and cultural practices that arose around it.[27] The producers of *Kingu* and *Ie no hikari* were able to envi-sion who the *masses* might be. This mass, furthermore, is contained in a conversation quite distinct from that concerning "high and low" culture commonly associated with literary and artistic production. The concern here is explicitly not about "low" as opposed to "high" culture,

---

26 永嶺, 雑誌と読者の近代 (*Modern Magazines and Readers*), 238–9.
27 The closest thing that could be said to have borne any resemblance would be the precursor to the Japanese masses embodied by the public of the early modern period as configured by Mary Elizabeth Berry; see *Japan in Print*.

but rather the genesis of mass culture itself, which encompassed both to some extent within the world of Japanese magazines.[28] Through the imagined audience, a *mass* was fashioned in reality; this group of people was merged together by the producers of these magazines from the various sectors which embraced the overwhelming majority of the population of Japan and its imperium. Kōdansha and the Kumiai were fixated on an audience that included *everyone*, bridging age, gender, class, occupation, location, and education.

To provide more concrete figures about this Japanese audience, *Ie no hikari*'s circulation was quite extensive with subscriptions from all prefectures of Japan, including 19,320 subscriptions even in remote northern Hokkaidō in 1937, for example. Between 1932 and 1935 there was a nearly fourfold increase in the number of households receiving *Ie no hikari*, whose total subscription rates were higher than those of any other magazine of the period, crossing the million mark in 1937. To contextualize, that same year the second most popular magazine was *Shufu no tomo* (Housewife's Friend) with 850,000 issues sold.[29]

Another issue that surfaces in the discussion of magazines (and some other forms of print media from these years) in the face of such statistics is that circulation numbers present some problems. First, it is generally recognized that circulation figures were commonly kept secret by the publishing houses and not regularly advertised in any public forum. Setting this difficulty aside for the moment, the larger issue at hand stems from *how* these magazines circulated among the Japanese populace. Publications like *Ie no hikari* and *Kingu*, more often than not, were consumed in group settings; thus, even accurate circulation statistics would be only a small percentage of the actual number of people who were exposed to their content.

To illustrate why this point bears elaboration: circulation figures would generally (when they can be had at all) list numbers of

---

28 One scholar traces the creation of categories of culture at the turn of the twentieth century and the ends to which these divisions were used in the American context: "because the primary categories of culture have been the products of ideologies which were always subject to modifications and transformations, the perimeters of our cultural divisions have been permeable and shifting rather than fixed and immutable" (Levine, *Highbrow/Lowbrow*, 8).

29 板垣, 昭和戦前・戦中期の農村生活 (*Rural Life in Showa during and after the War*), ii–iii, 55; 北村, 家の光の四十年 (*Forty Years of "Light of the Home"*), 34–5; 北村, 家の光六十年史 (*The Sixty-Year History of "Ie No Hikari"*), 39.

subscribing households (in the case of *Ie no hikari*) or single copies sold in urban markets (for magazines like *Kingu* or, say, *Shufu no tomo*). However, for every household subscription or individual issue sold, more than one person would "consume" the publication. When figures count households or issues, one could reasonably multiply that number by a factor of at least five, but perhaps upwards to ten, to approximate the actual number of *people* who saw each issue. When each of the members of a household would share in the consumption of a magazine, counting the impact of a publication based on figures that only concern who shelled out the money to purchase it fails to fully encapsulate the enormity of the magazine's impact.

The creation of this mass is remarkable enough, but the fact that those who worked to forge this demographic also saw themselves as the disseminators of values which could lead to the cultural development and advancement of the Japanese empire is exceedingly significant. Since these magazines were consumed by so many Japanese, anyone who wants to understand the discourses available to the masses would be well served by paging through these publications. To put this in more explicitly cultural terms: *Kingu* and *Ie no hikari* were some of the largest meaning makers in Japan. Those at the Kumiai and Kōdansha were explicitly self-aware of their magazines as conveyors of values. In the first issue of *Kingu*, the editors said:

> *King* is a godsend of mental nourishment for our seventy million citizens. This is not a property to be neglected on even one page, or in one line. In the same way that Rai Sanyō [1780–1832, author of *Nihon gaishi* (Unofficial History of Japan)][,] grasping the shoot of a brush in hand[,] had a powerful influence on the world[,] we firmly believe that our present job in the world for good or evil is to have this awakening influence too.[30]

It would be difficult indeed to deny that the editors of these magazines were aware of or interested in the influence they could have over their audience.

This process is, furthermore, about opting in and voluntary participation rather than about brainwashing, cooptation, or suasion. Japanese

---

30 「キング」編輯局同人, "『キング』が世に出るまでの苦心 (The Agony Until *King* Appeared)," 280. For more on Rai Sanyō, see De Bary, *Sources of East Asian Tradition*, 2:322–5.

people in the transwar years generally had the ability to choose how to spend their leisure time and they were roped into spending it differently, collectively.

Concluding Thoughts

People did not *have* to read magazines; rather, they *chose* to do so. In many cases they chose to read magazines instead of partaking in some other form of entertainment or leisure. Even if this choice was one that was restricted by the peculiarities of the market and other factors that determined what choices were available to an individual, it was nonetheless a decision made by people to spend their time and money in a particular way. Too many people in Japan during the years before, during, and after the Pacific War *chose* to consume these magazines for us to assume that they were in complete opposition to the content therein.

In the middle decades of the twentieth century, radio, film, newspapers, novels, festivals, sumo, kimono, sushi, and theatre all failed to achieve what magazines did in terms of cultural significance and the power to create an audience or modify social practice, though these practices did conglomerate and reinforce each other. Media interactions and the milieu of an increasingly complex and diverse set of media options over the course of the twentieth century were certainly present in Japan as elsewhere in the world.

These magazines had a gravitational pull – a power to draw the audience into their world. Instead of employing *wakon yōsai* (Japanese spirituality, Western technology) as Meiji-era nationalists did to bolster support for Westernization, modernization, and militarization more generally, these magazine publishers used a kind of "Japanese spirit, cultural technology" to rally their readers into a mass audience. When *Ie no hikari* managed to capture the hearts and mind of the rural population by centring itself on the specifically rural home, and when *Kingu* wooed the Japanese family in both urban and rural settings, a truly novel category of commodity was created. And it flourished. Since the previous focus of the publishing industry at large centred in and on urban areas, *Kingu* and then *Ie no hikari* became flagships for a new form of entertainment in these transitional years. This is most assuredly *not* to say that other forms of cultural production are valueless topics of study, or that they did not contribute to mass culture in their own ways; but to understand how mass culture was formed and the significance of its mechanisms we must look to the magazines, and *Kingu* and *Ie no hikari* in particular.

Chapter Two

The Splendid Power of Being in Perfect Harmony: How Two Publishers Made a Mass Japanese Audience

Literary production has been central to elite Japanese culture since the introduction of writing forms via Chinese intermediaries around the fifth century. The way in which written and (much later) printed texts circulated both physically and culturally among various audiences has changed throughout the long centuries of their presence in Japan and bears a brief survey here.

Historical Background

Buddhism made its way into Japan via Korea and China in the seventh century, originally being adopted among the nobility. But during and after the classical period, the general trend moved from obscure, elite, esoteric forms of Buddhism to ones that opened to more people through easier praxis, like the study of mandalas, ritual hand gestures, and meditation, which was not limited to monks and did not require any degree of literacy, wealth, or social standing. Copied for monks, nuns, and lay people alike, Buddhist sutras and texts expanded popular access to practices and understandings of the world through religion. Initially prompted by the spread of texts from the Asian continent, enlightenment and freedom from suffering became available to an ever-widening portion of the population. These practices show a major transformation over time in the relationship of Japanese Buddhism to its audience, but also worked to transform ideas about human nature and reality among elites in cultural and population centres as well as among commoners spread throughout Japan. This process connected print culture to religious practices and beliefs in lasting ways.

Throughout centuries of elite literacy in Japan, various forms of nonreligious writing existed in print form as well. Amidst the flourishing of elite literature and poetry in the classical era from the eighth to the twelfth centuries, for example, the *Genji monogatari* (*The Tale of Genji*), written by Murasaki Shikibu in the vernacular syllabary (*onnate*; lit. "woman's hand") and popular among courtly women of the time, is among the world's first novels. This type of literature created a shared sense of aesthetics and ideals by spreading courtly norms outward to a diffuse population of nobles. This genteel literature was replaced in popularity by war tales, such as the *Hōgen monogatari*, *Heiji monogatari*, and the most widely performed *Heike monogatari* (Tales of the Hōgen, Heiji, and Heike, respectively). These epics heralded the prowess and plights of the military class of samurai, who originated as retainers in the provinces, removed from the courtly life in the imperial capital, and helped this class define its own identity, aesthetics, and values as it rose to prominence and eventually wrested political control of the entire country from the hands of the imperial institution.

The peace of the Tokugawa shogunate (1600–1867) saw several new kinds of writing and expanded options for producing, printing, and distributing those materials. These early modern advances and innovations among publishers allowed for the creation of a popular audience, far broader than any that had existed before, that was profoundly tethered to notions about being Japanese – in terms of "us," "our people," "everybody." Created specifically for this audience, the gazetteers and guides, encyclopedias and excerpted travelogues, focused on novelty through the investigation of everyday life and regional variation. They addressed their imagined (later fully realized) audience collectively in friendly, intimate, and useful ways, shifting social identities and business practices in the process. "Making society visible to itself, they conspired in the making of society," as Mary Elizabeth Berry eloquently elucidates. The industry and its audience were unexpectedly created, in part, because of the government's refusal to share its extensive information with the population at large; so as public thirst for knowledge about roads, travel, lodging, etc., grew, commercial publishers stepped in to fill the role that the Shogunate failed to satisfy. Since the publishers did not question the legitimacy of power structures, or other aspects of officialdom itself, the state took no offence at their activities, even though, in actual fact, the publishers undermined the stability of the shogun's system: "in exploring the reaches of social activity for this audience, writers and publishers not only obscured the primacy of the polity but disturbed its values." These texts – about travel, sightseeing, food, humour, souvenirs, entertainers, and cartography – circulated widely, thanks to a new *public* that valued cultural literacy or "common sense" above class distinctions, and the commercial publishing industry gratified its new audience by educating and entertaining them as it simultaneously reinforced "an economic system of value."[1] This sophisticated yet subtle decentring and devaluing of the state in the popular early modern audience is reproduced with the creation of a Japanese *mass* audience as well.

There had been common publications aimed directly at farmers, the largest sector of the population, in the early modern period, referred to generally as *nōsho*. *Nōsho* can best be defined as "the generic term for books, tracts, diaries, prose-poems, chronicles, memoranda, and catalogues dealing with agricultural and rural affairs," which were written to be accessible and based upon notions about practical learning (*jitsugaku*).[2] Farm manual titles numbered in the hundreds by the 1700s and were ordinarily illustrated extensively. These volumes were confined to practical agricultural matters in terms of both conception and content. *Nōsho* were primers and guides not meant to delight and entertain, though they also contributed to the expansion of literacy in rural areas well before the twentieth century.[3]

By the 1920s amidst the literati of Japan, there was a flourishing of production and experiments in new forms and modes of artistic writing. The so-called I novels important to writers like Shiga Naoya and others of the White Birch School (*Shirakaba*) held sway among literati of the time. Natsume Sōseki, Kikuchi Kan, Tanizaki Junichirō, Nagai Kafū, and Akutagawa Ryūnosuke are among the best-known writers from the Taishō years, many of whom have since been translated and read around the world, in addition to their large domestic exposure and popularity during their (sometimes brief) lifetimes. Novels of the time addressed the widest range of themes: from dissatisfaction with modernity, civilization, and enlightenment; to yearning for genuine love and connection with other humans, however difficult that task might have been perceived to be; through erotic, grotesque, and bizarre explorations of darker aspects of the psyche; past comedic or existentialist critiques of class struggle and division; and on to many varieties of more straightforward historical, romantic, and hero tales that had been popular in earlier years. Many authors benefited from the increased demands from publishers for materials, and stories were often serialized in larger newspapers.

---

1 Berry, *Japan in Print*, 17–18, 208–12.
2 Robertson, "Sexy Rice," 233; Rubinger, *Popular Literacy in Early Modern Japan*, 88.
3 Rubinger, *Popular Literacy in Early Modern Japan*, 89–90.

Regional newspapers also existed in many areas of Japan, with small readerships in each prefecture, as did the "national" dailies centred in Tokyo and Osaka. Indeed, studies suggest trends in the 1920s of growing class diversity in newspaper readerships in the cities as larger numbers of workers and less educated folk were choosing to buy and read the dailies.[4] These publications were widely read in urban areas. However, as John Embree explains about the village he studied in Kumamoto, even by 1935–6 "the newspaper has come to the *mura* [village] of recent years and is subscribed to by about one household in ten. It is delivered by a boy from a magazine shop in Menda. More households subscribe to the National Agricultural Association magazine, *Ie no hikari*, than to a newspaper." He goes on to add that "the women's magazines, such as *Fuji* and *Shufunotomo* [Housewife's Companion], so much read in urban Japan, have very few subscribers on the farm."[5] By the 1930s, then, rural areas showed some disparity in their level of participation with urban media like newspapers.

Although no single newspaper could compare to individual magazines' circulations, newspapers had collectively reached a very large sector of the populace. James Huffman details the rise of newspapers in Japan from the Meiji years forward, saying, "the newspapers, in other words, turned people into citizens; the people turned the papers into mass media." However, there is a problem with asserting that something is mass when "the people" is restricted mostly to (middle-class) men in urban areas, and mainly those in Tokyo at that.[6]

Newspapers that were available to farming communities had editorial agendas simply less interested in the reimagining of Japanese society than magazines and their producers were. This was the case even if newspapers were inducing a nested identity of the farm community

---

4   I am thankful to Andrew Gordon for clarifying my understanding about the class breakdown of urban readership and refreshing my memory about the work of Yamamoto Taketoshi. For statistically rich work that breaks down the increasing numbers of workers, women, and the unschooled who were reading various newspapers in Tokyo and Osaka, see 山本, 近代日本の新聞読者層 (*Newspaper Readers of Modern Japan*).

5   Embree, *Suye Mura, A Japanese Village*, 76.

6   Huffman's work is otherwise careful and thorough. He notes that even the largest dailies had numbers of about 150,000 at the turn of the century, and in 1915 only one publication topped 300,000 (*Creating a Public*, 4, 9, 228, 387).

as a part of Japan and its empire.[7] In contrast, mass family magazines provided a homogenous content across the *entire country*, in both urban and rural areas.

The "family magazine" (*katei zasshi*) category that *Kingu* and *Ie no hikari* reengineered had been in existence since the turn of the century. In 1903, publications like *Katei no tomo* (The Family's Friend) and *Katei zasshi* (Family Magazine) were released and followed by *Fujo shinbun* (Women's Newspaper) in 1905 and *Fujin sekai* (Women's World) in 1906, which all had at least sections related to the household and its management. Even *Chūō kōron* (Central Review, a well-known intellectual journal) began a household column in 1905. But these titles, just as with other well-known publications like *Taiyō* (The Sun), left far more people out of their audiences than they included, due to the price and content of those publications; those excluded were predominantly the uneducated, the poor, and the rural. As Mark Jones notes: "early twentieth-century print culture functioned to exclude as much as to include."[8] These publications and their content were, thus, limited in their conception of the "household" and focused on women in middle- and upper-class families in urban areas, who comprised a small sliver of the Japanese population.

After its introduction in March of 1925, radio reached a relatively small audience, was heavily censored, had no advertising, and simply cost too much (in terms of equipment and subscription fees) during this period to become a common household good. But, while radio was a limited enterprise in the interwar years, popular music and the debates that arose around it did help to define middle-class values and reflected broader political changes in the pre- and postwar years.[9] Film, similarly, was not available enough in rural regions to become a mass medium until the postwar years, when it grew to be profoundly influential.[10]

---

7 A future study would do well to address the complicated interaction and cross-promotion of the various forms of media in these years, and particularly the vast variety and number of small regional papers in Japan.

8 Jones, *Children as Treasures*, 44, 57, 142.

9 For an insightful investigation of the discourses on popular music and vulgarity, see Nagahara, "Unpopular Music."

10 Though not mass, clearly pre–Second World War cinema has much to tell us about Japanese modernity at the very least. For both pre- and postwar cinema histories, see Wada-Marciano, *Nippon Modern*; Gerow, *Visions of Japanese Modernity*; Kitamura, *Screening Enlightenment*; 四方田, 日本映画史 100年 (*100 Years of Japanese Film History*).

Embree's fieldwork vividly describes one case of rural relations to film and radio into the mid-1930s:

> A more recent type of amusement is the movie. Movies come to the *mura* [village] two or three times in summer. A small movie-house owner of Taragi comes over and shows the films in the evening either at the school or in some vacant space outdoors. They are long, often historical, dramas of feudal times, with many a sword battle. Admission is ten *sen*, five *sen* for children. In Menda and Taragi are small movie houses showing pictures three times a week. Occasionally some villagers, mostly young people, go. Compared to the songs and dances of the villagers at parties or special celebrations, the movies are unimportant. They are, however, becoming more common as the years go by. The radio owned by the broker is always turned on but rarely listened to. The one at school is used chiefly for radio exercises. When the 1936 Olympic games were broadcast, less than five young men bothered to go to the school to listen at 9:00 P.M.[11]

The setting painted by this description indicates that movies and radio were known but not yet robustly incorporated into the life of rural Japanese.

These non-print media were, in contrast, quite popular in urban areas and made inroads even in the interwar era, but there were limitations to the spread of electronic goods so desired in the burgeoning middle-class lifestyle. Andrew Gordon summarizes that "of the products of modern machine civilization, only the bicycle was truly an item of mass consumption by the end of the 1920s," and among the fourteen million Japanese households from 1910 to 1930, bicycles rose in use from five hundred thousand to almost eight million in just those two decades.[12] It would not be until the 1960s, however, that rural folk (or poorer urban ones) would have regular access to the benefits of the modern industrialized economy, particularly as embodied by appliances and other electronics. Until then, print media and specifically magazines were the primary means by which mass culture was created.

Some Taishō elites and politicians bemoaned the expansion and naturalization of mass print media (especially in the case of women's

---

11   Embree, *Suye Mura, A Japanese Village*, 111.
12   Gordon, "Consumption, Leisure and the Middle Class in Transwar Japan," 5. My current project is on this very technology; see my forthcoming work, *Freewheeling in Japan: Bicycles and the Social History of Leisure*.

magazines) because critics saw the initial popularity as being frivolous and ephemeral at best.[13] Who, though, can we praise (or blame) for creating mass magazines, the first two "million-sellers," for the Japanese?

In the case of *Ie no hikari*, select members of the Central Committee of the Sangyō Kumiai initiated the project. At *Kingu*, Seiji Noma was the most influential person involved, but his staff at Kōdansha contributed to the magazine as well. Both the Kumiai and Kōdansha had produced magazines prior to the new additions in 1925, but those projects were not nearly as successful as *Kingu* or *Ie no hikari*. This was in part due to the style of the previous magazines and in part due to the way in which the newer projects were conceived, advertised, and promoted. Before getting into the details of how each magazine became so popular, it will first be necessary to understand the organizational commitments and ideologies that drove these institutions and their publishing plans as well as the differences in their institutional structures.

The Industrial Cooperative

As a direct result of the February 1900 *Sangyō Kumiaihō* (Industrial Cooperative Law) passed by the Diet, the Japanese government founded the Sangyō Kumiai (Industrial Cooperative). It was an organization that supported agricultural union members though education, mutual assistance programs, and financial services that simultaneously allowed for the encouragement of increased production, price regulation, and subsidies or grants for the upkeep of rural policies and governance more generally. Note that though the name "Sangyō Kumiai" is most commonly translated as "Industrial Cooperative" (for *sangyō* meaning "industrial" and *kumiai* meaning "cooperative" or "union"), it is a cooperative for farmers; it was agrarian industriousness that was the core of the organization, not to be confused with (largely urban) labour unions in light and heavy industry, for example.[14]

By 1925 there were roughly eleven thousand branches throughout Japan with a total of more than five million members. Co-op programs

---

13 Various versions of critiques offered about magazines generally and women's magazines specifically can be found throughout Sato's study. See Sato, *The New Japanese Woman*, passim; Sato, "An Alternate Informant," 150.

14 For a full treatment of the philosophical and ideological underpinnings underlying the creation of this organization (and how it differed from its predecessors), see Havens, *Farm and Nation in Modern Japan*, chapter 3. See also Yagi, "The Second Three-Year Expansion Plan of the Co-Operative Movement."

included savings, financing, and loan services through credit unions, sales and purchasing of farming-related implements and supplies, building and staffing of Kumiai schools, and annual rallies and events.[15] These cooperatives became central to the lives of many farming communities across Japan. A clear description of the organization and its place in a village in Kumamoto Prefecture as it existed in its slightly reorganized state in 1935–6 is provided by Embree. It reads as follows:

> The agricultural association is a local branch of a national organization. It is a farmers' cooperative organization working in harmony with the government agricultural policy. Most *mura* [villages] have one. There are four divisions: (1) co-operative buying, (2) co-operative selling, (3) credit, and (4) co-operative utilization. Only the first three are active in Suye. The utilization association covers such things as an association store or grain mill. Fukada, the next *mura*, has such a co-operative utilization association. In the association buildings are stored grains to be sold through the association when the best price comes. Meanwhile farmers are given a down payment … Rubber work shoes (*jika tabi*), soap, and some medicines are also purchased at the association office. The credit association acts as a village bank … Each *buraku* [community of about twenty households] has a branch association (*kokumiai*). The chief function of these branch associations is to encourage progressive farming, as noted above. The branch association head in many *buraku* is replacing the old native *buraku* head or *nushidōri*.[16]

Membership was restricted to dues-paying farmers, and the heads of the local branches (*kokumiaichō*) slowly took over the duties previously performed by village heads as the cooperative gained influence and membership.[17] The overwhelming majority of these branches were located in rural areas, with denser representation in Nagano, Fukuoka, Hokkaidō, and Niigata prefectures.

To make this slightly more concrete, one should note that the percentage of Japanese households engaged in agriculture was immense,

---

15 There were 11,160 branches in 1914, with 650,000 members by 1912, according to Havens. 奥原, 家の光の二十五年 (*Twenty-Five Years of "Light of the Home"*), 8–9.

16 Embree, *Suye Mura, A Japanese Village*, 63–5.

17 For a more details on average village leadership and the breakdown of cities, town, hamlets, etc., see ibid., 27, 32, 304. For a description in Japanese of the details of a village in wartime Gunma Prefecture, see 森, "戦時経済体制下における産業組合 (Industrial Cooperatives within the Wartime Economy)."

ranging from more than 80 per cent in 1920 to roughly 75 per cent in 1930.[18] To be sure, the practice of varied employments or bi-employment was common enough that not all of these rural residents were purely or only farmers, but certainly all those living in the countryside were at least immersed in the agricultural lifestyle that surrounded them, even if they only participated in actual farming part-time, as was often enough the case.

In 1905, the Cooperative started publishing a magazine called *Sangyō Kumiai* (*The Cooperation*, as its editors chose for the official English alternative title). Still being published into the early 1920s, the magazine never achieved substantial circulation numbers and was criticized by those in farming communities because it failed to be accessible by all but a few educated union administrators or village heads, those historically the most literate among the rural populace. Moreover, *Sangyō Kumiai* was never intended to be a popular magazine. It was written and edited accordingly. There were, for example, no pronunciation guides for the kanji; the articles were dry and practical.

Sangyō Kumiai was aimed at those village elites literate enough to wade through the dense, sensible, and concrete articles most definitely not written for their entertainment value. These villages elites had been the focus of much of the Cooperative's activities since the turn of the century when it was founded. This publication's content centred on institutional matters and management of the cooperative and was more of a report or bulletin than a magazine in the most general sense.[19] It seems clear that those in the Central Committee had modelled the magazine on existing publications targeting elites (either urban or rural) and catering to highly specialized demographics, such as *Shimin* (The People), a national publication directed primarily at village heads and rural male elites.[20]

The lack of popularity of its magazine was just one among a number of concerns facing the Cooperative. At one point, there had been

---

18 "According to Minami, 18.1 percent of the populace lived in the cities in 1920; this figure rose to 21.7 percent five years later and to 24.1 percent by 1930" (Silverberg, *Erotic Grotesque Nonsense*, 277). She is citing 南博 and 社会心理研究所, 昭和文化: 1925–1945 (*Showa Culture: 1925–1945*), 10 April, 19.

19 For comments on the older publication see 北村, 家の光の四十年 (*Forty Years of "Light of the Home"*), 5, 10.

20 As discussed in Wilson, "Bureaucrats and Villagers in Japan." (*The People* is Wilson's translation of the publication's title. Havens translates the same publication as *These People* in *Farm and Nation in Modern Japan*, 94.)

more than 13,000 branches of the Kumiai throughout Japan, but, in 1920 alone, 696 had dissolved. There were problems collecting dues from members, and in general there was a slow decline in support for the organization.[21] By the early 1920s, those at the Cooperative felt that something had to be done to reach out to new and former members to help foster the social change they saw as required for the betterment of Japan.

Shimura Gentarō (1867–1930), a graduate of Tokyo Imperial University and the second president of the Co-op, wanted to change the status of the organization, push to attract more members, and expand plans to assist rural communities. There were discussions about how best to accomplish this, but, at around the same time, plans for the establishment of Kumiai schools were being formulated, showing a general trend towards the support of educationally focused projects. Arimoto Hideo, a graduate of Sapporo Agricultural College (now Hokkaidō University), a former newspaper reporter and magazine enthusiast, was pushing for the creation of a popular Co-op family magazine. Arimoto had created the magazine called *Nōka no tomo* (Friend of the Farm Home) before coming to work at the Cooperative and serving as *Ie no hikari*'s editor for many years. These committee members recognized that magazines were becoming a more popular medium, and while it might have been possible to revamp *Sangyō Kumiai* to make it more accessible to members, Arimoto's suggestion for a wholly new project was convincing to important members of the Kumiai.[22]

Ie no hikari was introduced following much debate within the Cooperative. After Shimura decided that he wanted the Kumiai to produce a family magazine, three years passed before *Ie no hikari* was actually published.[23] Initial proposals for the new magazine were presented at the twenty-third annual national meeting in 1923 and encountered strong opposition from the generally conservative members. The timing of this proposal also might suggest a kind of preparation for competition with *Kingu*, which had originally been slated for release in 1923 until the Great Kantō Earthquake delayed its publication, though there is no explicit mention acknowledging this fact.

---

21 北村, 家の光の四十年 (*Forty Years of "Light of the Home"*), 2, 14.
22 Ibid., 4, 7.
23 家の光協会 (Ie no Hikari Kyōkai), 家の光五十年の人と動きと (*Fifty Years of the People and Developments of "Light of the Home"*), 7.

The proposal detailed the new publication's core style and goals:

Prospectus for the Popular Family Magazine "Light of the Home" …
Name: *Ie no hikari*. To be published on the first of the month every month.

For every issue, there will be about seventy pages of advertising, we
have about twenty pages already scheduled to be used for the first five
issues; with *furigana* included, the covers will be a refined expert three-
colour printing.

Content: fully loaded with general and easy articles about agricultural
commerce and industry, side jobs, the industrial cooperative, household
economy, life's necessities, hygiene, education, chemistry, economics,
public finance, law, religion, society, etc. Additionally, articles on hobbies,
leisure, beneficial novels, story-telling, *waka*, *haiku*, and children's readings for example, will, moreover, be included with novel pictorials and
comics each month.

The goal is to create articles matching the preferences of and providing actual benefits to even housewives, youths, children, and the elderly,
on the basis of real-life examples, that can be read with peace of mind
by offering ways to improve the spirit of co-prosperity and coexistence,
industrial development in the life of the people, and to provide wealth
and prosperity for the readers.

Price: one issue is twenty sen; one year is two yen forty sen with
advanced payment not requiring postage

Subscription application: if possible for Kumiai members one year subscriptions should be paid via postal savings transfer or money order. For
those committing to 10 issues or more a gift of one issue will be given as
a present.[24]

There are several things about this proposal that are worth disen-
tangling. Connecting to the preferences of the readers while providing
"actual benefits" to them is an important strategy in what made *Ie no
hikari* so successful. These benefits, of course, were synonymous with
the flourishing of the cooperative itself and the values it espoused. The
proposal also clearly shows that education about the cooperative and
its ideals was to be at the very heart of the magazine. Conspicuously,
education and pedagogical techniques were also present in the mission
behind *Kingu*. These ideas, furthermore, were to be presented in such

---

24 北村, 家の光の四十年 (*Forty Years of "Light of the Home"*), 10–11.

a way that *all* members of the family could find them interesting and useful.

The strong focus on being interesting and accessible to the readers of the Cooperative's new publication came from Shimura and the editors' desire to include a wider audience in the Kumiai's efforts and programs more generally. The reason it was so essential to interest and engage the readers was simple: if you couldn't reach them you couldn't teach them, no matter what ideas you wished to impart. This is expressed succinctly in a commonly repeated saying from Shimura Gentarō: "The spring of the spirit of cooperation is in the family. Our ideal society is cultivated in the homes of Co-op members."[25] The Central Committee believed that educational outreach about the cooperative and its mission was key to bringing about social change. Thus, the new magazine had to be able to win the hearts and minds of its readers in a way that the earlier publication *The Cooperation* had failed to do.

And it was social change, ultimately, that those at the Kumiai desired. The lives of rural Japanese were difficult during much of the twentieth century, and many at the Cooperative speculated that significant changes would be required to address the problems villages faced. Social transformation included the raising of living standards for the rural populace, a central role for women in the home as educators of children and managers of the household economy, and the devoted support from all subjects for the Japanese empire, for a start. The depression that gripped rural areas in the 1930s and the hardship that existed for many farming families became a focus over the twentieth century and concerned many policy makers and social commentators. Opposing imperialism or some more radical program, however, was beyond inconceivable for these men, so their desired social change worked neatly within the confines of the Meiji Constitution, but it required modification to rural culture nonetheless.

At this early stage of the project, many cooperative members opposed it. Their criticism was born of the belief that magazines were at best a shallow, ephemeral form of leisure entertainment and at worst a bad business investment and a corrupting influence. Most union members, like Mr Yamada from Toyama, quoted in chapter 1, and indeed the Japanese public at large were unable to see the potential profits a

---

25 家の光協会 (Ie no Hikari Kyōkai), 家の光五十年の人と動きと (*Fifty Years of the People and Developments of "Light of the Home"*), 6.

widely circulated magazine could have. Moreover, only a few pioneer-
ing members, like Shimura and Arimoto, were able to envision exactly
how big an impact *Ie no hikari* might actually have. They worked long
hours over the initial years of the magazine's formulation and production to argue, plead, and finally prove the merit of *Light of the Home*.

Diaries and records from those involved in the process suggest
that those most committed to the potential *Ie no hikari* possessed, like
Shimura, suffered and agonized over their pet project. The twenty
people on the editorial staff who weeded through the manuscripts collected for the inaugural issue, deciding what would be kept and what
would be cut, were well aware of the declining membership and the
resultant losses in revenue and influence for the Cooperative. Shimura
is reported to have said that, if the Central Committee was unwilling to
provide the capital for the magazine, he would pay for it out of his own
pocket, since he was so dedicated to the realization of *Ie no hikari*.[26] Okuhara Kiyoshi explained the situation of the late 1920s in these terms:

> Since the issue of *Ie no hikari* started with no capital it was a plan that was
> truly in the red. The salary of all the principal personnel was in its entirety
> expended from the Kumiai's full-scale operations and, just as with the per-
> sonnel labour costs of the magazine, there was no end in sight to the fixed
> price of twenty sen per issue. That is, by issuing the magazine they were
> taking a loss. Even so, the mission of the publication was thought to be
> important and by facing down the opposition through every hardship and
> sacrifice the publication continued.[27]

Were it not for the unswerving dedication of these editors in the early days,
it is unlikely that the publication would ever have gotten off the ground.
As we will see, Kōdansha and *Kingu* were under no such fiscal constraints,
but this financial uncertainty was clearly an issue for *Ie no hikari*.

By February of 1925, a table of contents, cover, and reference materials were all that existed of *Ie no hikari*, but there was enough impetus for
the project and agitation from those like Shimura that permission was
granted by the Central Committee to move forward. However, even
the originally proposed cover was under scrutiny. From the outset of

---

26 One editor, a Mr Kitayama, had a diary from the time called *Bitter Memories* (暗い思
い出), for example. 北村, 家の光の四十年 (*Forty Years of "Light of the Home"*), 14–15.
27 奥原, 家の光の二十五年 (*Twenty-Five Years of "Light of the Home"*), 32.

the project, there were ongoing discussions about the use of images on and in the magazine.

The first cover picture drafted by the well-known Tanaka Ryō was critiqued for several reasons. The depiction of a woman in the image with hair styled in a short cut, wearing a kimono, and holding a bundle of blossoms seemed at the time too similar to an actress of the day named Mizutani Yaeko.[28] Since promoting the appreciation of average Japanese was one goal of the magazine, not glorifying celebrities, Tanaka's cover was scrapped.[29] Tanaka drafted a new cover as a second attempt, but records of it and what it represented have since been lost.[30]

Because of the debates surrounding this decision, Tanaka's stylish image seems not to have been what those at the Cooperative, more generally, envisioned when they thought of how they wanted to represent their values on this their first colour magazine cover. This feeling was once succinctly explained by one chronicler of the magazine: "*Ie no hikari* was a family magazine ... you have to think of it as starting the publication of a *plain* and popular magazine."[31] So actress lookalikes did not pass muster.

There is an apology of sorts in the first issue of *Ie no hikari* that explains that, despite the preliminary announcements and the great anticipation of a cover by the renowned Tanaka, the actual cover was changed at the last minute to an image created by the artist Tashiro Seibi.[32] The originally intended Tanaka Ryō cover was included in the initial publication, but simply under the title "Spring," inserted discreetly after the front matter and advertisements and before the pictorial section. There is no explanation in the magazine itself of why this change occurred, but the record suggests that, because of the disagreement about the image, something more in line with the mission of the magazine and cooperative seemed fitting.

The actual inaugural cover image has several stylistic and compositional differences from the originally presented sketch (see figure 2.1). In

---

28 Not to be mistaken for her daughter, who is also an actress of the same name. The mother was born in 1905 and was featured in such films as the 1921 *Kantsubaki* (Winter Camellia) and *Jōriku dai ippō* (First Steps Ashore) in 1932.

29 北村, 家の光の四十年 (*Forty Years of "Light of the Home"*), 9–10.

30 Ibid., 9.

31 Emphasis added. 奥原, 家の光の二十五年 (*Twenty-Five Years of "Light of the Home"*), 13, 16.

32 "編輯部より (From the Editors)," 11.

Figure 2.1. Inaugural cover image, *Ie no hikari*

general, it is a more pastoral scene in which a woman, whose hair is up and covered, stoops to place flowers in a vase. The name of the magazine stretches across the top of the cover in a fluid calligraphic font (read right to left, as with most prewar vertical titles), in contrast to the blocky font (read vertically top to bottom) listing the volume number on the bottom left and a motto of the Cooperative, "Coexistence and Mutual Prosperity," in Minchō font at the top. Green fields, trees, and something suggestive of a stream running through the image evoke a tranquil scene of rural fertility. The carp flags flying in the distance also lend a sense of family because of their association with the May holiday of *Kodomo no hi* (Children's Day). So instead of a portrait of a refined and stylish woman alone on the cover, the editors decided that the image and ideals they most wanted to associate with their magazine, from the very beginning, were those of the farm and family, portrayed in a romanticized fashion. From the outset, *Light of the Home* was designed to be a magazine rooted in the rural household and the mission of the Cooperative, helping to show its audience just how many positive possibilities existed for that family and their everyday life.

Kōdansha and Noma Seiji

Kingu was the brainchild of Noma Seiji, then president of publishing giant Kōdansha International (Dai Nihon Yūbenkai Kōdansha). Writer and playwright Kishi Yamaji claimed that *Kingu* was equivalent to Kōdansha, and Kōdansha to Noma Seiji.[33] Kishi, a former journalist probably best known for his "proletarian literature," was likely not the only public figure to make that connection, as it was generally understood among publishers, journalists, and advertisers of the day that Noma was the company's driving force and the source of its vision. All major decisions and most minor ones required his exacting approval. His eccentric personality and ruthless business ideology allowed Kōdansha to forge new markets and undertake projects no other publisher in Japan could have risked.

How did his editors describe Noma? A section of the first *Kingu*, titled "Our Tireless President Noma," is worth quoting at length:

> President Noma works diligently enduring hardships just as his employees, just like the head of an extended family. In a steadfast mission, the

---

33 See 貴司, "「キング」論 (Discourse on *King*)," 163.

spirit of our President is expressed through a corporate culture of collective consensus coming from the fellowship of being in complete harmony. Put another way, one can see how virtuous our President is. The President has no political ambitions, no desire for greater social standing, but rather a determination to devote all of his strength to the achievement of his current mission of spirited cultural endeavours. Consequently, his every action germinates from being an enthusiastic moral conscience, suitably guiding with morals and sentiments, in order to bring the light of a moral path to everyday life … The creations of morals at our company all come from this point of departure. And in the first publication of *Kingu* – the efforts of the President were no easy task … As one member of this extended family – those of us who pale in comparison alongside the head of our company – [we] continually think of our President as the soul of our body and desire to help him in his enterprise. Because of this, the unveiled result is a true benefit to the nation that embodies Noma's acts of public service.[34]

Evidently the editors thought highly of their boss. Nor was this level of gushing uncommon about Noma. He was wealthy, educated, and came from an illustrious family, and he likely could have made his way into politics had he so chosen. But what is of more significance here is the attitude that he is the moral exemplar and father not only to the company that he headed but also to the nation at large.

Noma was more than willing to speak for and about himself as well. If we can extract even a modicum of truth from his self-aggrandizing statements, we are faced with the model of a marvellously virtuous enterprise. Noma described his core business methods thus:

We have three principles by which all of us, Dai-Nippon-Yubenkai-Kodansha, are implicitly bound. They are taken from Chinese phraseology … The first is what we call "Konzen-ittai," which means more than "perfect co-operation," for literally it stands for one soul with diverse bodies; the second is "Seijitsu-kinben[,]" that is, "sincerity and perseverance," and the third is "Juwo-koryo," which you may render into "initiative and hard-thinking." It has cost us three years to evolve these principles, and to us these words contain a meaning far deeper and more precious than you can ever read into them.[35]

---

34 「キング」編輯局同人, "『キング』が世に出るまでの苦心 (The Agony Until *King* Appeared)," 283.
35 Akimoto, *Seiji Noma "Magazine King" of Japan*, 26.

Here we see at least the public face of Kōdansha's operation: harmony, perseverance, and hard work. The inaugural issue of *Kingu* also touted these norms, going so far as to say,

> The self as the company and the company as the self, forged together in a huge flash furnace, firmly fused, heart to heart. The outcome of a fight to the finish is decided by the tight formation of the assault troops. These forces are united, becoming a unitary force of the present moment displaying an astonishing power. At our company, not only is there a fierce intensity to each individual employee, but an unnaturally close formation that is fashioned; now that the charge has begun, our collective mobilization, this general fellowship, a truly united power, has unleashed an almost mystical and unimaginable power.[36]

Obviously, such harmony and tenacity are only ideals, just as the ideals in the pages of the magazines were not the reality of Japanese society. Nonetheless, these powerful visions reveal underlying assumptions about the goals for which Noma thought he and his people should be striving. Even if all this heartwarming rhetoric was in service of a profit-driven publishing house, the point here is what these people publicly *said* they were doing. Notably as well, Noma's publishing activities were not presented in public discourses as capitalist enterprises, greedy ploys for profits, or entrepreneurial selfishness; many seemed to believe he was truly doing the public the moral service for which he strove. Clearly the heavy-handed PR worked.

In a later section of the same article, the readers are told:

> Indeed, if there is a place where democracy exists as an ideal, we do not hesitate to say that it is here at our company. Namely, there is no distinction in rank at our company, no high and low status, no distinction in age, our roughly two hundred employees become entirely as one, quite freely, openheartedly, and cheerfully express their views and goals together, assuring a beautifully spirited enterprise ... The highest goal in our company's policy is genuine service to the nation.[37]

---

36 「キング」編輯局同人, "『キング』が世に出るまでの苦心 (The Agony Until *King* Appeared)," 282.
37 Ibid., 281.

His was a company where harmony, cooperation, dedication, initiative, and all the various values Noma upheld for sustaining managerial and operational practices also propelled the content of the magazines. The conception invoked here is one of little-"d" democracy viewed as harmony and social equality, rather than big-"D" democracy in the sense of a distinct political practice per se. By extension, the rest of Japan would be best served, as Noma saw it, by getting on board with this grand project. Kōdansha's bottom line unquestionably benefited as well.

Cooperation was a common ideal held among many business elites throughout the 1920s and 1930s and was an outgrowth of ideas circulating since the days of rising entrepreneurs in the early Meiji years. The paradigm presented most frequently was that of capitalist enterprises created not for the acquisition of personal wealth, but rather to forward the interests of the nation. Those at the huge *zaibatsu*, like Mitsui, Sumitomo, Yasuda, and Mitsubishi, as well as at newer financial conglomerates that appeared in the first decades of the twentieth century, frequently promoted archetypes of harmony and duty to the nation. The president of the Kanegafuchi Spinning Mills was quoted as asserting, "I am not a capitalist. I am an employee of the company and a servant of society." Business leaders from most sectors readily boasted about their own hard work as a model for others, especially youths, to follow.[38]

These discourses about capitalism and the working world that disdained material compensation for its own sake while promoting duty and cooperation were present at Kōdansha as well. Noma consistently voiced opinions (in exceedingly creative and boisterous ways) which fell in line with overarching values among his peers, though he frequently pushed individuals to be ambitious. This emphasis on individual ambition, reflected in Noma's own behaviour, may have been part of why he had earned his reputation as an aggressive and idiosyncratic personage.

More so than his contemporaries, moreover, Noma was keenly enough attuned to the habits of the masses that he could envision how to appeal to their interests through advertising and entertainment. By the late 1920s, Noma's nine monthly magazines had a combined

---

38 The quote is from a Tsuda Shingo (Marshall, *Capitalism and Nationalism in Prewar Japan*, 98–101).

estimated circulation of around ten million (at a time when Japan's population was roughly sixty million) and were responsible for somewhere
between 70 and 80 per cent of the magazines titles sold at bookstores
throughout Japan and its colonies. Kōdansha dominated the publishing industry in Japan. This huge share of the market led to Kōdansha
being, far and away, the principal user of ink and paper in prewar Japan
(second being the Japanese government itself). Indeed, because of this
success, Noma was personally among the most heavily taxed individuals in Tokyo.[39]

While the Industrial Cooperative was driven by the desire to educate
and enrich their audience as a move to bolster union membership and
participation in Co-op efforts, and thereby effect change in Japanese
society, Noma pushed for social change through entertainment and
panache. This is not to say that Noma was uninterested in the earnest
business of educating the populace.

Noma started his adult life as a primary- and then middle-school
teacher, and many of his attitudes about how best to communicate with
average Japanese were coloured by his pedagogical leanings:

> the lessons are given at school in a cut-and-dried pedagogical manner,
> which often defeats its own end ...When I was a teacher, I was popular,
> if you permit my little vanity, for I always tried to teach in an interesting
> manner, telling them stories of warriors and saints, for instance, instead of
> cramming their heads with chronological tables or merely explaining hard
> passages in the text-books. In this way, the children can best be taught
> important lessons in ethics. It is the same to some extent in educating
> adults. We learn best from what interests us most. To make the virtues
> interesting and irresistible ought to be the aim of teachers and writers, and
> that is what I am aiming at in all our publications. So, you see that I am still
> guided by the spirit of the teacher that was within me thirty years ago![40]

Here not only is there evidence of Noma's conviction that he was
teacher for the masses, but also an admission that moral education was
the subject of his lectures. Moreover, Noma saw the goal of his publications as teaching ethics and virtues to the adult reading public. When
he was a teacher, he inculcated morals in his students with heroic tales.

---

39 Akimoto, *Seiji Noma "Magazine King" of Japan*, 3–4, 25.
40 Ibid., 13.

As a publishing giant, Noma sought to instil values in his many readers with content that engaged and inspired them. Because Noma's publications were omnipresent, so were his beliefs.

Moral education has a somewhat religious provenance in Japan, with connections to spreading the ideas and practices of Buddhism and Confucianism under the guise of what can also be called "moral suasion" (*kyōka*).[41] Noma himself was not overtly religious in his philosophizing about his publications, though he wholeheartedly took up the mantle of providing what he saw as social "good" and Japanese cultural development that sat comfortably amidst the history of Tokugawa moralizers, Meiji reformers, and modern bureaucrats alike.

Thus, making lessons stimulating, motivating, and attention-grabbing drove the content creation process at *Kingu*. Noma wished to teach all citizens of the Japanese empire these ideals: striving for self-improvement; bettering (monogamous, heterosexual) home life; being honest, hardworking, filial, and loyal; all for the sake of Japan. These values are present in vast numbers of public statements from Noma about his enterprises, in addition to being explicitly printed in the publications he managed. The magazines from Kōdansha, especially *Kingu*, defined what "broad appeal" *meant*. For Kōdansha, this appeal was housed squarely in the lower classes.

In reference to his ideas about *Kingu*, Noma once said, "I want to create a magazine that is interesting – truly interesting – to old people, young people, men, and women, and one that educators, workers, housewives, alike yearn to read at any age, profession and location."[42] Noma's iconic statements are frequently shortened to pithy quips like "something interesting for anyone to read" and "aiming at the masses," as are the sayings proudly displayed on the Kōdansha website even today: Kōdansha, publishing "entertainment and edification."[43] Recently, Kōdansha's homepage still prominently displayed both a quotation (in the top banner) from the founder and a bust of Noma Seiji among the links featured along the sidebar.

Noma's business savvy included the understanding that general magazines previously on the market were still modelled on "intellectual"

---

41 Garon, *Molding Japanese Minds*, 7, 28, 229.
42 Originally from Noma's autobiography, quoted in 永嶺, 雑誌と読者の近代 (*Modern Magazines and Readers*), 204; 野間, 私の半生 (*My Early Life*).
43 In the original: "講談社「おもしろくて ためになる」出版を," homepage.

publications like *Chūō kōron* (Central Review) or *Taiyō* (The Sun) and expected readers to come from the educated middle and upper classes. He had seen the decline of more erudite publishers like Iwanami Shoten who catered to educated and literary audiences. Their publications were not, furthermore, designed to engage more than one or two members in any given household. Certainly, in many rural households, such magazines failed to engage anyone.

Top of the Bottom

Noma viewed class as a pyramid. In this configuration, elites and the wealthy sit at the top, the growing class of white-collar workers form the middle, and farmers, labourers, and the poor subsist at the bottom. The top of the pyramid is a small sliver of the populace, while the bottom encompasses millions upon millions. In envisaging his audience, Noma aimed for the "top of the bottom."[44] *King* created subscribers out of those who previously were not reading magazines, simply by making the reading interesting and accessible for the largest and most diverse audience. This meant trawling for the poor and the lower class who encompassed the clear majority of the Japanese population in the 1920s and 1930s – the "top of the bottom" of the pyramid of class. This combined the lower classes, comprised largely of farmers, labourers, and white-collar workers, with whatever middle-class individuals happened to be collected in the widely cast net as well. Those at *Ie no hikari*, too, envisioned this same massive varied demographic as their audience. Thus, the production of these two magazines, at more or less the same time, was a first in Japan.

Lifestyles in Japan had reached a point where this "top of the bottom" group – literally tens of millions of people – were able to have some degree of leisure. Disposable income might not have been much for them, but it was sufficient to support the growth and expansion of these publications. Both Kōdansha and the Kumiai had the prescience to consider not only the market potential of tapping the masses, but also the cultural capital they could marshal once those masses had been captivated. They were able to envision a market sized to mirror the whole of the Japanese empire. Both publishers recognized, in advance, that their magazines

---

44 社史編纂委員会 (Committee for the Compilation of the Company History), 講談社の歩んだ五十年 (*The Path of Kōdansha's First Fifty Years*), 666–7.

could reach larger audiences than ever before and, furthermore, that they could generate cultural change through the ideals presented within. By aiming at the "top of the bottom," these organizations generated and maintained discourses that reached down and through to the very foundations of society. More importantly, they created the very mechanisms for captivating and sustaining that audience once it was created.

These magazines were low cost and widely available, either via subscription or at bookstores, with content accessible and engaging to an eclectic swathe of readers. Not only did these magazines have content for the rural poor and working class, but they also appealed to the educated, the elites, and white-collar workers (as the Tokyo surveys support). Noma was not, nor were those at the Cooperative, opposed to the "top" of the pyramid buying the publications as well, even though they were not the focus of promotional efforts, just as the middle class was not excluded from the audience either. Family magazines' broad appeal allowed for the normalization of consuming media on a mass scale. At their heart, these magazines were designed to reach a huge audience, but also to convey their producers' respective ideals and solidify a Japanese readership. The rapid spread of the practice of buying and reading magazines derives from this core nature of the publications.

Of course, a more cynical reading of the espoused ideals might lead one to conclude that, whatever the packaging, Kōdansha was after profits and the Co-op was after members for their dues. Noma did, after all, admit:

> The truth is that we have been too preoccupied in the past with the immediate requirements of our magazines to think of the character of certain of our published material. To make them interesting so as to secure larger sales was our chief concern, but having now obtained certain standard circulations, we shall henceforth give greater attention to the improvement of the contents of each.[45]

This is an acknowledgment that not every detail conformed to the high ideals Noma espoused, but, considering the variety of materials in the nine different magazines Kōdansha published, this is hardly surprising. Nor does it undercut the stated missions, since profits and moral improvement are not necessarily mutually exclusive. People did

---

45 Akimoto, *Seiji Noma "Magazine King" of Japan*, 32.

actually seem to enjoy these publications as a bit of respite in a life of hard work, so the leisure and entertainment *Ie no hikari* and *Kingu* provided for Japanese people was not all toxic.

Gotō Shinpei, one-time mayor of Tokyo and all-round social policy enthusiast, once said in praise of *Kingu*, "Mr. Noma has done us a great service. I had thought that there would be no good institution to guide the populace of Japan, but here is a good organization [for doing so]."[46] Gotō described Kōdansha as a vehicle for guiding the people in accord with ideals of the government. Respected historian Ishida Takeshi has also said, "Kōdansha was jokingly called 'the private ministry of education.'"[47] In effect, Kōdansha served as an extra-official educational institution of the government, at least in Gotō's mind, and in that way functioned similarly to the Industrial Cooperative.[48] Of course, seeking wider circulation stemmed from desiring greater revenues, but Noma, and thus Kōdansha, had a serious and genuine concern about Japanese society and its possibilities in the future.

Cynics may cry foul at this, however. In the same way that Gotō was a statesman and diplomat while simultaneously embodying an obscured role of drug dealer and human trafficker, the publishers were also guilty of duplicity. Noma claimed to be investing agency and self-determination among his readers while concomitantly enmeshing them more fully in the consumer culture that robbed them of exactly those kinds of prerogatives. The Cooperative as well was hoping to raise the daily lives of those in the countryside, but was simultaneously undermining the agricultural economy and household model on which they depended.

Noma, nevertheless, took his role as moral educator of the people quite seriously. This is evidenced in part by the way he ran Kōdansha. He pushed his employees to be effective in reaching out to the *moga* and *mobo* – "modern" young urban women and men often portrayed as self-indulgent, decadent drains on society. He did this to inculcate in them desirable virtues like loyalty to the emperor, filial piety more generally, and self-improvement, and to motivate *risshin shusse* (rising in the world) because they too could be contributing parts of a better

---

46 The quotation is from 丸山, 現代政治の思想と行動 (*Thought and Behaviour in Modern Japanese Politics*). Cited in 永嶺, 雑誌と読者の近代 (*Modern Magazines and Readers*), 227.
47 Ishida, *Japanese Society*, 90.
48 Driscoll, *Absolute Erotic, Absolute Grotesque*. He deals with Gotō skilfully, if rather unflatteringly, throughout part 1.

Japan as he saw it. Noma flatly stated, "how to propagate among the youths and flappers of Japan the virtues of filial piety and loyalty to the Emperor and inspire them with the ambition to become great is the aim of my magazines, in which I believe all my co-workers unite," in order to explain the relationship of his ideals and the aims of his company.[49] This was the response Noma gave when asked, "What is your idea of greatness?" and confirms that within his publishing empire he viewed magazines specifically as central to his mission.

In such attitudes about nationalism and ideas about *moga*, some journalists might have found statements in *Ie no hikari* and *Kingu* rather conservative. For example, those of the Seikyōsha (of the *Nihonjin* and *Nihon oyobi Nihonjin* publications) had, by the time of *Kingu's* publications, backed down from the critique of the individualism of youth because of the objectionable way in which the military was capitalizing on such criticisms' counter-effects.[50] Noma's ideals aimed at creating loyal Japanese subjects who worked to better their country's standing in the international community; he saw this work as starting with changing the attitudes and values of his audience.

Youth and the promise it held also particularly fascinated Noma. It is possible that this preoccupation with youth was exacerbated by the untimely death of one of his sons and his reported devotion to Hisashi, his surviving heir. Nevertheless, he was once given the advice that "The work of the Meiji Restoration was done by young men, and the future of Japan rests also on young men. Therefore, if you keep up your present spirit of working for and with young men, you will be a success."[51] The advice came from Marquis Okuma Shigenobu. Interestingly, Kōdansha's publications did not solely focus on men, however, but gave equal attention to women and men, boys and girls alike, as is evidenced by the variety of titles aimed at each group and the varied content of *Kingu* itself; this inclusivity was both forward-thinking and essential to the creation of its mass audience.

Noma took both this advice and his optimism about youth seriously and hired employees accordingly; he also spent much time among the young boys affiliated with various *kendō* organizations his family

---

49 Akimoto, *Seiji Noma "Magazine King" of Japan*, 12–13.
50 I thank Tak Matsusaka for his enlightening take on these issues ("Nationalist Journalism and Foreign Policy Crises in Meiji and Early Taisho Japan").
51 笛木, 私の見た野間清治 (*The Noma Seiji I Saw*).

supported. Among the workers at Kōdansha in the late 1920s, the vast majority were around the age of twenty, far younger than the average age of most publishing industry professionals and certainly of those working as editors and marketers at *Ie no hikari*, for example. Within Kōdansha's workforce there were supposedly more than 350 such young men in Noma's employ out of the roughly 400 total employees, making them roughly 87 per cent of the company.[52]

Getting the Magazines to the Audience

How do you convince a factory worker, or farmer, or flapper to buy your magazine? While both *Kingu* and *Ie no hikari* achieved unprecedented sales in the late 1920s and 1930s, their sales strategies were quite dissimilar. There were many in the marketing department at *Ie no hikari* who argued with the editors that, no matter how good the magazine was, if no one read it, it obviously could not succeed in fulfilling its role of promoting the values of the cooperative, boosting membership, and building a better Japan.[53] The expansion of *Kingu* and *Ie no hikari* alike was a process of drawing in an audience by making the content interesting and beneficial to a wide swathe of the populace, so that the principles underlying the project could reach an ever expanding group of readers. Such ideals were present from the beginning, as is clear from the discussions about designing these magazines.

One interesting feature of the expansion of these two institutions was how different Kōdansha and the Kumiai were in their approach to persuading Japanese to buy their periodicals. For example, Noma is said to be the progenitor of the full-page advertisement in Japan and was known for causing furor among his competitors for the enormous amount of money he spent on advertising.[54] He created unprecedented hype around Kōdansha's publication plans, especially in anticipation of *Kingu*'s first issue.

Full-page advertisements were not inexpensive, especially in newspapers, and one hundred thousand yen (the cost of a full-page

---

52 Akimoto, *Seiji Noma "Magazine King" of Japan*, 23–4, 27, 36. In the first issue of *Kingu* a more modest estimate was given at more than 100 young men and the total number of employees being slightly less than the figures given for 1927, see 「キング」編輯局同人, "『キング』が世に出るまでの苦心 (The Agony Until *King* Appeared)," 282.
53 奥原, 家の光の二十五年 (*Twenty-Five Years of "Light of the Home"*), 41.
54 Akimoto, *Seiji Noma "Magazine King" of Japan*, 6.

advertisement in some newspapers) might seem an exorbitant amount to pay for the advertising of just one issue of a single publication. The full-page advertisement for *Kingu*'s January 1926 issue (see figure 2.2) as seen in *Yomiuri Shinbun* read, in part: "Advance notice for the New Year's Issue of *Kingu* … Extraordinarily interesting! Exceedingly beneficial! There's no reason this magazine should be less than one yen …" This New Year's edition advertisement for *Kingu* even claimed it was "Japan's only national magazine."[55]

Advertisements for the inaugural issue included such pitches as "The day for the first issue of the grand world-famous magazine *Kingu* is approaching!"; "Choose your magazine now!"; "Tremendous popularity the world over! A flood of orders! Voices of praise from the whole country!"; "Behold! A magazine only seen before in dreams. A new magazine for the benefit of our beloved brethren!"; and "One copy for every family: See the new magazine sensation!"[56] This last slogan in particular seems to be the one that is most commonly remembered and associated with the magazine. The original Japanese ("一家一冊　大評判の新雑誌キングをご覧!") more fully invokes not just the idea of one magazine for the whole family, but also the intent that there be one issue in *every* household. Statements like "choose your magazine now" also suggest a clear knowledge of the fact that most families purchased only one publication, either by choice or because of economic necessity.

There is no evidence to suggest that any other commercial publisher advertised as heavily or widely as did Kōdansha. Even with the expense of all this publicity, Noma found that aggressively advertising his magazine, in other print media and elsewhere, did in fact pay, as his sales continually increased over the late 1920s and early 1930s. The first issue alone sold nearly three-quarters of a million copies. It was not long before each subsequent issue was selling over a million copies. It is worth noting for comparative purposes that *Shufu no tomo* (Housewife's Friend), the leading women's magazine of these years, printed 340,000 issues for its first run (though some were returned to the publishers unsold), and the Veterans' Association had *Our House* (*Waga ie*), which sold about 100,000 copies at five sen a piece in the mid-1920s.[57]

---

55 "キング新年号予告 (Advance Notice for the New Year's Issue of *Kingu*)."
56 Quoted in 佐藤, 「キング」の時代 (*The Era of "King"*), 6–7.
57 奥原, 家の光の二十五年 (*Twenty-Five Years of "Light of the Home"*), 13.

Figure 2.2. Advertisement, for *Kingu*'s January 1926 issue

One must understand that Noma's advertising techniques were suited to his largely urban distribution system. Because there were not bookstores in appreciable numbers in small towns and villages throughout Japan, this kind of advertising would have been less effective in the hamlets where *Ie no hikari* thrived through subscriptions. Diversity of purchasing options for urban readers was far superior to that of their rural counterparts, and thus arguably induced a greater potential for suasion by advertising for a particular publication among the urban readers' available choices.

Regrettably, there is no direct method for tracking whether any households received both magazines, but based on disparate statistics and anecdotal evidence it is safe to assume that at least some households in Japan purchased both publications. For example, *Ie no hikari* does list sales for the magazine in cities: monthly Tokyo averages of 3,832 subscriptions in 1933; 4,986 in 1934; 6,717 in 1935; 8,448 in 1936; and 9,025 in 1937; with Osaka having similar averages of 1,782 in 1933; 3,738 in 1934; 6,672 in 1935; 9,606 in 1936; and 10,581 in 1937.[58] Since the number of people purchasing *Kingu* in the cities over these years was far higher than these tallies, at least some people must have read both. There are also the occasional mentions of people bringing *Kingu* into the countryside after issues were purchased elsewhere. *Kingu* similarly did have a readership in smaller towns and hamlets, even if *Ie no hikari* was favoured in these locations.[59]

Readers of both publications could be described as those at the outskirts of the cities who were still interacting with or participating in agricultural communities but with enough connection to the city and disposable income that they could afford both or knew people who could. Another possibility is people living in cities who also owned farming lands. Even though they most often did not themselves farm

---

58 Ibid., 39.

59 Nagamine explains the differences in regional preferences more specifically, saying: "In farming villages the surveys showed that subscribers of magazines like *Kingu* were substantially less common than in the cities. For example, they show that of the 358 households surveyed [in Fukuyama] only 61 were subscribers in 1931 … of 84 households [in Kanagawa] only 16 were; and … in 1932 of 64 households [in Saitama] only 8 were. Even in places where subscription numbers were low, *Kingu* was near the top of the list – places further from Tokyo also show *Ie no hikari* as being among the big sellers and outranked *Kingu* at least once." 永嶺, 雑誌と読者の近代 (*Modern Magazines and Readers*), 215.

that land, landlords would nonetheless have been interested in the information the Cooperative had to offer their tenants. The stark dividing line that often gets drawn between the city and the countryside during this period of Japanese history is in some ways overemphasized, as are the lines between the classes. Class, and culture more generally, are more fluid than such compartmentalization would suggest.

The disparity between lifestyles that existed in densely populated cities and out in the rustic hamlets has been the centre of many debates both at the time and in the scholarship on Japan since then. What the statistics and reports we have about these magazines seem to suggest is that some differences were undeniable; rural lives were challenging and lacked access to many of the wonders of the modern world flourishing in cities by the 1920s in Japan. But that did not prevent significant shared experiences via media. Culture was not simply produced in a unidirectional manner out of the cities and urban centres and into the rural hinterlands. People who went into cities brought their sense of the world and attitudes about it with them from the countryside when they did. Moreover, variety manifested in different cities (Tokyo is not the only city in Japan, after all) and thrived in different villages (warm fishing villages on the coasts compared to mountainous, field-cultivating frigid ones, to name one simple contrast). The unsophisticated binary of urban-rural tends not only to overemphasize Tokyo but also to ignore variation more generally.[60]

The commonality of the mass audience does in fact partially hide difference (thus the value in uncovering this process and revealing erasure), but it also explains the ways in which readers themselves envisioned their own sameness. Despite rhetoric and stereotypes about the backwardness of the countryside, the audiences of these magazines were able to look past their differences (regional, social, economic, educational, etc.) in order to participate in a collectively imagined community that transcended those disparities even as the mechanism by which they did so often helped to reinforce lived inequities.

Unlike Kōdansha, at the Cooperative money was not readily available for advertising campaigns. The editors and marketing divisions responsible for vending *Ie no hikari* were aware that publicity might

---

60 Louise Young succeeds in teasing out the complicated tensions present in the urban/rural binary and the discourses and scholarship about it (*Beyond the Metropolis*, chapters 3–4).

very well help sell magazines, but decided that because of the enormous expense of advertising, especially in newspapers, it was not an option for them.[61] Instead, they relied on word of mouth and *Ie no hikari* rallies (public events for entertainment and education) to promote the Co-op's new publication. They nonetheless achieved circulation results similar to what was achieved by the seemingly endless yen Kōdansha poured into advertising.

The Cooperative had one advantage over Kōdansha in this regard; in the mid-1920s, far more of the population lived in rural areas, and there simply were not many publications making it into those areas. Furthermore, the Cooperative already had lines of communication throughout all of Japan. Even though the membership numbers had dropped, the Cooperative still had techniques for getting the word out about their new magazine to many homes in remote areas that Kōdansha could not reach so easily, and, even better, such publicity was free of charge.

The Cooperative used rallies throughout the 1920s and 1930s to educate members and promote the organization more generally, and these rallies were a core advertising technique for the marketing of *Ie no hikari*. Through lectures, film showings, and demonstrations, members of farming communities came together at rally events hosted by the Kumiai and left more informed about various aspects of the Co-op's projects, yes, but also knowing how to place their orders for *Ie no hikari* through the local branch. By the early 1930s, these rallies with their movies, frequently *bidan* (literally "beautiful stories," but more generally understood as "inspirational tales") adapted into short films, and other forms of entertainment would have been exceptionally exciting for rural folk who did not have easy access to movie theatres and department stores.[62]

In this regard, Noma and the Kumiai used similar blanket appeal methods; both wished to attract wide audiences with parables that entertained but also served as moral guides. Thus, though their approaches to distribution and sales were dissimilar, they both used such stories in order to attract more readers and thereby promote their respective visions of an ideal Japan.

---

61 奥原, 家の光の二十五年 (*Twenty-Five Years of "Light of the Home"*), 43.
62 Ibid., 23–5. Chapter 4 of this book deals extensively with the rallies and their significance.

Concluding Thoughts

Divergences in their approaches to advertising were but one contrast between the two publications. For example, *Kingu* and many other magazines in the 1920s were sold on consignment basis; namely, a bookstore would be given a certain number of copies of each issue, and any of the magazines that were not sold before the next issue came out could be returned to the publisher for a refund. Upwards of 30 per cent of each month's copies of many different publications frequently went unsold.[63] *Ie no hikari*, in contrast, was sold through subscriptions only. Copies of the magazine were obtained through the union itself, and subscription fees were collected through the individual branches, often by volunteer boys who went door to door. At the local branches in 1935–6, Embree explained how this looked in terms of purchasing and popularity, explaining that "from its offices can be bought the association magazine, *Ie no hikari*, a cheap twenty-sen magazine of fiction and agricultural advice. More people in the *mura* [village] (sixty houses) read this than any other periodical."[64] These two methods were each successful in their respective locations, as cities and towns had bookstores available, where most villages and hamlets likely did not.

Pricing was another point of divergence between the two publications. *Kingu* sold for fifty sen a copy, as did most other, though much slimmer, contemporary monthlies. For a magazine that was several hundred pages long, this was not a bad price. According to several national surveys of the day, the average cost of living per farming family member per day was reported to be eight sen.[65] *Ie no hikari*'s producers also knew their audience and, thus, did one better: the cover price for each issue was only twenty sen. The price of *Ie no hikari* was put into place as an essential component of its circulation.

The person at the Cooperative placed in charge of deciding initial pricing was Furuse Denzō.[66] In the planning stages and into the early years of the magazine's publication, he and the *Ie no hikari* publicists made the case to local members that the content actually helped to bring down household expenses and economized spending in general; seen as a kind of investment, subscribing was explained as a net financial

---

63 Ibid., 43.
64 Embree, *Suye Mura, A Japanese Village*, 64.
65 奥原, 家の光の二十五年 (*Twenty-Five Years of "Light of the Home"*), 19.
66 Ibid., 21.

gain for the readers. Moreover, whereas a small number of free issues were previously distributed to the branches in order to help woo new subscribers, by the end of the 1920s the union was offering bulk discounts through the branches instead. The more member-subscribers in a locale, the lower the cost for each subscriber. This changed as rallies became the core of the promotional plan to boost circulation.

In the widespread and burdensome increases in prices during the 1920s, the *Ie no hikari* discount system worked such that the cost of each magazine was reduced for branches with more subscribers. The price of each issue could drop as low as thirteen sen.[67] The discount worked like this: starting in March of 1926, branches with more than fifty subscribers got 20 per cent off per issue and branches with more than one hundred subscribers got 25 per cent off. In 1928, the discount system was slightly changed so that branches with more than twenty subscribers got 15 per cent off per issue, those with more than thirty got 20 per cent off, and those with more than fifty got 25 per cent off. As circulation numbers approached one million, these discounts were eventually abolished, but even charging full price for these publications clearly did not hurt their circulation figures.

The decision to purchase these magazines was not one that was made lightly by many families or individuals living in farming communities. In the 1930s, rural residents were suffering a time of crisis when daily living expenses were pushed to extremes.[68] One anecdote explains,

> In the ending years of Taishō and the beginning years of Shōwa, rural areas were in a time of crisis. The prefectural agricultural association had been entrusted to assess the household account book of one farming household at this time. When they asked the household head if it was not a mistake that "one block of tofu roughly 5 sen" had been entered as an item under "medical expenses," he responded that it was only natural that they might see it as a mistake. However, in his household, because conditions were so dire that they were unable to give an infirm member of the household any medicine or other beneficial sustenance, they gave tofu instead of medicine, so that was why he had entered "one block of tofu roughly 5 sen" as an item under "medical expenses."[69]

---

67 北村, 家の光の四十年 (*Forty Years of "Light of the Home"*), 16.
68 For a most detailed and careful investigation of the policies directed at these suffering farming villages, see Smith, *A Time of Crisis.*
69 奥原, 家の光の二十五年 (*Twenty-Five Years of "Light of the Home"*), 17.

The subtext here is that tofu would be a splurge that the rest of the family would not regularly get to have. This one example is neatly representative of the larger situation throughout Japan, where the depression had severely curtailed the standard of living for most Japanese. In such circumstances, the desire for a bit of leisurely diversion is absolutely reasonable, especially when that entertainment offered as a benefit to the household in return.

Numbers for *Ie no hikari* subscriptions for the late 1920s hovered around 40,000, but then steadily grew through the early 1930s. This increase can be directly connected to the *Ie no hikari* rallies (detailed in chapter 4) beginning in 1928. The yearly average was 254,907 subscriptions for 1932, 478,261 for 1934, 925,569 for 1936, and 1,000,087 for 1937. These numbers indicate issues sold to recipient households and only begin to express the true reach the publication actually had because of the multiple people in most households and the variety of social reading practices previously mentioned.

Despite these differences, both these magazines ultimately achieved a level of parity in terms of their popularity, together becoming the first two magazines to reach circulations of over one million copies. They became nationwide phenomena. Both were read by people from every walk of life, throughout the nation, and were created, in part, to present a set of values that would promote the ideal of Japan fostered by each producer. These ideals were not identical, but their overlap is striking. *Ie no hikari* and *Kingu* sought to define how Japan ought to be, and they tried to show their audiences how to achieve that goal.

In effect, these magazines presented and advocated for possible realities for Japan. Moreover, readers of the magazines seemed to find these entertaining, useful, educational visions of Japan desirable. This desire, or collective imagining, was one mechanism by which the magazines both appealed to the populace and also created a mass culture that naturalized consumerism. The next chapter starts with a close reading of the first issue of each magazine, followed by a discussion of who was reading them, how they were reading them, and what impact they had on cultural practices.

Chapter Three

"We Came, We Saw, We Astonished": How a Japanese Mass Was Won

On the covers and in the pages of these magazines, there unfolded a process of inclusion where individual Japanese people could join a community of readers and fellow countrymen. The mechanism that the magazines embodied was supported by the content within. The stories and articles provided examples and models for emulation by any Japanese citizen and, by doing so, taught the audience how magazines could seamlessly incorporate themselves into the lives and social practices of the readers as well. Once members of this mass audience, Japanese individuals experienced increasing exposure to the ideas and norms of the world of magazines. The goals might have been to make Japan better as a nation, but the publishers of the magazines were not interested in the state or politics as such – they were in the business of incorporating families and households into their audience. If change was necessary and possible, as the editors certainly thought it was, that change had to happen at the individual level in the families across Japan.

Historical Background

For Japan, full freedom of the press (as we understand it in the contemporary sense) was not guaranteed until after the Second World War. As one scholar put it, "the 1889 Constitution guaranteed the freedom of the press only 'within the limits of the law,' which meant within the limits of the existing press laws."[1] Such laws progressively became more lenient in the decades surrounding the turn of the twentieth century,

---

1 Westney, *Imitation and Innovation*, 157.

seeing amendments in 1887, 1900, and 1909. However, this meant that all of the materials that made it into publications were subject to governmental regulations placed on content. Remarkably, in the case of the thousands of pages of *Ie no hikari* and *Kingu*, there is nothing to suggest that the content was in fact censored.

The Peace Preservation Law (*Chian iji hō*) was enacted in Japan in May of 1925 and strengthened in 1941 as a mechanism for the government and imperial institution to entrench itself against a growing left wing. It forbade conspiracy or revolt against the national essence (*kokutai*) of Japan and effectively criminalized socialism, communism, and other ideologies that would threaten Japan's emperor-centred social order. The law is considered to have been conjured by the Ministry of Justice and "set ideological limits for individuals and organizations and served as the framework for the creation of special techniques for handling 'thought criminals' (*shisōhan*)." Such criminals were the under the purview of the Special Higher Police. Called *Tokubetsu Kōtō Keisatsu* (or *Tokkō*, for short), this organization of "secret" police was established to observe and regulate election campaigns and public meetings, as well as all media. Treated as rehabilitatable through "conversion" (*tenkō*), thought crimes (*shisō hanzai*) came to be understood after 1927 as those "not limited to violations of the Peace Preservation Law but extended to any criminal action in which ideology played a role."[2] Considered to be unique to Japan, the *kokutai* was a political system embodied in the imperial line and the institutions supporting it, blending politics and ethics, turning dissent into a moral as well as a legal issue.

Work on censorship and state policy in Japan done by Gregory Kasza extensively documents transitions from Meiji era debates, to the height of party politics, and into wartime mobilization. While he views the interwar era as particularly significant as a turning point in state control, his research also makes clear that the brunt of state censorship regarding periodical publications fell most squarely on small journals and political outliers, namely the radical Left. More generally, censorship was primarily driven by the guidelines of "public order and manners and morals," up until the end of the Second World War.[3]

This meant that publications like *Kingu* and *Ie no hikari*, ones that so heavily stressed moral cultivation along with social duties and

---

2   Kōdansha, *Kodansha Encyclopedia of Japan*, 6:168–9.
3   Kasza, *The State and the Mass Media in Japan, 1918–1945*, 9.

obedience, would not have had much trouble with government interference, since their missions sought to maintain public order, promote patriotism, and advance Japanese interests in the world, even if they were attempting some degree of social change. In this way, the content of *Ie no hikari* and *Kingu* can also be viewed as a mirror of what was satisfactory and comfortable for the Japanese state in these years. In a fashion similar to the shogunal permission of the proliferation of inoffensive popular print media before the Meiji Restoration, the content of these two magazines over the decades of their publication was sufficiently palatable to the state that no evidence of censorship was ever recorded for either publication.

The reality of state influence in the first half of the twentieth century should nevertheless inform our understanding of these Japanese publications. As Miriam Silverberg explains it, "Japanese consumers were always simultaneously imperial subjects."[4] While I am sympathetic to Silverberg's emphasis on differences masked by the category of "consumer," and appreciative of the nuance the concept of "consumer-subject" brings to bear, the process of creating a *mass* in Japan was not focused on the emperor system per se, but, rather, on the population that lived within it. Moreover, the mass that was born in the interwar years continued into the postwar era less because of the *subject* part of their identity and more because of the *consumer*. The commonality of the mass audience did not require empire, even though it was created and coexisted comfortably within it.

The government applauded magazines like *Kingu* and *Ie no hikari* because the explicit values they espoused overlapped neatly with government policies and agendas during these years.[5] After all, these magazines reached people more intimately and willingly than the government could hope to, and they did so while exhibiting ideas that straightforwardly reinforced support of the nation and aims for its betterment. Why would the government interfere with such a blessing? Moreover, these editors would have been aware of the restrictions placed on publishers and may have steered clear of any potentially "dangerous" topics.

---

4 Silverberg, *Erotic Grotesque Nonsense*, 25.
5 Gotō Shimpei's approval has been mentioned above, and the policies which allowed for only these magazines in barracks and other government-run institutions will be covered in the next chapter.

There were no documented concerns from writers or editors that any censor would excise the values and ideas they wished to pen, nor proof that *Ie no hikari* or *Kingu* editors or writers felt unduly burdened by the laws in place. Scholars have mined texts that were censored to better understand what was suppressed and *not* permissible; conversely, these magazines are the less explored counterparts of what was both *acceptable* and *accessible*. The social disparities concealed and realities constrained through these pervasive publications constitute core features of the transwar culture of Japan worth highlighting more broadly.

It was said that in the late 1920s, the world of magazines had shifted from Hakubunkan to Kōdansha. Hakubunkan was a publishing company established in 1887 that issued such periodical titles as *Taiyō* (The Sun) and *Bungei kurabu* (Literature Club), selling an average of 56,000 copies per journal around the turn of the century, compared to *Kingu*'s roughly 740,000 printed issues each month in its initial years. In Hakubunkan's heyday, popular appeal meant covering scandals from the pleasure quarters and other varieties of society gossip, topics that understandably earned it the uncultured reputation it seemed to have. But Kōdansha's editorial policies completely re-envisioned the meaning of mass as something not needlessly crass or lowbrow, but rather and simply *accessible*, and the so-called Kōdansha style was born. The magazines Noma's publishing house produced were qualitatively distinct from what came before, with radical differences both in terms of the physical and formal features and in terms of the content and audience.[6]

There were, moreover, quite a few technological advances that allowed for the production of such large quantities of magazines. The rising success of various newspapers, and then magazines, caused an importation of higher-speed rotary presses in the early decades of the twentieth century. A domestic typesetting machine was also invented in 1920 for Japanese-language publications.[7] The advances in printing

---

6   奥原, 家の光の二十五年 (*Twenty-Five Years of "Light of the Home"*), 13.
7   Useful information and anecdotes from the publishing world can be found in Westney's scholarship, but there is also a problematic tendency to explain phenomena by alluding to "Japanese" cultural habits or frames of mind, frequently linked to "a Confucian tradition," which dampen the otherwise useful and well-documented technical information. Additionally, Westney's overemphasis on Western influences on business practices, as if in the absence of Western models Japanese were simply at a loss for what to do, seems a bit passé. However, see Westney, *Imitation and Innovation*, 183.

technology came conveniently in concert with a marked decrease in the cost of paper. Oji Paper Company, Fuji Paper Manufacturing, Hokuetsu Kishu Paper Company, and others had overproduced in the mid- to late 1920s and, consequently, the price of paper fell noticeably. Because of this, various publishing companies were able to buy paper at more than 20 per cent off the prices from the turn of the previous decade. The magazine world obviously benefited from this, especially those at the Industrial Cooperative, who did not make a profit on the publication until several years into the enterprise in the early 1930s.[8]

The mission of these publications was established early on and carried through the decades of their production in steadfast and unrevised devotion. To show the articulation of those missions, a close investigation of the first few issues of the magazines is required. The point of this chapter is not, however, to meticulously catalogue the depth and breadth of the thousands upon thousands of pages of these two publications, though it does sketch what the content of these periodicals looked like more generally, to provide a sampling of what people were so smitten with in these Japanese family magazines.

Kingu

"Caesar may have said 'I came, I saw, I conquered,' but all at our company proclaim in wondrous unison 'we came, we saw, we astonished.'" With these words in the first issue of *Kingu*, the editors set forth their bold new project, "not like soap or face powder and other such products," but "food for the soul."[9] Associating the quote from Caesar about his famous victories on the battlefield with the avowed mission at the release of the first issue of *Kingu* is ironic.[10] Here was a magazine that claimed to provide not just entertainment, but self-betterment for its readers; *Kingu* conquered its audience with entertainment. *Ie no hikari* took the development of ethics and principles of the audience as the centrepiece of its mission as well, though perhaps it expressed this with less ostentation.

---

8 奥原, 家の光の二十五年 (*Twenty-Five Years of "Light of the Home"*), 14.
9 「キング」編輯局同人, "『キング』が世に出るまでの苦心 (The Agony Until *King* Appeared)," 280.
10 *Julius Caesar* was also the first Shakespearian play to be translated into Japanese (Quinn, "Political Theatre").

The inaugural issue of *Kingu* was released 1 January 1925 and boasted close to four hundred pages in total with all of the front matter, advertising, and back matter included. The cover of the first *Kingu* was emblazoned with a rising sun as a backdrop to a winged, naked woman, arms crossed to cover her chest, holding a rose (see figure 3.1). Wada Eisaku, a notable enthusiast of Western painting techniques, created it. The title is printed as both *KING*, in a capitalized bold roman typeface, across the top (read left to right) and *Kingu*, in a sharp *katakana* script, down the right side (read top to bottom).[11]

If the title was an attempt to counter the world of women's magazines with a masculine-sounding name, the image is reminiscent of neoclassical portraiture in the European tradition. The cover evokes an ethereal feminine messenger with an even gaze at the viewer, a flower in her hand, and dark hair and eyes. A messenger of the empire, suggested by the sun's rays in the background, has come. The cover provides the possibility of a number of different readings of the image's meaning, which is also in line with *King*'s style: concrete enough to grab one's attention yet ambiguous enough to be multiply interpreted and enjoyed.

The first piece of writing in the magazine, after the scores of advertisements and notices functioning as wishes for a successful venture from various industry and business leaders, is an opinion piece from Sawayanagi Masatarō (1865–1927). His "Notable Opinion" explains how the value of military prowess in the international community had declined after the First World War, and, though such power still had its place, the equilibrium of power that was present before the war had ceased to exist, according to Sawayanagi. He goes on to say that Japan was in fact not far behind the world's naval leaders (Britain and the US) and could reasonably be considered to have the third best navy in the world. Through this security and the progress of its culture, claimed Sawayanagi, Japan could one day take its place among the Five Powers and avoid being subordinated to first world nations as had happened with so many other countries.[12]

On a slightly tangential note, the editors of *Kingu* made an interesting decision about the way they used typeface. This article provides

---

11 Typefaces are as important a visual component of magazine cover design as any of the other elements. For a discussion of some ideologically charged fonts, see Weisenfeld, "Japanese Typographic Design and the Art of Letterforms."

12 澤柳, "名家一説 (A Notable Opinion)," 1.

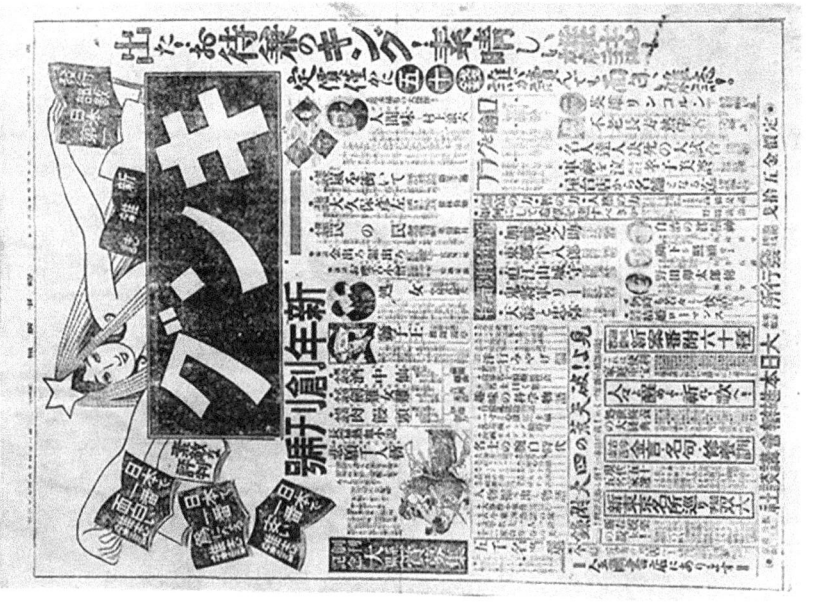

Figure 3.1. Inaugural cover image, *Kingu*

a perfect representative example. The phrase "balance of powers" in Sawayanagi's article is written in the Japanese kanji as per common usage (*kenryoku no heikō*); however, the pronunciation guide (*rubi*) used to gloss these words for the reader is given in *katakana* (the type of *kana* normally used for foreign words, animal noises, and sounds not native to the Japanese vernacular) and is an approximation of the English pronunciation for "balance of powers" (*baransu obu pawāsu*).[13] This is done not once but twice for the phrase in this article, and such glosses are provided for various words and phrases throughout every issue of *King*.

Sometimes it appears that the choice to use a non-vernacular transliteration of a perfectly ordinary Japanese expression is meant to be evocative of the wider world in which Japan is a part. Sometimes it is an attempt to educate readers about terms from foreign languages (usually English) in common parlance among intellectuals and elites more "in the know." But most importantly, the unusual use of the vocabulary with pronunciation guides shows remarkable expectations about and attention to the "common" knowledge of the audience. The producers of these magazines thought to teach their audience down to even this most subtle of methods.[14]

---

13 In the original: 権力の平衡 and バランス、オブ、パワース respectively. See ibid., line 1–2, 5.

14 While an exhaustive study of *furigana* usage in print media is beyond the capacities of the author, my general familiarity with newspapers and other publications of this era suggests that extensive manipulations of *kana* were unusual in post-Tokugawa years (if not a prerogative of Noma's publications). Ariga claims that "Publications, including newspapers, magazines, government documents, official proclamations, and literary works, often appeared with *sō-rubi*. For example, *kōshimbun* 小新聞 ('small newspapers'), which did not include political news and were aimed at a general readership, always came out with *sō-rubi* in *hiragana*. Even *ōshimbun* 大新聞, or 'big newspapers' intended for more educated readers, used *rubi*" in order to help un- or under-educated readers, but "the Police Bureau of the Home Ministry in 1938 urged the editors of magazines for children and school pupils not to use *rubi* in their publications. After World War II, both the cabinet and the Ministry of Education issued a list of 1,850 *tōyō kanji* 当用漢字 on 16 November 1946, stipulating that only these characters should be employed in legal and official documents, magazines, newspapers, and other public writings. The instructions accompanying the list stated that, as a rule, *rubi* were not to be used. *Rubi* today are employed only sparingly in certain publications, such as technical and scholarly writings, literature, and commercial books and magazines for children." See Ariga, "The Playful Gloss," 317, 320.

The prefatory editorial then goes on to explain that among the leading countries of the world there is a notable degree of similarity in terms of the maintenance of infrastructural systems of railway, roads, and harbours, but that Japan's efforts, in contrast to fitting in with those of other nations, should be focused on the advancement of culture and the prevention of infectious disease, infant mortality, and similar "embarrassments" for advanced civilizations. According to Sawayanagi, thinking broadly about how to advance Japan's place in the world, including more holistic aspects of its development, should be the focus of everyone's efforts.[15] This is a call to the masses of Japan to contribute to the cultural advancement of their nation by shining their collective, civilized light for global society.

To put these ideas in context, some background on Sawayanagi is useful. He was an educator and reformist of considerable note. He worked in both public and private capacities ranging from the Ministry of Education, the First Higher School, and Tōhoku Imperial University, to Kyoto Imperial University, Seijō Middle School, and the Imperial Education Association (*Teikoku Kyōikukai*). He was an avid supporter of Japan's imperial projects in the colonies, if not of strong governmental control over education, and saw Japan as being a uniquely prepared leader that needed to promote Asian civilization in the rest of the world through the advancement of Japanese culture on the world stage. He advocated for an educated but obedient citizenry domestically, endorsing a mixture of cultural development that simultaneously promoted "modernism" and the advancement of Western liberal ideas while also demeaning non-Japanese Asian people (including the Ainu and Okinawans) in his "civilizing" project.[16] Readers might not have known him by name, but they likely would have encountered, if not his words themselves, his ideas, since they seemed to be relatively common in the public discourse and popular press of the day.

Such ideas of "Asia for the Asians," pan-Asianism, and the like were not new and had connections to the well-known debates and discussions in the years surrounding the turn of the nineteenth century by

---

15 澤柳, "名家一説 (A Notable Opinion)," 1.
16 For a more complete treatment on Sawayanagi and his ideas and politics, see Lincicome, *Imperial Subjects as Global Citizens*, 34–71; 新田, 澤柳政太郎: 随時随所楽シ マザルナシ. Also, for a brief mention of his writings about women within the realm of women's magazines, see Frederick, *Turning Pages*, 40, 41, 43–4.

prominent figures like Fukuzawa Yukichi, Okakura Tenshin, and Ōkawa Shūmei, for example. However, the specific flavour of discourse present in Sawayanagi's editorial for *Kingu* is also representative of the principles of the magazine at large. Noma's commitment to his role as teacher is mirrored in the choice to have a prominent educator – not a politician, or actor, or farmer – speak first to the audience. Further, this particular educator was a vocal patriot who believed that Japan's advancement in the world was only possible through the raising of cultural standards throughout the Japanese empire, quite in line with Noma's overarching philosophy central to the project of *Kingu* as well.

Immediately following Sawayanagi's piece, one finds the second article, *"King's* Brilliant Arrival," which begins: "Beloved Ladies and Gentlemen! This is indeed the very magazine for you – the ideal magazine – the pride of our country's publishing world."[17] The ideal magazine for me? How could a reader not be intrigued by such a bold claim, even if just in curious scepticism? So, one reads on.

In reference to the magazine's name, we are told, *"Kingu* is the king of the publishing world. A stately character, with an easy manner, as a dashing figure of a king astride a white horse, this king adapts himself to the circumstances perfectly without obstacles, a leader among leaders, commanding an army one million strong."[18] The personification of the magazine's name in the figure of a dashing monarch astride a snowy steed, marshalling those under his command, seems quite in step with Noma's visions of his publications in the world. He clearly saw himself as being a moral exemplar standing tall for all to emulate. Indeed, this kind of image did not change much as, in 1943, when the title of the publication was changed to *Fuji* and the cover showed the famed statue of samurai and celebrated imperial loyalist Kusunoki Masashige located near the Imperial Palace (see figure 3.2).

But what visions are in store for the audience? What are the stakes? The article claims, "this King is not medieval, but modern, not despotic, but of the masses, plentiful with luminous pastimes, lightheartedly masquerading as occasion calls, everywhere appearing and disappearing, and always keeping you guessing."[19] Since the content was always varied, the suggestion goes, readers might think they knew what the

---

17 "燦たりキングの出現 (*King's* Brilliant Arrival)," 2.
18 Ibid.
19 Ibid.

Figure 3.2. Inaugural cover image, *Fuji*

magazine was about, but would always find new surprises. These surprises, simultaneously modern and mass, are presented thus:

> You can experience the marvellous wonder of becoming an infinite variety of people: telling the mysterious truths as the figure of the philosopher, extolling the mysteries of existence as the figure of the poet, mapping out hundred-year plans for our country, debating the urgent issues of national defence as a soldier, being the compass on the sea route for the sailor, thinking of the trends in economic and morals as a merchant, finding traces of the divine timeless and transitory as an artist, kneeling in offering to the absolute being in devotedly earnest prayer as a believer; or becoming an old man, or a pure youth, or a lovely maiden, or an energetic student, becoming a saint or the common man, ancient folk, or the people of today.[20]

---

20 Ibid., 3.

In Noma's vision, *Kingu* provided a smorgasbord of content, allowing the audience to be entertained through their own imaginations prompted by what they encountered on the pages before them. Through fiction and articles ranging widely in topic, consumers of *Kingu* did indeed gain exposure to a surprising variety of images, stories, and entertainments. These amusements were all provided in the context of being "we Japanese" and participating in "our country" or "the nation," etc.[21] The perspective of the magazine articles was almost always that of "us" and "our," promoting a sense of community and shared knowledge, values, and culture specific to Japan.

"*King* is the National Park of the magazine world" (another example of code-switching vocabulary, normally printed in kanji and pronounced *kokuritsu kōen*, but glossed here in kana as *nashon'naru pāku*, mimicking "national park" in English) is a section of the same article, again speaking to the grandeurs and wonders in store:

> In the shade of lofty trees, praising the dew at daybreak on an unnamed white flower. The bird sings. The insects chirp. Snow, the moon, flowers, sunshine, rainfall, rustling wind, the natural features and varied weather from season to season all proceed in due course. Our *Kingu* is truly a huge natural park. Furthermore, our *Kingu* is the very wonder of the magazine world. Painting natural vistas, every when and where, by means of the unselfishness of civilization, to truly give meaning to the surprise of the heart and spirit ... Isn't there one great realm pregnant with <u>every possible thing</u> in any form, catching <u>everything in existence</u> in its nets? *Kingu* is that great realm. What is this grand wonder in the first place? Indeed! *Kingu* receives the honour of this ringing call! This grandiose and splendid national park! The grand wonder of this radiant civilization! AH, our beloved magazine *Kingu*![22]

Seeking to convey the vastness and splendour of the interesting content to unfold, the language is profoundly self-important. But it also uses the metaphor of a national park. This can be read in a few ways.

First, national parks are constructed spaces designed to conserve "nature" within the framework of national pride and ownership of the

---

21 In the original as: 我々日本人, 我が国, 国家, etc.
22 Emphasis appears in the original. "燦たりキングの出現 (*King*'s Brilliant Arrival),"
    3–4.

environment.[23] Second, the analogy that the magazine content provides all things in existence is not just absurd or impossible boasting. Rather, it speaks to the publishers' conception of what there *is* in existence. *They* determined what the world was and what it comprised, then provided a representative sample of it for the audience. Topics excluded from these publications simply mattered not. And for most of the audience it was unlikely that what went missing was missed.

In seeking to find the ways in which cultural practices are normalized and the process by which it happened was obscured, language like this should be an enormous red flag. The selection process required for editing *King* and the principles that informed it were also concealed in this manner of talking. Steeped in the idiom of flowers, sunshine, snow, and the moon, such language evoked a natural world untouched by human intervention. Natural laws of the universe exist and are largely to be unquestioned. The magazine was the exact opposite of a natural occurrence, since it was created by interested human parties.[24] These publishers were, thus, world-defining meaning makers for the masses.

The article does mention the editorial efforts involved, but does so in a value-laden, self-congratulating way, not in any sense demystifying the process for the readers. It says:

> As for the management of our magazine *Kingu*, we have concentrated all of our efforts on decisive action, completely transcending selfishness in a very important heroic attempt. We beseech every single citizen, without discriminating based on occupation, class, regardless of wealth, men and women of all ages, those who are learned and those who are not, with one accord, gathered here, in the middle of reading absorbed with interest, naturally noble refinement, cultivating a solid moral sense; and we've changed people's attitudes. Throughout all of Japan, just as in every house there is a National Flag, our *Kingu* is treasured because it contributes to cultivation of the mind and it indeed serves as our flag.[25]

---

23 For a relatively recent work discussing natural history museum projects, with the accompanying "complete" collection of natural things, presented for edutainment purposes and the like, see Havens, *Parkscapes*.

24 For one discussion of ways in which naturalistic and scientific discourse works to impose power on colonial subjects, see Pratt, *Imperial Eyes*, 164–5, 215–16.

25 "燦たりキングの出現 (*King*'s Brilliant Arrival)," 5.

Kingu did come onto the scene with quite a bit of fanfare, due to the wide-spread advertising Kōdansha lavished upon it. But the explicit announcement of the inclusive nature of the publication is also important.

Amidst the new category of "family magazine" that these publications had created, readers would have been able to see themselves included as a target audience – the magazine spoke to them directly, be they man, woman, or child, educated or not, poor or elite, rural or urban. Moreover, though, equating the publication with the national flag (*kokki*) and assuming its natural inclusion in every household conflates patriotism and its display with consumption of the magazine.[26] The value implicit here is that everyone should display their national pride with flags (and magazines) and participate, as well, in the collective culture that *King* can offer.

The themes purportedly allowing audience patriotism, refinement, and education come bundled together with participation in the collective audience and were present from the first issue; they also continued throughout *Kingu*'s publication. Claiming that "we've changed people's attitudes" in the first issue puts the cart before the horse, but in the decades of publication that followed, and as its influence spread, *Kingu* did in fact impact attitudes and Japanese culture more generally.

According to the article, moreover, "*Kingu* has raised the bar and reached greater numbers than any of its brethren; contributing to morals and sentiments is our ardent desire and the concurrent result."[27] The editors' devotion to the project of improving the audience's moral and cultural life is the avowed impetus of all policies for *Kingu*. Such examples are too numerous to ignore, and the ideological bent of this project is obvious and explicit from the outset. The article concludes:

> We've got a burning passion [for this project] within our organization and a surprising demand for the birth of such things outside our doors. Thus, we venture to honour this king, this grandiose and splendid national park, and this grand and brilliantly shining wonder. We proclaim in our loudest voice: "Indeed, this is our beloved *Kingu*." This is for the well-being of our seventy million fellows and for the very happiness of mankind.[28]

---

26 This usage for "national flag" (国旗), as opposed to 日の丸 (*hi no maru*) or 日章旗 (*nisshōki*, more commonly used for the "the flag of the rising sun"), is perhaps notable.

27 "燦たりキングの出現 (*King's* Brilliant Arrival)," 5.

28 Ibid.

Here, especially, the language suggests that not only is *King* a wholesome and beneficial enterprise, but one for which the masses themselves have been clamouring. Kōdansha is simply giving the people what they want, according to its editors, and thereby promoting the betterment of Japan and the world at large.

Noma once flatly mused, "the luxuries of material life are fast becoming the universal need of the masses."[29] This was certainly the case with magazines; a commodity once viewed as a luxury (due to price or erudition) was rapidly establishing itself as essential leisure material for the vast majority of the populace. Nobody *needs* a magazine in the sense that they need sustenance and shelter, but the integration of a commodity in everyday life can shift people's desires towards the more common inclusion of new products within their daily practices. More important is the shift in the understanding of one's needs.

Advertisements that appeared in print media for commodities like toothpaste, watches, dyes, cosmetics, radios, and sewing machines all enhanced the manufacturing of this kind of desire, or there would have been no visible increases in the sales of such commodities. The creation of desire was certainly part and parcel of the publishing practices at Kōdansha, and the success of *Kingu* derived in part from their ability to make their product (along with the lifestyles and products advertised within) desirable.

Among the pieces included in the first issue of *Kingu* was one penned by Noma himself. In it he lays out a method for happiness that strikes all of the same chords present in his comments on his mission and methods. The article is worth relating in detail. It begins:

> I ask you not to seek lofty knowledge and scholarship in vain. Truly knowledgeable seekers of the path know the most valuable thing is personal experience. It is seriousness. It is perseverance. [You] must embrace hope for the journey ahead. [You] must establish a philosophy of life. On one hand [you] must then commit yourself to being courageous. And on the other [you] must spend your life in gratitude and appreciation with a humble heart. And when you internalize this path, you will be able to have the pleasures of a free and pious life.[30]

Making knowledge relevant and useful to daily life is a part of Noma's personal philosophy that fitted neatly with his magazine enterprises.

---

29 Akimoto, *Seiji Noma "Magazine King" of Japan*, 32.
30 野間, "如何にして希望を達すべき呼 (How You Should Reach Your Dreams)," 17.

Diligence, self-control and self-improvement, and eschewing book learning all not only manifested in Noma's various writings and statements but also provided the general tone for *Kingu* and Kōdansha's magazines more generally.

Noma continues by explaining,

> I ask you not to seek lofty knowledge and scholarship in vain. In the world, we seek erudition and genius and are overly captivated by it. The study of today can bestow the knowledge of the so-called mechanical culture, but it does not have the power to cultivate people. Studying for the sake of study takes one ever higher, but often further and further from actual life.
>
> So, then what should we be thinking about? We should be thinking about the fact that the path is near. The ancients have long argued, "awareness comes only through practice." "Practice" is "personal experience." True learning is not obtained from books. It exists in a place from personal experience. It exists in ordinary rooms, where religion, morals, society, and the nation all live. This is a microcosm of the world; it's a training *dōjō*, heaven's laboratory for the whole universe.
>
> Inside this room where ordinary affairs take place, devoting oneself to contemplation, a dedication to spiritual improvement, is working up to the place of gaining experience through one's actual life; truly the study of living opens the door to all of the experiences of one's lifetime. The path is near; we just must simply experience the unexpected.[31]

Kingu presents itself not just as a magazine – solely fluffy entertainment, as the critics of the day might have complained – but a life manual, a guide to better living. In addition, a plea for less academic pursuits from a former schoolteacher is a poignant one, but makes sense in light of who was being targeted as the audience.

In order to make the magazine accessible to the "top of the bottom," such a strategy was successful on several levels. First, it assured readers that they were already sufficiently schooled to understand and benefit from the publication. Second, the nation, society, and morals are comprised of the individual efforts of ordinary people in their pursuit of personal betterment, the article intimates. And last, it complimented the audience by suggesting that the power to make themselves happier was easily obtainable without the formal education and institutions of

---

31 Ibid., 17–18.

higher learning that society overemphasized and that excluded so many from the "top of the bottom." Since many of the readers would have received only minimal schooling, this is obviously a clever approach to take.

Noma understood who the masses were and how to convincingly address them. He saw the ways in which this huge group of people was not being satisfied by other media. The minimal growth of disposable time and income among so many people during this era primed that demographic for the entertainment and values that family magazines could provide. These publishers had remarkable insight into embryonic social shifts that had not yet fully taken shape but that responded well to spurs urging their consolidation.

Kingu's first issue also advertised the more mundane merits of the publications and explained the price point and length.

> We have embarked on the most audacious venture dared in terms of the three aspects of quality, quantity, and price. We've solicited manuscripts from far and wide the country over, and from among this surprising number, we've carefully selected a surprisingly select few of the superior ones so that our excellent quality wrangled the entrance of only the brilliantly shining few. The number of copies in circulation is truly an unprecedentedly huge amount; it was unavoidable that we started printing nearly half a year ago. Moreover, each issue contains more than three hundred pages, a vast amount; the price is a real miracle.[32]

King was a volume with substantial heft. One made it scores of pages into the publication before even reaching the first article. There were pages of photos intermixed with the advertising in the front matter that went under the moniker *Kingu gurafu* (from "graph" in English, for the pictorial section). Four or five hundred pages were the average for each issue. Most other fifty-sen monthlies of the day were not nearly as lengthy; newspapers were far shorter and as much as eighty sen for a monthly subscription.

In order to provide this huge amount of content, Kōdansha used a number of methods to produce and obtain manuscripts. A significant portion of the magazine was filled with serialized and illustrated fiction: Murakami Namiroku, Kan (Hiroshi) Kikuchi, Maeda Shozan,

---

32 "燦たりキングの出現 (*King*'s Brilliant Arrival)," 5.

Tsunoda Kikuo, Watanebe Katei, Shirai Kyoji, Masao Kume, Nomura Aisei, Kawaguchi Matsutarō, Katō Takeo, Takeda Toshihiko, the list of contributors goes on and on. These fictional pieces were varied in topic and style. There was historical fiction (*jidai shōsetsu*) with tales of samurai, courtesans, and monks, modelled on classical pieces of literature (at least in topic) for those who enjoyed envisioning days long past. This included authors like Yoshikawa Eiji, who made his name through his writings in *King* and later went on to pen the beloved *Musashi* series along with his modernizations of classical tales.

For those with more current tastes, each issue also included two or three serialized contemporary novels (*gendai shōsetsu*), frequently from the most notable authors of the day. These ranged from detective fiction by the likes of Nomura Kodō (née Nomura Osakazu) to the erotic, grotesque, and nonsensical (or *ero-guro-nansensu* as the genre was later titled) authored by Edogawa Ranpō (this *nom de plume* of Hirai Tarō was a phonetic play on his muse Edgar Allen Poe's name). The contemporary fiction ran the gamut from titillating or romantic to contemplative and brooding as a reflection of the flourishing of literary production in Japan more generally at this time. No matter the preferred type of fiction, readers would be satisfied by something on offer in each issue.

The variety continued. There were tales of wanderers and gamblers (*matabi mono*) that were stories about those freed from social constraints, travellers who sought their own paths through virtuous actions, providing both escapism and exemplars of morals overcoming poverty.[33] Newly written *rakugo* stories were placed alongside the others. *Rakugo* is an originally oral tradition of comical storytelling about one or two main protagonists; it is well known in Japan and still televised to this day. Poetry, as *waka* or *haiku*, was often sandwiched between the fiction and articles as well.

The entertainment provided was not restricted to fiction, either. There were comics sprinkled throughout each issue, some in black and white and some in two- or three-colour spreads (see figure 3.3), many based on silly puns or physical comedy that were easy to understand and produced an instant giggle. There were games and comments about games, with sudoku grids and strategies for *go* (a game of black and white stones) and *shogi* (Japanese chess). Children and adults alike would

---

33 For some commentary on *matabi mono*, see Alan Tansman's chapter in Washburn and Cavanaugh, eds., *Word and Image in Japanese Cinema*, 150.

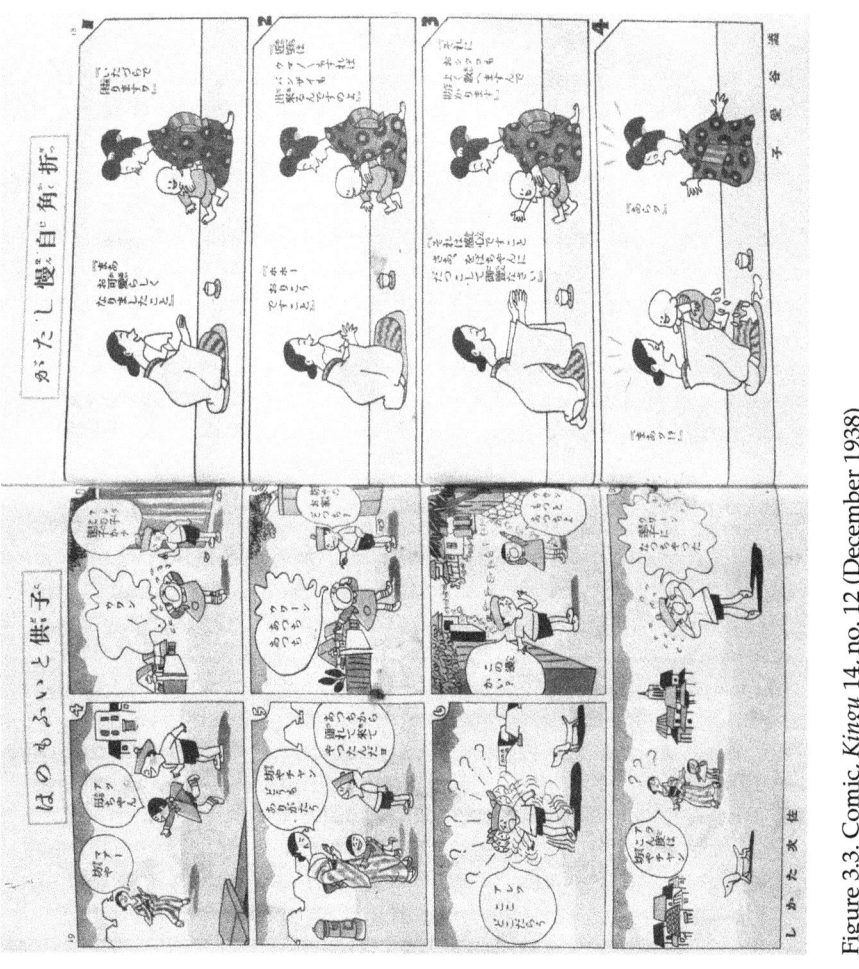

Figure 3.3. Comic, *Kingu* 14, no. 12 (December 1938)

find instructions for small projects (paper airplanes, spinners, bug nets, birdhouses, kites, etc.) that were easily made with common household items and that would provide leisure opportunities through both their construction and use. When Noma said he could provide something interesting for anyone, the content of *Kingu* certainly reflected a concerted effort at the hodgepodge approach, and there were very likely at least one or two things that anyone would find of interest in every issue.

For nonfiction pieces, there were in-house writers employed full time by Kōdansha and then a vast number of contracted writers from whom "copy" was purchased. Noma himself says that an attempt to rationalize the process of the payment of such writers was underway by 1927, explaining how the committee established for buying copy worked:

> We need such a tremendous amount of "copy" that we must have a regular and abundant supply. We consider all MSS. carefully and buy them, if we think them good, though we may have no immediate use for them. Last year, for instance, we bought ¥100,000 worth of articles … Some of them may be published someday, but the great majority will go to the limbo of unused MSS. In actual payment, too, the conditions differ. In some cases, we pay in exchange for the "copy," and in others we pay on publication.[34]

Thus, the process of collecting articles on the variety of topics included in a given issue of *Kingu* was, as this statement suggests, an involved one.

Were it possible to see what articles got winnowed from the pile, we would indeed have a more detailed idea of the editorial understanding of value. However, there appears to be no record of what got condemned to Kōdansha's midden heap. What is clear is that the expense of maintaining a diverse and regular supply of material for their over four-hundred-page monthly magazines was considerable.

It is worth noting as well that it was not simply obscure columnists who filled the non-fiction pages of *Kingu*. Articles, as with the fiction, were often not just about notable figures of the day, but written by them as well. The payments for these services rendered were not conditioned by the rationalized system developed for standard copy acquisitions. Noma clarified, "for contributions made by Ministers of State and prominent businessmen, who are too busy to write and therefore contribute their views orally, which involves some trouble in writing out,

---

34 Akimoto, *Seiji Noma "Magazine King" of Japan*, 29–30.

correcting, etc., we may not pay in cash, but will express our appreciation in some fitting form."[35] One wonders what type of appreciation
would be considered fitting, but we are left, at least, with a general
understanding of where and how the content of the magazine was produced when not penned by his employees or Noma himself.

Ie no hikari

For the first year of its publication, each issue of *Ie no hikari* was only
about one hundred pages long. The magazine increased in length as
it became more profitable, growing to two hundred plus pages in the
1930s. The initial pages were filled with various advertisements, while
the first piece of actual content that appears in each issue of *Light of the
Home* is a one-page preface with an illustration. This prefatory piece in
many issues speaks about ideals – for the cooperative and society.

In the inaugural issue this preface was written by Shimura Gentarō
and titled "The Spring of the Spirit of Cooperation." In it, he explains
that realizing a better life and creating an ideal society is all possible simply by using resources the readers already have: by working together
and fostering a spirit of cooperation and mutual assistance, families can
improve their lives and thereby "make this ideal into reality in everyday life."[36] He continues, "The place where this spirit is cultivated is in
the home of our members. Parents and children, husbands and wives,
understanding each other, working together, comforting each other,
with sincere cooperation and harmony ..." and, notably, that with this
ideal in mind, "The purpose of this magazine is to support the cultivation of the spring of the spirit of cooperation – the family."[37] As in the
Noma editorial in the first issue in *Kingu*, the readers are complimented
about the skills they already possess and given hope about the ways in
which their lives can be improved (in a tone that is directly connected
to the espoused values of the publication). These were likely attractive
ideas for farmers, often living difficult and grinding lives with little
means at their disposal.

The first full article in that issue is about the education of children in
the home and respect for mothers in their important fulfilment of this

---

35 Ibid., 30–1.
36 志村源, "共同心の泉 (The Spring of the Spirit of Cooperation)," 1.
37 Ibid.

task. In it, we are told that despite the successes of the formal education system, the teaching that goes on in the home, even before a child is of school age, is of utmost importance to Japan. Experiments about the importance of early education for children from a British educator are mentioned to bring to light the fact that Britain had daycares to promote early childhood development but Japan had no such facilities.[38] And since children did not formally enter school until they were six years old, the duty of early childhood education in Japan fell to the parents, especially mothers. As such, the article tells readers that mothers had two extremely important tasks; Japanese mothers needed not only to help children learn and to provide an environment for good language acquisition and the like but also to promote psychological development (精神発達, lit. psychogenesis), so that their hearts, mysterious though they were, could be cultivated alongside their intellect. These efforts were all towards the economic and political betterment of society at large, according to the author. Thus, the article argues, advocating respect for motherhood and promoting motherly domestic pursuits in Japan helped mothers to accomplish their important duties, ones that they were particularly able to perform.[39] Indicative of the inclusivity of the editorial tone, this article speaks to males so as to advance the status of women within the family and communicates to females so as to clarify how they can better perform their central domestic roles.

It is notable that the author is in fact Sawayanagi Masatarō – the very same figure chosen as a leadoff author for the first issue of *Kingu*. The kind of education being promoted here is not book learning; rather, it is more fluid, informal, and based in moral education and the transmission of values. This is evidence for an overlap between the two publications; even if they diverge on the particulars of their respective ideals, the result of their impact is a common cultural vehicle created through these media and a participatory and comprehensive audience. Moreover, *Ie no hikari* was a channel stressing the moral and cultural development of its readers that regularly provided suggestions for possible lessons on moral and cultural attitudes. These magazines created "common sense" as they simultaneously created the audience that possessed it.

---

38 It is unclear exactly who this British educator, Mrs McMillan or MacMillan, might have been.

39 澤柳, "母性尊重と家庭教育 (Home Education and Respect for Motherhood)," 2–5.

Part of the article is presented on the same page as an illustration and a small inset of the first instalment of a story titled *The Strange Glow* by Kawahara Nadeshiko. The story, serialized over several issues and doled out in paragraph-length sections scattered throughout each issue, is about a woman who glances at the newspaper left spread open on the desk only to have the eyes of her "angelically beautiful face" become mysteriously transfixed by the print, which draws her in, line by line. This segment of the story ends with the declaration, "Oh my! Even such things [can happen]."[40] The captionless illustration seems to do double duty on the page. Primarily, the image of a kimono-clad woman reading a newspaper is intended to accompany the story, which is described in the inset box as being an illustrated short story. But secondarily, it is a visual representation of a reading woman that is included on the final page of an article discussing motherly duties in early childhood education in the home. As such, this example is instructive about one peculiarity of the format of magazines more generally.

One wonders how we are to read the combination in this example. First, reading the article about mothers providing for the spiritual and mental development of their children and then seeing an image of a female perusing a newspaper might conjure images of momma educating herself in order to better educate her offspring. But when paired with the serial fiction that it illustrates, the illustration takes on a very different cast. Kawahara's story about an otherworldly possession by a newspaper suggests that newspapers can be dangerous, so the status of newspapers and women reading them is left undecided. (Such opaque integration is discussed more fully in chapter 5, but it is worth mentioning briefly here.) This one example is not meant to demonstrate a rule about the relationship between the various components of a magazine, but it is meant to suggest that attention to the interplay (including the ambiguities) of all aspects of this kind of media is required.

Each issue was divided in the table of contents into sections based on the type of content: lectures, economics, popular science, household side-jobs, hobbies and "real life," children's articles, etc. The rest of *Light of the Home*'s first issue is filled with this variety of content. It included articles about farm life that centre on the family, mutual assistance, and the Cooperative. Examples include "Rural Women in Denmark," "The Household and the Farm," "Guidebook for Governing the

---

40 河原, "異様な輝き (The Strange Glow)," 5.

Family," "Toward the Cooperative Purchase of Fertilizers," and "The Question of Rural Financing and Thoroughgoing Trade Unionism." All of these articles are written in an unpretentious and straightforward style meant to be enjoyable to read, understandable, and beneficial to even the most uneducated person.

Of all the articles in this inaugural issue, "Light of the Home, Light of the Nation," however, provides the clearest articulation of the mission of the project at hand. It pushes the audience to participate socially in a manner that integrates politics as promoted by the Cooperative into the daily activities of rural folk. We are told,

> It is not sufficient to describe our lives as disconnected from politics ... because we engage in private life construed as separate [from the political or social]. But in this private life we do not carry on by ourselves. The rice we eat, the clothes we wear, the roof we all live under, it's all gotten by mutual cooperation. This is what we call economic solidarity.[41]

If the cornerstone of society is the family, the family's purpose is participation in the larger community, the personal and political allied and made manifest, claims the author. The collective advancement that the Sangyō Kumiai sought for Japan was based on generalized cultural improvement among the rural populace.

The article continues by saying,

> The Industrial Cooperative was first started and is managed by culturally minded individuals and we aim to advance the economic profit of the middle and lower classes and expand their protections. At the crossroads of whether or not we achieve this goal are rural economic survival and the source of destiny for deciding local political autonomy. More lectures will come successively from this Industrial Cooperative, but we will omit them today, for now just saying one word of congratulations that *Light of the Home* has been published.[42]

The protection of farmers and the advancement of their cause is the heart of what the Cooperative was about, as is clarified in this statement. The editors at *Ie no hikari* intuited, similarly to Noma at Kōdansha,

---

41 岡, "家の光、国の光 (Light of the Home, Light of the Nation)," 23.
42 Ibid.

that *combining* the middle and lower classes together made it easier to achieve their aims.

The article also positions the publication as facilitating the Cooperative in making these social changes. This is made clear again in a section called "Don't be envious, work hard!"

A Western poet once mused – what do you envy? Thriving industry, splendid steamships, hotels constructed of granite and iron, fortresses, warships? Stop! ... we should not envy the city simply because of its form. True peace and happiness are in the countryside – home is in the countryside – and home is the birthplace of a secure and blessed livelihood. The security of that livelihood begins with self-help and diligence, and advances because of cooperation with others. Thus, the dark night will only be illuminated because of *Light of the Home*'s transmission of diligence communicating the spark of cooperation.[43]

Those at the Cooperative who wanted to expand the reach and influence of the organization's efforts made these ideals about the farming family the forefront of the publication. The magazine was a vehicle to help achieve this goal. With less flash and bravado than *Kingu*, *Ie no hikari* nevertheless offered its readers hope for the future along with their magazine subscriptions.

The prefatory article of the second issue of *Light of the Home* offers a critique of stale entertainments:

We are not just calling for an out of touch, old style of rural woman. This is a women's magazine that should be read. The ideal rural woman creates her family; the ideal women's magazine provides the means and most trusted source for the most effective way to do this. This is the exact, significant goal of this magazine.[44]

This piece reiterates the importance of the home and family, with women as the keystone of the family. It is interesting to note the use of the descriptor of "women's magazine," since all of the planning documentation speaks of *Ie no hikari* as a "family magazine." Those at the Kumiai who were savvier about promotion and advertising realized

---

43 Ibid., 24.
44 "農村と婦人雑誌 (Farming Villages and Women's Magazines)," 1.

that their audience would know what a women's magazine (*fujin zasshi*) was and thus sought to capitalize on that familiarity in order to promote their own publication. Rather than representing any shift in attitudes about the focus and mission of the magazine, they were comparing *Ie no hikari* to other women's magazines and thus used the phrase in a somewhat sardonic fashion. But more importantly, this passage echoes the importance of women, via their participation in the Cooperative's activities, in making changes for the betterment of Japan.

In this vein, another article continues and further articulates the importance of the Cooperative within a larger framework. It reads:

> We have been blindly obedient to customs and habits of the past several hundred years, and the precious splendour of the self has dulled; we need a complete change in the pessimistic attitude of the so-called village mood, even though the current situation of our farmers is extremely bad.
>
> Within this hidden power of the self – a progressive, advanced self – is the very best development of self-improvement. If we continue to make this effort, your light will become the light of the home, and the light of the home will become the light of society, allowing for the first time the flower of our country's beautiful culture to bloom.
>
> In a word, the light of the nation is in the home, the light of the home is in the self. In debating big national or social problems, the development of our rural communities naturally weighs heavily, but more than that, our urgent current business is the existence of the farmer's self. I think there is the opportunity to illuminate that inner light aplenty in an organization [like ours] fit to carry out such improvement.
>
> And thus, if we act positively, then this light will spread. Assistance or cooperation is an important means of social evolution; the development of every kind of cooperative is an extremely important foundation for individuals and the national society.[45]

If individuals within each home took the lessons of the Cooperative to heart, then families would benefit, the reader is told; when families worked together, hamlets and villages could prosper, according to this ideal. Once villages were combined in collective efforts, the nation, by this line of thinking, also prospered, and the purpose behind the existence of unions would be made manifest. To requote Shimura Gentarō,

---

45 森本, "家の光は自己にあり (The Light of the Home is in the Self)," 7.

"The spring of the spirit of cooperation is in the family. Our ideal society is cultivated in the homes of Co-op members."[46] Here is the heart of the *Ie no hikari* project: to combine all the households of Japan in a voluntary and common effort.

While profits were naturally on the minds of the editors on the one hand, that balanced with their obvious concern over getting people to actually engage with their product and to consume the information it contained. This is made clear in the discussions that surrounded the issue of pricing the magazine. One summary of such a debate went thus:

> It would have been natural for *Ie no hikari* to be a free publication since it was in essence an advertisement for the Cooperative. However, it was common for free publications to be discarded without being read. This would have made the publication meaningless. So, if there were a charge for the magazine, then at the very least people would read it. This was the thinking that formed the basis for charging for *Ie no hikari*.[47]

This suggests that promotional efforts by other means had already been made, though unsuccessfully. Since it was not simply the product (i.e., *Ie no hikari*) that the editors were concerned about hawking, those at the Cooperative were quite preoccupied with how to go about gaining their audience's interest and loyalty.

Along these lines, the editors of *Ie no hikari* understood the competition they had with other magazines and regularly referred to such publications, especially women's magazines, of the day. In one rather blunt estimation, "the contemporary *Shufu no tomo* was badmouthed as being a magazine for aristocratic housewives and [the publication] was compared to *nukamiso* [a salted rice-bran paste for pickling, used idiomatically to mean a homely or stodgy woman]."[48] Insults about the competition aside, members at the Cooperative were ready and willing to make the most of the prospects created by the growing readership of other publications; this became all the more clear as *Ie no hikari* outstripped *Kingu* in popularity.

---

46 家の光協会 (Ie no Hikari Kyōkai), 家の光五十年の人と動きと (*Fifty Years of the People and Developments of "Light of the Home"*), 6.

47 北村, 家の光の四十年 (*Forty Years of "Light of the Home"*), 12.

48 "ぬかみそ臭い女," to give the precise phrase. 奥原, 家の光の二十五年 (*Twenty-Five Years of "Light of the Home"*), 27.

Those at the Cooperative committed to their magazine project saw the combination of the depressed state of rural areas and a craving for leisure entertainments as a golden opportunity for spreading the values of the Cooperative and improving the lives of those in farming communities. The "one copy per house, all-purpose magazine" they hoped *Light of the Home* could become stemmed from the idea that rural villages were suffering in the difficulties of the economic situation; the editorial focus of *Ie no hikari* had to match this reality.[49]

The methods for trying to do just this developed into more concrete policies over time as *Ie no hikari* expanded its circulation. In the last years of the 1920s, Umeyama Ichirō in particular created "The principles for the development of *Ie no hikari*'s editing," which were listed as follows:

1. As a technique for polishing up the spirit, starts with the harmony and prosperity of each house in every village.
2. [We must] constantly touch on the news of the day and try never to be behind the trends.
3. [We must] remember the knowledge and craft of farming and aim for the prosperity of each home.
4. [We must] remember the knowledge and craft of the family and aim for the improvement of daily life.
5. [We must provide] articles of varied interests for the sufficient enjoyment of life.
6. [We must] satisfy children's desire for reading materials.[50]

The editors and writers of the magazine followed these principles of providing entertaining benefits in earnest. It meant that there was a fairly lengthy editing process for drafting and polishing the articles that made it into each issue. And it also consequently meant that there was a certain dedication to *bidan*-style parable writing, which was viewed by those at the Cooperative (as by Noma at Kōdansha) to be particularly efficacious for moral education. It meant that for women, men, children, young, and old alike, fresh entertainment was essential to the happiness and well-being of rural families; original art, *manga*, fiction, and the like were all included to address this need.

---

49 The quotation, originally from Umeyama Ichirō, is cited in ibid., 28.
50 Ibid., 29–30.

The aggregate efforts of the editors indicated their desire for the betterment of rural Japanese "in order to raise the spirits of rural folk."[51] Well-known agrarianists (often farmers themselves) from various parts of the country provided stories of their personal experiences and philosophies on life, and these were woven into the stories, biographies, and anecdotes in each issue. Agrarianism was a movement in Japan emphasizing the centrality of farming communities in national advancement with roots in the late 1800s, grown through figures like Shinagawa Yajirō, Tachibana Kōzaburō, Yokoi Tokiyoshi, Gondō Seikyō, Hirata Tōsuke, and later Yangita Kunio and Kawakami Hajime.[52]

This rural mood raising was achieved through changes to rather practical affairs in many modes. A chronicler of the Cooperative's history described the practicality of *Ie no hikari*'s methods in this way:

for economizing expenses on ceremonial occasions, and [cases like] thinking about illness, the Kumiai promoted Cooperative practices of various kinds for daily collaboration in people's lives. *Ie no hikari* came to life as the instructional magazine for the development of the Kumiai and in order to [help readers] economize daily expenses; the editors promoted childcare centres, cooperative cooking, shared gas usage, common use of funerary tools, shared crematorium and bath usage, kitchen and lavatory improvement, cooperative maternity clinics, joint food production, and shared use of sewing machines.[53]

These Co-op activities were promoted throughout the country and served to aid ailing farming communities with varying degrees of success during the interwar years and beyond. To put this slightly differently, as another article specified:

This is just as simple as the foundations for the important policies to revitalize the stalling world economy. It is to advance the everyday life skills of each individual. In particular, we must advance the efficiency of those farmers who have been significantly wasteful. To awaken the self-consciousness of each individual to the preciousness of their "self" that

---

51 Ibid.

52 Havens, *Farm and Nation in Modern Japan*, chapters 4–5; Shillony, review of *The Age of Hirohito*, 452.

53 奥原, 家の光の二十五年 (*Twenty-Five Years of "Light of the Home"*), 31.

is lying dormant, to nurture that power, to be able to brighten that light even more, which would easily increase their productive capacity two- or threefold.[54]

Here the Co-op is placed in the larger world setting, putting Japan within a global context, and individuals are shown to have agency over their lives. As should be clear by now from the articles and ideas from the Kumiai, raising the farmers' spirit went hand in hand with attempts to improve their material conditions. Furthermore, the magazine was, explicitly and from the very beginning, about getting more people to read the publication and participate in the projects of the Cooperative. If morale could be boosted along the way, all the better.

The editors were profoundly committed to the idea that *Ie no hikari* could help build a better Japan. The magazine was supposed to foster the core values of the Cooperative because, by expanding its reach and influence, it could help improve Japanese society. Understanding that this was the motivation for the magazine allows us to place subsequent activities and expansion within the context of this core moral project seeking the united cultural development of Japanese society.

It is clear as well that this was not the project of all magazines (not even all the publications from Kōdansha). The first issue of *Light of the Home* bemoans the state of the publishing world, saying,

It is a golden age of women's magazines in the publishing world. While it seems that some provide progress through the advancement of knowledge for rural women, many are simply spreading through the villages like a virus. Most are merely a publicity organ for the cities, stirring up the vanity of women and creating incentives for the concentration of women in the cities. We're concerned that this will bring about a truly dreadful result.[55]

This is a clear critique of the frivolity of the city and women's magazines against which *Ie no hikari* was setting itself, but it is also an indication that some women were enticed from the farm by urban glows. In the third issue of *Ie no hikari*, an article turns our attention to the media

54 森本, "家の光は自己にあり (The Light of the Home Is in the Self)," 6.
55 "農村と婦人雑誌 (Farming Villages and Women's Magazines)," 1.

at large in order to discuss the inherent abilities of the Japanese people and the dangers facing youths.

> In particular, the youths of our rural communities have the regrettable tendency to refer to new thought trends from the West they hear about in newspapers, magazines, and short lectures … The ideology of the Japanese people is particularly sound and possesses merits that display ideological and economical fellowship vertically from top to bottom. In these times of turbulent ideas and economies, our stable plan is essential.[56]

The general concern for the influence of media and ideas from outside Japan on young people of the day and on the purportedly "native Japanese" norms was not voiced by those at *Ie no hikari* alone. But what is clear from these kinds of statements is that the influence of media was expanding; the influence it had, furthermore, was not always in line with the values of the Cooperative, and thus the editors of *Ie no hikari* saw their task as serious.

In a plea to preserve the harmony that supposedly existed between top and bottom, this same article ends by saying, "viewed from this point, spreading the doctrine of the Industrial Cooperative is an important social policy, especially having the youth be the centre of these activities in the main body of society; we will not lose our course."[57] What they thought was needed was a communal stand for positive social change, rooted in youths staying in rural areas.

Another essay from the second issue repeats the values at the core of the project:

> There is nothing more important than the improvement of the lives of our farmers. Truly, our country has come to the end of its tether, but the salvation of our national power lies in promoting the well-being of our countrymen and doing the important planning to advance the agricultural community.
>
> The greatest inventions of the modern age are not the steam engine, nor electricity, or the radio. It was the discovery of "the self." It goes without saying that electric and steam power are not required for the well-being of people's everyday lives, although treasure and wealth is useful to all … even though there are many in the countryside wearing rags, the event of

---

56 馬場, "大和民族性と青年覚悟 (Japanese Ethnicity and Youth Preparedness)," 8.
57 Ibid., 9.

the modern age is the discovery of those "selves" whose personalities are more precious than diamonds or gold.[58]

The efforts of the Cooperative, the editors argue, are for the benefit of Japan. In the example given, electricity is meaningless without people, but people are valuable wherever they are. No technological advancements are enough if the capacities of individuals are not harnessed to capitalize on collective work, as this line of thought goes. A critique embedded here, significantly, is that even in the "modern age" inventions have not rid Japan of inequity; thus, the work of the Cooperative is, in part, an attempt to rectify this situation.

The article continues:

> Needless to say, the majority of the population are farmers. At the same time that they are scorned, the little peasant, or a farmer with a small holding, who comprise great numbers of our countrymen, exist as precious selves in great number in our rural villages. They have the right to enjoy a modern life just like the wealthy and influential individuals in the cities; if our famers aren't able to enjoy a life that is replete both materially and spiritually we cannot develop the culture of the whole nation. The inner light of these people is the light of humanity; *The Light of the Home* with that inner light can help materialize cultural development in society.[59]

The publication aspired to provide the means to address and solve the disparities between urban and rural areas and suggested that a modern lifestyle was not only within the realm of possibility for its audience but also a self-evident right. This spiritual and material development, moreover, impeccably supported the advancement of Japan in the global environment.

Two points are worth emphasizing here. All of these goals were assumed to be possible through the magazine's promotion of the cultural development and participation of its audience along the lines spelled out in the Cooperative's mission more generally. Inequity in the lives of Japanese existed and modernization did not solve that. One of the transwar cultural continuities for *Ie no hikari*'s audience was that neither wartime imperialism nor postwar democracy did either.

---

58 森本, "家の光は自己にあり (The Light of the Home Is in the Self)," 4.
59 Ibid.

Second, this group identity (suggested by the unremitting references to "community," "our ...," and "the Japanese people") is significant for the audience of both *Ie no hikari* and *Kingu*. The publishers of these magazines saw the masses as unambiguously Japanese. These media were for the good of the nation, and the community created by a mass audience was embedded within that context. This, too, was a transwar social stability. The "spoked wheel" of propaganda production that comprised various sectors of Japanese society, including these publishers, allowed for a collective conception of Japan as positive, forward-looking, and innovative that translated smoothly from Taishō progress and expansion to wartime mobilization and on to postwar recovery.[60]

The long-term process of making social and cultural meanings and the naturalization of media among the Japanese population was integral to the missions of these publications. Membership in their noble collective identity and being proudly "Japanese" were core to these publications. As Jason Stanley explains, "group identities lead to the formation of beliefs that are difficult to rationally abandon, since abandoning them would lead them to challenge our self-worth," and "when our group affiliates are such as to lead us to these kinds of rigidly held beliefs, we become especially susceptible to propaganda."[61] Moreover, this susceptibility, sadly, reinforces acceptance of inequity, perpetuates ignorance or tolerance of injustice, and generally prevents masses from acting in their own genuine and legitimate self-interest. This phenomenon is alarming because the inclusionary nature of mass culture exacerbates the acceptance of defective understandings of the world, and it caused many Japanese to comply with activities that diluted their own (individual and collective) well-being.[62]

---

60 As Kushner usefully explains: "Advertising and media professionals, whose images of Japan postwar domestic audiences avidly consumed, were the same media technicians who had created wartime visions of Japanese modernity and leadership for Asia" (*The Thought War*, 186, 10, 16, passim).

61 Stanley, *How Propaganda Works*, 20.

62 As Stanley puts it, "Flawed ideology is an obstacle to realizing one's goals. On the one hand, those benefiting from large material inequalities will tend to adopt flawed ideologies in the form of false legitimation narratives. These false legitimation narratives will blind them to injustice, and hence from realizing their ethical goals. On the other hand, those suffering materially from large inequalities, via lack of land, access to high-status positions, or other obstacles to equality of opportunity and attainment, will be led to adopt a flawed ideology of their own inferiority. This will prevent them from realizing their material interests" (ibid., 7–8).

Editorial Content

Ie no hikari and *Kingu* both possessed their specific ideological bents prior to their very first issues going to press. For example, the ideals fundamental to the Cooperative itself – the family as the basic unit of society, the importance of communal work in support of Japan, the presentation of women as the centre of the household, the essential importance of farming communities within the empire – could be found in almost every article of every issue. The various contributors to the publication expressed these principles, with some variations in emphasis, as the years progressed, but at the core, the message was consistent.

The articles and essays of *Kingu* and *Ie no hikari* (unlike the advertisements, it should be mentioned) from the early 1930s onward present frequent and positive reportage on and support of Japan's military expansion. This has not gone unnoticed within the scholarship about these years; Sandra Wilson, to name an example, specifically addresses the way that articles in *Ie no hikari* blatantly toe the imperialistic, militaristic line regarding Japanese expansion into Manchuria, while Satō Takumi discusses *Kingu* in a similar context, though one more focused on the publication's manipulation of the public.[63] Specific details can more fully present the flavour of the discourse in these publications, though I am not particularly interested in, for example, the internal variations of opinion among the Cooperative members who contributed to *Ie no hikari*.

It would be difficult to fully expound on all of the intricacies of the editorial stances of these periodicals for the entirety of the 1930s, but, after sorting through volumes spanning two decades, one can see that certain trends were present in the pages of *Ie no hikari* and *Kingu*. One of these was an unswerving support of Japanese military projects and the expansion of the empire.

Pro-war content can be seen throughout the decade, though in much heavier doses in issues after the events of late 1931 and mid-1937. With articles like "Because of the Manchurian Incident, Japan Has Gained All This" in 1933 and "The Brilliantly Shining Japanese Navy" in 1934, the pro-military stance of the writers and publishers of *Ie no hikari* is

---

63 Wilson, "Bureaucrats and Villagers in Japan," 121, 127, 129; 佐藤, 「キング」の時代 (*The Era of "King"*).

easy to detect.[64] In April of 1937 there were articles such as "In Praise of the Esteemed Qualities of the Emperor" and "Japanese Spirit, Western Learning," which supported the Imperial Family and the use of technology to further Japan's glory in the world.[65] Similar articles continued with fervent calls to organize the kitchen ("Keeping the Wartime Kitchen: A General Mobilization of Housewives!"), to remember the Manchurian Incident ("We Cannot Forget the Manchurian Incident"), and to share expertise in the wartime crunch ("The Collective Knowledge of Our Countrymen in the Grips of the Wartime System"), to name only a few examples.[66]

Kingu, similarly, had regular articles and images that presented the Japanese military, government officials promoting Japanese military activities, the waving of the Japanese flag, the display of imperial naval vessels and equipment, and *bidan* promoting all of the above. Articles in the January issue from 1934 discuss the benefits of travel in Manchuria (thanks to the profits that Japanese settlers evidently reaped there), reasons to be proud of the "verifiable" antiquity of the Japanese nation, and compliments for the Imperial Navy's spirit and dedication in the "time of emergency."[67] The May issue of the same year displays a romanticized photograph in which the *Hi no maru* flutters high over a military installation strangely devoid of human presence. These sundry specific occurrences added up to a conglomerate whole: a vision of a communal, improving Japan with dedicated and upstanding people working in concert for the collective national good.

With the rise of less expensive means to produce and reproduce photos, each issue had a number of photographs from various points around the Japanese empire and other global locales. The December 1934 issue had several vessels from the naval fleet proudly displayed at sea. Every issue for the entire year of 1934 had articles about the military, usually the navy; a photographic example from 1937 shows soldiers posing with Chinese children, jumping rope, and hanging out

---

64 "満州事変によって日本はこれだけを得た," *Ie no hikari* 39 (October 1933): 176–7 and "輝く日本海軍," *Ie no hikari* 43 (May 1934): 54–9.

65 "正常陛下の御生得を配す," *Ie no hikari* 60 (April 1937): 34–5 and "和魂洋才," *Ie no hikari* 60 (April 1937): 36–7.

66 "戦時の台所を預かる: 主婦総動員！" *Ie no hikari* 63 (October 1937): 36–7; "忘れるな満州事変," *Ie no hikari* 63 (October 1937): 44; and "戦時体制州の国民心得集," *Ie no hikari* 63 (October 1937): 118–21.

67 キング (*King*), 1 January 1934, 80–1, 110–11, 326–7.

with their compatriots – a decidedly palatable depiction of war on the Asian mainland. These articles and images served to tutor the readers in the esteemed nature of the Imperial Forces and their efforts in expanding and supporting the Japanese imperium. The hawkish trends simply increased in both publications as the 1930s progressed.

In *Kingu*'s third issue (released in March of 1925), a list of "compliments received from various notable figures" was printed on the outer flaps enclosing the table of contents. This list of *King*'s supposed merits read:

1. Moral cultivation can be enjoyable for people who read *King*.
2. People who read *King* can develop common sense and feel no shame to go out among people in the world.
3. People who read *King* can improve their mind where they lack knowledge and develop a fine character.
4. People who read *King* get interesting, relaxing entertainment.
5. People who read *King* are roused to spirited action and can rise in the world.
6. The family that reads *King* will be happy and harmonious.
7. Towns and villages that read *King* will flourish with improved public morals.
8. *King* is the people's preference and energizes the advancement of culture.
9. *King* brings peace through its thoroughgoing morals.
10. *King* cleans the world of evil ideology.[68]

Even if these were not actually comments made by notable people of the day, they are obviously points the editors wished to highlight as being what made the publication special and valuable. The tone of the first few comments would have mirrored common attitudes among Japanese elites, who seemed predisposed to dismiss magazines and their assumed worthless frivolity. A magazine that was capable of enhancing common sense, moral decency, general knowledge, and self-improvement must have indeed been viewed as a new invention not to be as easily scorned in the cultural milieu of the day.

Again, this creation of "common sense" submerged the active construction of what was determined to be worth knowing, to merit

---

68 "キング十徳 (Ten Virtues of *King*)."

discussing, or to need seeing. These values more generally, though, focused on wholesome entertainment for the family with moral and cultural advancement for the benefit of the nation. The issues of *Kingu* from the 1920s and 1930s concentrated on these virtues, the ones that the first issue had explicitly established. The editorial stance from then on was loosely bundled around moral cultivation of the citizenry for the betterment of the nation.

One common technique used in *Kingu* for expressing these principles was the paragon. Important political, military, and artistic figures were presented as models to be emulated because of their bravery, determination, honesty, loyalty, and hard work. It was common in issues throughout these years to see leaders of industry as paradigms recognized for their service to Japan and its peoples. *Kingu* fans would have come to recognize Japanese elites as being a singularly industrious bunch, since articles disparaging leaders (from public or private spheres) were nonexistent. In one example that stressed such elite family ties, General Nogi Maresuke, famed for his successes and failures while serving in the Imperial Army during the Sino- and Russo-Japanese Wars as well as for his September 1912 suicide, is honoured in an article which mostly describes his home life and the devotion of his wife.[69] The consistent line in most if not all of these kinds of articles was the perseverance that allowed these men – it was always men, though supportive wives and families are often given due credit for their backing – to succeed.

This is not to suggest that the editors made no critiques at all, since they certainly did throughout the years of *Kingu*'s publication. The kinds of critiques presented in the editorials, however, were directed more generally at dangerous or undesirable ways of thinking or modes of behaving. For example, an article which calls into question governmental policies about trade and oil imports mentions no particular figure guilty of problematic conceptions of the world; rather, it stresses the growing need for oil for industrial use in the "age of the automobile." Thus, the author suggests, Middle Eastern locales held increasing significance, "from Baghdad to Damascus" (where such resources could be had), since Japan, and other places the world over, were moving from steam-powered technologies to those that used not just oil, but gasoline. The article explained for the readers in simple terms that, for those countries wishing to be leaders on the world stage, understanding

---

69 キング (*King*), 1 February 1925.

oil's strategic importance was as essential as the control of the resources themselves; otherwise Japan would perish, in the editorial's bleak estimation.[70] In addition to lacking any pointed political critique, the editorial stance here, common for *Kingu*, provides an example of generalized concern for Japan's international well-being and suggestions for what individual Japanese could contribute to the cause.

Another familiar writing technique used by the editors of *Kingu* was addressing particular people within the household. While the family unit was the centre of the world of *Kingu*, and the articles were written to be understandable by anyone, most often it was only specific members who were targeted by individual articles. This was part of the way in which the magazine was able to be the "one issue per household" magazine of preference, but in practice it meant that husbands/fathers were not spoken to directly by the editors with the same degree of frequency that wives/daughters/sons were. Examples of these kinds of articles can be found throughout issues of *King* in 1920s and 1930s. Overall, it seemed that while father's moral and cultural improvement was to be gained from the magazine in some generalized sense, the rest of the family had more specific lessons from the editors.

Accordingly, for example, when the editors wanted to include a list of maxims for respectable daily comportment, *Kingu* readers were given several lists. A list for boys included "the spring of your youth will never come again" and "there is no gain from nightlife"; a list for girls, "moderate makeup, thin rather than thick, is best" and "If you've got spare time, give your parents' shoulders a rub"; a list for a wife, "charm is more important than anything for a bride" and "express beauty through the heart rather than fashionable dress"; and a list for a mother-in-law, each item of which is an admonition to avoid interfering with her daughter-in-law's running of the household.[71] No such complementary list of suggestions is included for a father or grandfather, however.

The "commonsensical" values being modelled also represent the restrictive nature of these lists. For example, males apparently do not wear cosmetics, only females do; boys must resist the urge to be frivolous (drinking and carousing, it can be assumed) and waste their precious nights, while girls should dutifully see to the well-being of others

---

70 "油が無くなると国が滅びる (The Disappearance of Oil and the Ruin of Our Country)."
71 キング (*King*), 1 February 1925.

in their household, rather than taking part in some other more "selfish" activity. These admonitions and suggestions, aimed at people enacting these binary gender roles, were never-ending over the years of publication. The naturalization of such norms tied people down to these limited roles, even as it claimed to be encouraging them.

Sometimes these kinds of lessons were presented not in the form of lists but as imagined conversations among family members. "The World of a Mother and Her Daughter" in the March 1931 issue of *King* depicts a conversation between two women attempting to entertain themselves one afternoon. The conversation begins with a daughter telling her mother she wants to learn to dance, to which the mother responds by saying the daughter should talk about something more serious; she suggests hobbies for young women, other than dancing, that improve character, befriending the neighbours, and generally doing other things that contribute to a girl's charm.[72] This expresses not only editorial attitudes about the proper comportment of young females but also the expectations that mother is the coach on respectable behaviour and a major check on "undesirable" daughterly characteristics. Here the magazine could be tutor to both mother *and* daughter, in case either family member was in need of such guidance.

By 1931, those at *Kingu* were able to further refine the merits of the publication into a revised ten-item list similar to the one printed in the third issue of the magazine. The newer catalogue of *King*'s virtues ran thus:

1. We have the most interesting topics in the land.
2. Moral cultivation can be enjoyable.
3. We are always a wellspring of new thrills.
4. Not a single phrase is meaningless.
5. This is not the masterpiece of first-class experts.
6. No effort shall be spared for the sake of the readers.
7. We are constantly making new plans in order to surprise the world.
8. We are a delight to all people, women and men, young and old alike.
9. We improve the nation and brighten the home.
10. Since its launch, we have been the absolute king of the magazine world.[73]

---

72 キング (*King*), 1 March 1931.
73 "Advertisement," キング (*King*) no. 3 (1931).

Here are all of the ideals Noma had hoped for with *Kingu* laid bare once again: moral cultivation, benefiting the nation through the support of the family while explicitly concentrating on mass-focused content that was interesting to everyone. This list provides another succinct statement of what *Kingu* was all about and suggests that, six years into the publication, these principles were still driving the project as much as they were at the very beginning in 1925.

January of 1931, moreover, saw a reaffirmation of various ideals espoused by Noma himself through the publication of two special extra editions. These two commemorative supplements were sold alongside the New Year's edition of *Kingu* in 1931: one was a colourful and elaborate foldout illustrated history of roughly the previous sixty years, and one was a collection of articles, *The Cornerstone of Success*, written by Noma Seiji, compiled and bound in a single volume of just over two hundred pages.[74] Noma's essays and the ideas they contained were considered important enough not only to have been printed within the magazine issues originally, as regular copy among the pages of *Kingu* in the later 1920s, but also to be doubly emphasized by their proud separate republication. A quick survey of their tone and attitude is instructive on the editorial tenor of the magazine more generally, since Noma's guidance and ideals both established the magazine initially and then reinforced its general tone and outlook over the years it was published.

The topics of these essays (articles originally) vary across a wide range of subjects that all intend to promote moral cultivation and self-improvement in the reader. There is a consistent focus on youth and the importance of beginning early in life to provide models for children to emulate, on taking advantage of any opportunities available in one's youth, and on how the young are particularly capable of striving to develop Japan.[75] No matter what the topic, however, Noma's devotion to the Japanese empire and its transformation into a powerful world leader and cultural paragon was an obvious motivator behind all of his aphorisms and recommendations.

---

74 This illustrated history is discussed in greater detail in chapter 4. 淵田, 明治大正昭和大絵巻 (*The Illustrated Meiji Taishō Shōwa*); 野間, 出世の礎 (*The Cornerstone of Success*).

75 野間, 出世の礎 (*The Cornerstone of Success*), passim.

In an issue in 1939, after Noma's death the year before, these values were reiterated yet again:

- *Kingu* is a magazine that cultivates the healthy ideas of our citizens.
- *Kingu* is a magazine that raises the good morals and manners (pristine way of life/genial manners and laudable customs) of society.
- *Kingu* is a magazine that dazzlingly brightens the family.
- *Kingu* is a magazine that provides a guiding principle for disciplined conduct, a key to rising in the world.
- *Kingu* is a magazine that enriches and broadens common sense.[76]

The mission of *Kingu* never wavered from that presented at the outset of the project. Noma's vision of what his publications were remained and simply manifested in various topics over the years of his periodicals' publication.

For *Ie no hikari*, the attitudes present at the beginning of the project, never at odds with Japanese military expansion abroad, simply intensified as the years marched onward. Ideological articles appeared from the first issue of *Light of the Home,* and these kinds of charged pieces continued over the course of the 1930s and into the 1940s. The project that was established as the core of the Cooperative's efforts regarding this magazine involved moralizing to the audience. Sadly, this commitment actually undermined their other stated goal of protecting farming communities and the families they contained because the increasing support of wartime mobilization effectively caused greater suffering in rural areas (and across Japan) than it served to alleviate.

While the contents of articles were often presented under misleading titles in *Kingu* – Noma seemed to have a particular flair for giving his pieces strangely vague titles which had little or nothing to do with the actual topic under discussion – *Ie no hikari* was always far more straightforward, since the titles of its articles always mapped cleanly onto the text's content. Among several examples of the kinds of articles *Ie no hikari* published over the late 1920s and early 1930s, consider "Foundations for a Blessed Life" in May 1927, which was written by Inoue Tetsujirō, a philosopher interested in education and noted for his imperialistic preaching in support of things like the necessity of the

---

76 Untitled item, キング (*King*), 1 March 1939, 49.

Imperial Rescript on Education in schools; "Sightings of the Imperial Virtues of Emperor Meiji," written in August 1927 by a well-known poet, Chiba Taneaki; "The Encouragement of Farming Villages and Putting Education First" and "Making the Cooperative into a Family and Making the Family a Cooperative" in February and March of 1929, which continued to tout the importance of basic education and keeping the family at the heart of Kumiai activities; and "The Japanese Spirit Burning through the Entire Nation," written in April 1935 by right-wing General Sadao Araki, who served in different administrations as minister of war and minister of education, touting the wonderful determination of the Japanese people in support of their empire.[77] These were not articles attempting to undermine the legitimacy of the *kokutai* or questioning imperialist behaviour.

The January 1938 issue of *Ie no hikari* included a foldout supplement that was an elementary phonetic syllabary with a military theme centred on the "China Incident" (*Shina Jihen irohakaruta: Shina Jihen* was the official term in these years for the military engagement on the Chinese mainland, now called the Second Sino-Japanese War; *iroha karuta* means a syllabary chart game) (see figure 3.4). Syllabaries like these and other kana copybooks (*kanadehon*, phonetic guides used to teach basic literacy) were common and were often included in various kinds of publications, but the overtly military-imperialistic theme, specifically about the conflict in China, was unusual. This kind of content shows how lessons on simple non-normative subjects (learning to better read the Japanese vernacular) came inextricably bound together with ideologically saturated and partisan themes (like the romanticized glorification of the imperial military forces).

In November 1937, to provide yet another example, *Ie no hikari* had articles about soldiers' important work "protecting Japan's lifeline" in the conflict with China. The Japanese military efforts on the Asian mainland were presented as being a defensive activity essential for the survival of Japan in a hostile imperialistic world.[78] In an article about

---

77 井上, "幸福なる生活の基礎 (Foundations for a Blessed Life)"; 千葉, "明治天皇御聖徳の一斑 (Sightings of the Imperial Virtues of Emperor Meiji)"; 勝田, "農村振興と教育第一 (The Encouragement of Farming Villages and Putting Education First)"; 八條, "組合の家庭化と家庭に組合化 (Making the Cooperative into a Family and Making the Family a Cooperative)"; 荒木, "全国に燃え上がる日本精神 (The Japanese Spirit Burning through the Entire Nation)."

78 "日支事変第二報 (Second Report on the Conflict with China)."

Figure 3.4. Elementary syllabary with military theme, *Ie no hikari*, January 1938

the importance of mothers, there is a focus on the education of Japanese children while fathers were off on the battlefield. The mother's role as home educator of small children was presented as increasingly urgent, since fathers and brothers were more frequently absent due to the demands of the draft and general mobilization.[79]

Many articles like these were illustrated, and the editorial cartoons that accompanied such articles were also strikingly propagandistic. Paired with an article in the same November 1937 issue was an image that showed a Japanese soldier thwarting a northern "bandit" puppet, manipulated by a southern Chinese puppet ultimately controlled by Stalin (see figure 3.5).[80] The article text itself detailed the situation leading to the Marco Polo Bridge Incident and touted the presumed good intent of Japanese activities in Manchuria in line with *Ie no hikari*'s unflinching support of Japanese militarism abroad.

Another article in the same issue explained yet again how Japanese military action in the Far East stemmed from a duty to be leaders of their brethren and was simply the most expedient means to peace for all Asians.[81] It was accompanied by a cartoon of a Japanese soldier holding a rifle aloft with one hand while straddling the Taiwan Strait (see figure 3.6). In the other hand, the soldier waves a flag reading "Peace for the Orient," and the other Asian peoples are depicted around his feet as children now saved from a devil who is being driven away by Japan's light and peace (represented by the sun and doves).

These specific images graphically represent two common themes of rhetoric coming from the military: first, the Communist threat and interference in Japanese interests in China, and second, the idea of Japan creating an "Asia for the Asians." As John Dower and others have discussed, the Japanese press, following the military, often presented Japan as playing a paternal role towards other Asians, who were depicted as underdeveloped children in need of Japan's guidance and tutelage.[82] For those who did not bother to read the articles themselves, these images were at least as powerful in conveying meaning as any words.

---

79 大倉, "母の横顔とうしろ姿 (Mother's Profile and the Figure Behind)."
80 "遂に日支事変へ (Finally towards the Conflict in China!)."
81 "皇軍奮起の目標 (The Goals of Our Inspiring Imperial Army)."
82 One visual example is an image from *Jiji shinpō* comic from 18 February 1902, "Concerning the Anglo-Japanese Alliance." Here the "children" are China and Korea. "The principal declared object of the Alliance is to guard Chinese and Korean integrity." See Richards, *Guarding Childish Feet*; Dower, *War without Mercy*.

Figure 3.5. "Finally towards the Conflict in China!" *Ie no hikari*, November 1937

十一　皇軍奮起の目標は

北支に上海に銃砲火はうなり、皇軍は暴戻なる支那兵を相手に、極東戦史上空前の壮烈な立體戰を演じ、空に陸に海に膺懲の爆撃をつゞけてゐる。

そのはじめ、わが國は東洋平和のため『事件不擴大』をつくしたのにも拘らず南京政府はすべてを無視し蹂躙するばかりか、着々戰備を整へて挑戰してきた。かくなるからには徹底的な膺懲あるのみだ。

排日抗日侮日によつて全國を統一しようとする南京政府、その南京政府を傀儡として踊らしてゐる赤化共産主義の禍根こそ、皇軍の敵なのである。日本は一刻も早く共産赤化の妖魔を粉砕、支那民衆四億の眞の幸福をめざして、東洋永遠の平和を確立しなければならない。

これぞ皇軍奮起の目標。東洋民族の盟主としての、皇國民の義務は益々重大である。

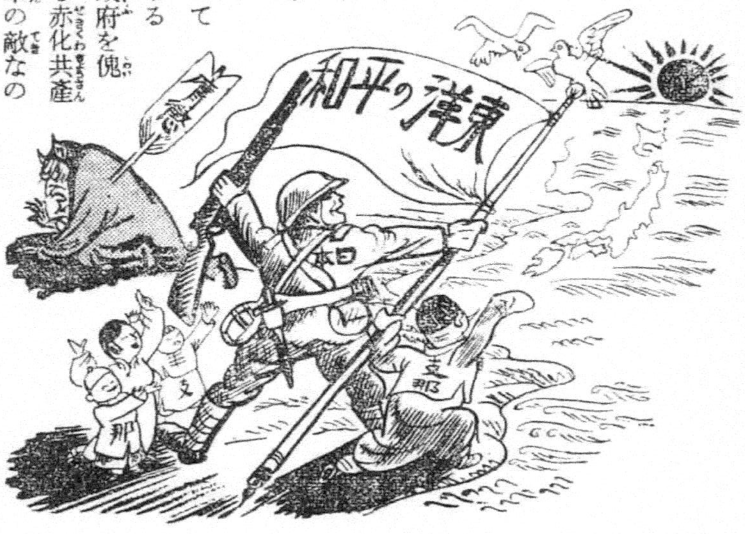

Figure 3.6. "The Goals of Our Inspiring Imperial Army," *Ie no hikari*, November 1937

The Children's Section

How children specifically fitted into this picture is also important – these images and words communicated directly with the youths who would grow up to be the adults of the postwar years. One commonality between *Kingu* and *Ie no hikari* was the importance of youth to the publishers, and many children were indeed exposed to the magazines because of their ubiquity and their content explicitly and specifically directed at children. The child-targeted content of both *Kingu* and *Ie no hikari* was similar to the editorial materials and the magazines' higher dispersion of wartime rhetoric after the early 1930s. What is interesting to note is how barefaced the children's section is in its presentation of ideological material in support of the Japanese empire.

Beginning in June of 1931 and throughout the 1930s, at the back of *Ie no hikari*, readers found a children's section: *Kodomo no ie no hikari* (Children's Light of the Home). This section began as the "Children's Page" in the first issue of the magazine and ran until volume 2, number 2 under that title. After that issue, there was a hiatus in child-specific material until "Children's Hall," which began in volume 6, number 11, then the "Children's Column," and finally the one-page "Children's Playroom." Each of these ran for only two issues and was replaced once *Kodomo no ie no hikari* became a permanent fixture.

By the late 1930s, the children's section had entered into the war effort wholeheartedly. One frightening example is a two-page spread devoted to various weapons, under the title "Various Armaments" (see figure 3.7).[83] Turn the page and the title reads, "City Air Defences" (see figure 3.8). This particular graphic, which is accompanied by text explanations, enlightened child readers about the means of defending cities from air raids and attacks from the sky.[84] Sadly, there is no mention of any type of fire-suppression system. In addition, the bottoms of the pages contained elucidations of what kind of payload would be required for destroying what size building. This portion reads from largest to smallest payload, beginning with a one-thousand-kilo bomb, said to be roughly three times the height of an adult (depicted as a male in a suit) and capable of destroying an eight-story building, and so on down the line to a fifty-kilo missile, about the height of a child

---

83 "いろいろの兵器 (Various Armaments)."
84 "都市の防空 (City Air Defences)."

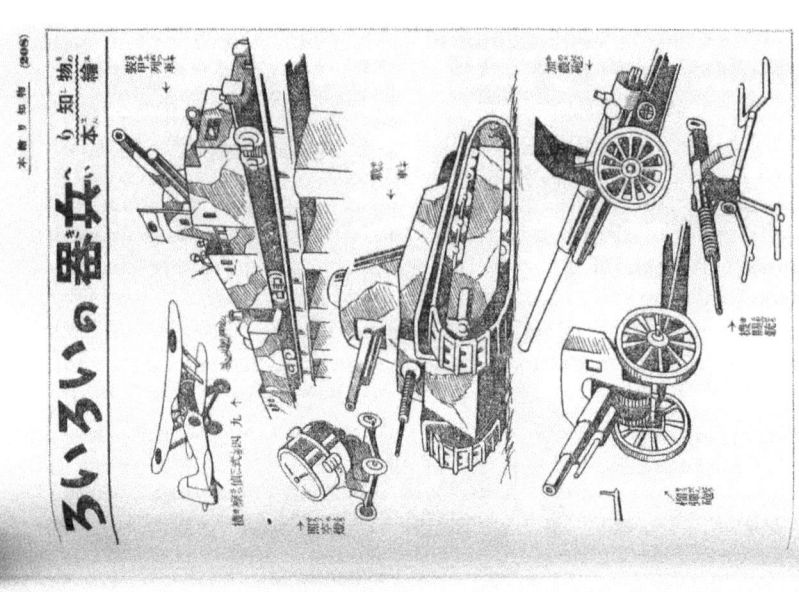

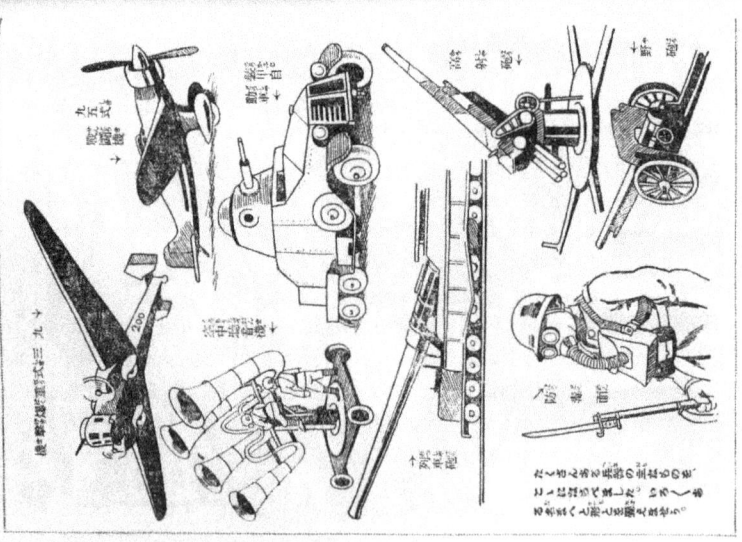

Figure 3.7. "Various Weapons," *Ie no hikari* 65, no. 2 (February 1938)

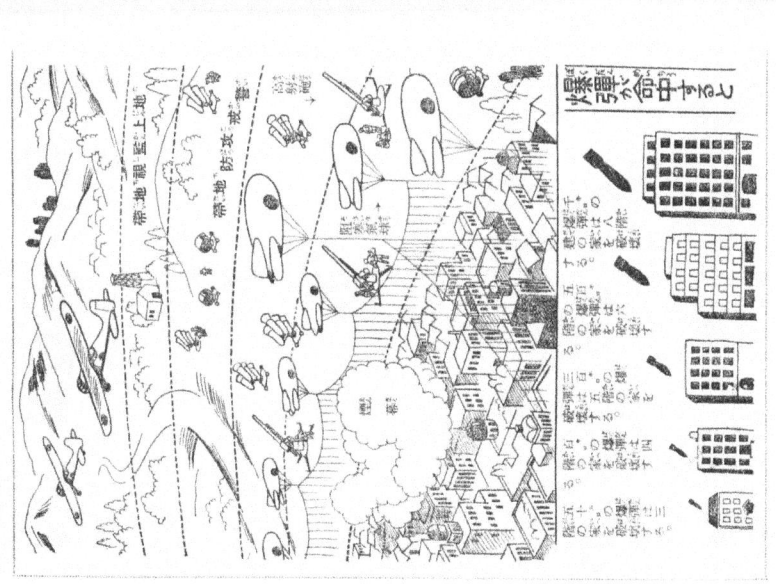

Figure 3.8. "City Air Defences," *Ie no hikari* 65, no. 2 (February 1938)

(depicted as a female dressed in a school uniform), able to reduce a three-story house to rubble.[85] Stories about soldiers, mention of military equipment and behaviour, and repeated inclusion of the Japanese flag in drawings and cartoons occur in the *Kodomo no ie no hikari* section of the magazine from the mid-1930s onward.

One serial cartoon contained in the children's section had a main character named after the Japanese flag, *Hinomaru Tarō*, and involved a small boy exploring nature and learning about different environments. This cartoon was replaced by another serial named for its main characters, *Sankichi fujiko*, a small girl and boy. It presented the children in a gunship-shaped plane decorated with the Japanese flag, touring various locales, fighting pirates, dealing with dark-skinned, spear-toting primitives, and making a triumphal return to Japan. *Sankichi fujiko* was in turn replaced by *Shirochun Kurochun* (White Mouse, Black Mouse), which has an even larger number of guns, tanks, and military men peppered throughout.[86] By 1938, the content of the children's section was frighteningly saturated with militaristic imagery and content.

These few examples are representative of the whole decade. The editorial and feature writing of *Ie no hikari* and the children's section within it frequently, overtly, and consistently supported Japanese military expansion and imperialistic behaviour throughout the 1930s and beyond. The imagery and stories in *Children's Light of the Home* and the sections directed at children in *Kingu* or Kōdansha's youth magazines (like *Shonen kurabu*) deserve a closer look as instances of popular media aimed at children. Such a study might help us to better understand the more general relationship of media to the children of Japan in the 1930s.[87]

Concluding Thoughts

The wider media world during these years supported the war effort and Japan's imperial project as well. After the Manchurian Incident and

---

85 Apparently toys based on these warlike tendencies were not unheard of outside Japan either, as one example from the Cold War years shows: Doctorow, "Old Toy for Teaching Children to Accurately Drop Atom Bombs – Boing Boing."

86 *Ie no hikari* 57, no. 9 (September 1936): 218–21, no. 10 (October 1936): 220–3; 59, no. 1 (January 1937): 218–21, no. 2 (February 1937): 220–3; 61, no. 5 (May 1937): 224–7, no. 6 (June 1937): 222–5; 65, no. 1 (January 1938): 224–7, no. 2 (February 1938): 222–5.

87 One scholar who has attempted to delve into the world of children deserves note here; see Jones, *Children as Treasures*.

Japan's military expansion onto the Asian continent, the general populace viewed Manchuria as important for Japanese security in the region and more generally. Moving pictures and on-site reporting (through telegraph and air travel) also led to increased media competition among the different outlets. The Three Human Bombs (*Nikudan Sanyūshi*) story, for example, popularized the supposed heroics of men involved in that fateful incident. Scholars like Louise Young have written well about this topic, explaining that the popularity, in films, songs, and articles, of such wartime "heroes" not only shows public investment in the war and the incremental and incidental imperialism that prevailed but also helps us to track the new kinds of media produced and circulating at the time.[88]

State and businesses worked together on several levels to promote and reinforce popular support of the militaristic imperialism to which Japanese leaders had committed the country by the 1930s. This created a generalized atmosphere of collective participation in, if not implicit advocacy of, the ventures of the Japanese empire. And it should be reasonably clear now what was in these magazines. These magazines represent the omnipresent, acceptable "common sense" from this period.

Some might claim, "Yes, that's all well and good, but what of the reader's response to these publications?" Miriam Silverberg obviously gave much thought to this quandary, and her opinion on the issue is similar to mine:

> For those who demand an account of the reader's response to media representations, my response is that the producers of modern Japanese culture *were* consumers: all were privy to the imagery being circulated. In other words, production presumes consumption, and vice versa. In has never been possible to document the actual response of the café waitress reading *Shufu no tomo* or the housewife examining the pictures in *Shūkan Asahi* or the white-collar worker turning the pages of *Kingu* because of the way consciousness is layered from the time of original reception through its reformulations in memory. Instead I attempt to provide close textual readings that can give a good idea of how meaning was produced and circulated.[89]

---

88 Young, *Japan's Total Empire*, 77–8, 427, 430, passim.
89 Silverberg, *Erotic Grotesque Nonsense*, 6.

The production and circulation of meaning should be the primary focus for historians, partly because reader responses and contributions to the publications were indelibly mediated. However, it is possible to glean some information about audience responses by piecing together records of who was reading these magazines and what they had to say about them (without over-psychologizing the readers in the process). This can teach us about social and cultural practices from a slightly different angle, which is the topic of the next chapter.

Chapter Four

Reading Together: How the Audience Participated

The mass audience, whether urban or rural, could now imagine what was possible for their world. The editorial voice of these publications encouraged them to feel as if they already possessed the skills to make their will and desires manifest in their lives. Moreover, the moralizing aspects of the magazines created a sense of duty, or at least a motivation, to attempt to do so. The tension underlying this new-found ambition, however, was that the ideals were unattainable, disguising the conditions inhibiting people in Japan during these years.

There is a feedback loop in which media offers the supposed means to obtain one's hopes and desires at the same time that it creates unfulfillable needs that push one to continue searching in media. As media and the models they provide are normalized in everyday practices, so too are the beliefs that their desirable ideals are possible, whatever the audience perceives those models to be. The degree of flexibility in interpretation allows for an inclusivity that had not manifested in other forms of literature, entertainment, or leisure.

Magazines provided commonality in a shared experience, since the content of each issue of *Kingu* or *Ie no hikari* was the same for everyone (just as, today, everyone experiences the same taste of Kikkoman soy sauce, Coca-Cola, or McDonald's). But this also fractured into the individual imagined experiences of each person exposed, as an example of the ways in which mass culture is simultaneously collective/participatory *and* isolating/individualistic. It could be both at once. Magazines helped to morph the pre-existing sociability to new and more commercial ends, impacting the nature of those social practices while also helping to continue them. These tensions present in the lives of the masses, whether by themselves as individuals or amid others in a group, exhibit the paradox of everyday life in mass culture where we are always simultaneously included *and* alone, participating *and* isolated.

Contexts

Many Japanese scholars and scholars of Japan of the first postwar decades saw the collapse of more democratic trends and the ensuing rise of fascism as an inevitable consequence of fundamental social deficiencies dating back to the 1868 Meiji Restoration, and indeed continuing into their postwar present. However, as the Introduction previously addressed, it is unproductive to depict the 1930s as a "dark valley." Certainly, for Japan during the 1930s and 1940s, dark days did exist. However, there were also hopeful lives being lived with continued interest in and popularity of foreign goods and ideas, a persistent consumer culture, and broad popular attentiveness to politics, even as there were simultaneously increasing social controls, countless government-initiated demands for mobilization, failing diplomatic practices, and growing isolation for Japan internationally.

During the last years of Emperor Taishō's reign and the beginning of Emperor Shōwa's, Japanese leaders and citizens alike struggled with fears and aspirations tied to the tremendous societal shifts taking place, spurred by increasing modernity and Japan's place in the new global order. Trying to personally make their way in the world, and habituating themselves to new practices and realities, people from all sectors of Japan had different ideas about how best to participate and cope. Andrew Gordon's concept of "imperial democracy" neatly encapsulates a number of seeming contradictions as this process unfolded in class consciousness, nationalism, and imperialism amidst the social and political changes in the early decades of the twentieth century. Further, visual representations from this period reflect widespread and varied attempts at political agency, partly through protest and riots.[1] These popular activities suggest a populace not cowed by their government, but actively struggling to assert their notions of (democratic) rights and privileges even as they simultaneously valued the imperial institution and Japanese nationalism more broadly.

---

1   Gordon, *Labor and Imperial Democracy in Prewar Japan*; Gordon, "Social Protest in Imperial Japan"; Gerteis, "Political Protest in Interwar Japan."

While magazines provided a novel spare-time activity amid the erupting varieties of collective participatory leisure in the cities, in rural areas they faced only limited competition for the recreational attention of farming communities. Magazines as a new, shared pastime fostered socializing with one's neighbours and community-gathering activities that reinforced a sense of involvement and belonging in both villages and cities across Japan. Group entertainments that had historically filled the lives of most non-urban Japanese almost immediately gave way to new events that centred on magazines, like fan clubs and reader rallies, and reinscribed collective behaviours with different meanings.

As one Japanese reader of *Ie no hikari* bemoaned in 1925, "We rural residents are starved for entertainment."[2] An *Ie no hikari* reader from Nagano likewise exclaimed (in the same issue),

> I am just one farming housewife of modest achievements with no opinions, but I have seen the preliminary announcement of these plans to publish *Ie no hikari* as a commemorative project of the Industrial Cooperative and I spontaneously leapt for joy with grateful acceptance. We farm women and children don't really see [many] magazines, but presently the magazines that are available for sale at shop fronts are unexceptional – they have only lots of pages and a high price. Reading material for rural women and children is rather scarce, but I think now, with *Ie no hikari*, we truly have something to read that can clearly be a guide in our actual lives. I feel like we've truly gained a friend.[3]

Suffice it to say that the lives of rural Japanese were not filled with many spectacles or fancy diversions in these years. The cycle of festivals and other celebratory events that dotted the calendar for most rural residents had persisted from decades past, and inventions like the radio and movies were only unevenly making it into hamlets and villages by the 1920s and 1930s, as we have seen.[4]

Part of the story of the success of these magazines must have lain in their ability to offer their audience something new. So how did the mass audience of Japan come to participate?

---

2 "読者講談室 (Reader's Lecture Room)," 88. The "dearth of entertainment in local villages" is also discussed in" Kushner, *The Thought War*, 31.

3 "読者講談室 (Reader's Lecture Room)," 88.

4 Partner, *Assembled in Japan*; Gordon, "Consumption, Leisure and the Middle Class in Transwar Japan"; Kasza, *The State and the Mass Media in Japan, 1918–1945*.

Readers

Surveys demonstrate that people were not only reading these magazines but also rereading them. What's more, some reports detail *Kingu*'s
popularity among a broad range of demographics, specifically ones not
often associated with mass publications. For instance, after 1925, educated youths in cities who had more commonly subscribed in the past
to intellectual journals like *Chūō kōron* (Central Review), or in earlier
years to publications like *Taiyō* (The Sun), now reported their regular consumption of *Kingu*. The breakdown of the reporting was thus:
according to the surveys from these years, there were "magazines for
scholarly reading," most notably among them *Chūō kōron*, and "magazines read for leisure." It was the ones for leisure, like *Kingu* and *Ie
no hikari*, that were reread multiple times. The second most popular
magazine in this category was the well-known *Bungeishunjū*. Students
thought of different magazines as serving different purposes, either
educational or entertaining, and spent more time revisiting those publications that they viewed as providing leisure and enjoyment.[5]

Nagamine Shigetoshi has done excellent work illuminating survey
data that details the demographic breakdown of the readership of a
number of publications from the interwar years. His data is mostly
from surveys done in the late 1920s and early 1930s by the Tokyo
Imperial University (which are now housed in the Faculty of Law collections and not publicly available). This work centres on a concern for
class and age differences in the readership of various magazines and
sets out to recapture magazines from the perspective of the readers, as
he puts it. Moreover, the data compiled also makes clear a number of
other realities about the practice of reading among various groups of
people, and the evidence for institutional reinforcement of that reading accentuates the special role that these magazines played in creating
mass culture.

5　学術的に読む雑誌 and 趣味的に読む雑誌 in the original Japanese. 永嶺, 雑誌と読
者の近代 (*Modern Magazines and Readers*), 236. My interest in Nagamine's work is
partly because of the value of his thesis, but also because of the wealth of the hitherto
inaccessible data his monograph makes available. Since his sources were not directly
obtainable, I mined his reproduction of the surveys and questionnaires to provide
evidence for some claims I make about readership. (I had an extensive conversation
in 2010 with Shigetoshi about his work, these materials, and his support for my
project.)

To give some specific numbers, 50 per cent of the youths interviewed in 1930 subscribed to *Kingu*, making it the most popular among this demographic; it was also the number-one-selling periodical for all categories in 1928. Nagamine quotes some examples from contemporary readers' comments about their habits:

> Previously where young men would be reading things like *Chūō kōron* or *Kaizō* [Reconstruction], by the beginning of the Shōwa period *Kingu* had taken its place at the core of what the vast majority of young men were reading ... In a survey done by Tokyo Imperial University Library in October 1927, *Kingu* was named as being the second most widely read magazine. This was especially the case among middle school boys and girls and *Kingu* took its place at the top of subscription magazines.
>
> "I'm a girls' school fourth year student but *King* is really popular among middle-school students and in my class, you'll find many avid subscribers." Kyūshū's Biggest *Kingu* fan, March 1925.
>
> "[*Boku wa*, used to denote a male speaker] I am a high school freshman. If you were to ask me, *Kingu* seems to be the most widely read magazine." Kashita Yoshio, Hyōgo Prefecture, September 1925.
>
> "There are 150 students in my class and 130 of them read *Kingu*." First-grade student from Shizuoka, November 1928.[6]

Here is clear evidence of the penetration of Kōdansha's favoured publication into the lives of students throughout Japan within a very short period of time.

Even if students (from those at primary schools up through higher educational institutions) divided their reading into categories based on function, it seems clear that those people who did less reading overall did not make such explicit distinctions about their interactions with magazines. Farmers and urban labourers, for example, read less overall than their urban or student counterparts. It is patently difficult to make comparisons among your reading materials when you are only reading a single publication, as was most of the rural population. The superfluity of these distinctions is also evidenced by the success of the category of blended "family magazine" itself that *Kingu* and *Ie no hikari* so successfully engineered – the overwhelmingly preferred category of periodical that explicitly attempted to incorporate educational and

---

6 Ibid., 214.

entertainment materials in one publication. In all cases, however, family magazines reached to all corners of the empire and happily encouraged collective involvement in their community of readers.

It is notable that in cities (especially Tokyo), as well, that *Kingu* managed to be the *only* magazine that appealed to readers across all of the various demographics accounted for in the surveys. These groups were broken down from the main categories of elementary school children, middle school children, vocational school students, high school students, college students, youth association members, labourers, farmers, Koreans, etc. into smaller units of extraction; in the case of labourers, they were broken down into manufacturing or sales. Within the urban populace, *Kingu* managed to attract readers of all varieties, whereas *Ie no hikari* is mentioned among the responses from only the farmers (men and women) and young urban boys.

The variety of readers who were exposed to the content and ideas in these magazines was tremendously broad – in terms of geography, education, and age. These magazines not only captured the interest and loyalty of readers already accustomed to buying periodicals, but they also garnered force through people who, as Nagamine describes them, "likely did not subscribe to *King* but rather picked up a copy to read at the library or listened in when someone else was reading it at the house or in the neighborhood."[7] The process of broadening the audience of *Ie no hikari* and *Kingu* continued to incorporate and normalize magazines among the empire's population by pasting various demographic groups together.

King was replaced over time by *Ie no hikari* in rural locations, and the latter continued to be as successful there as *Kingu* was in the urban centres. This conclusion is supported again and again in accounts from merchants and booksellers in the transition from the latter years of Taishō to the early years of Shōwa. For all their success in rural areas when magazines like *Shufu no tomo* and *King* had really taken hold, by 1932 a clear transformation was under way. Nagamine stresses the

---

7 Nagamine explains: "*Kingu* readers can largely be divided into two groups. The first group was already established readers of magazines and among this group *Kingu* was secondary to their previous reading preferences. Women and students [in cities] were the main base of this group ... The second group was readers who were the main subscribers of *Kingu* and could roughly be called the [urban] working class, but also among them were young men and farmers ... Thus the million readers of *Kingu* were pieced together from all these different groups" (ibid., 220–1).

novelty of this shift, saying "*Ie no hikari* has to be declared as the first entertainment magazine aimed at farmers; since this category of magazine had not previously existed, *Kingu* had managed to fill this void before *Ie no hikari* came to take its place."[8] As the Industrial Cooperative released and promoted *Light of the Home* in rural areas, it became top in terms of number of subscriptions, bumping *King* to second.

Magazines were both popular and significant, especially in the rural context. Ella Wiswell's field notes describe this phenomenon in the mid-1930s:

> Only with our generation [of people in their twenties] has schooling reached its present universal level, at least in this part of the country. Nevertheless, many households subscribed to illustrated magazines. The most popular was *Ie no hikari* [Light of the Home], followed by *Fujin Kurabu* [Women's Club], *Shufu no Tomo* [Housewife's Companion], *Kingu* [King], *Haiyu* [Actors and Actresses], and various other movie magazines bought by young men for the pictures of the women actresses. Few families subscribed to newspapers. Even those young women who could not write were able to read these magazines, and the older ones who could not read could enjoy the pictures.[9]

Here again is evidence in rural areas that magazines were the preferable form of entertainment. Simon Partner, as well, reports of twentieth-century Japanese village life that his subject received magazines from a brother who mailed them to her village from Tokyo, and "these magazines were Toshié's greatest pleasure."[10] This kind of reporting highlights and confirms the popularity of *Ie no hikari* in farming villages and hamlets, as well as the concurrent presence of *Kingu*, and marks both magazines as different in kind from what had come before. But one other significant feature of these publications was their devotion to producing a community out of their readers, and it is essential to how they produced a mass audience.

---

8 A useful chart comparing *Kingu* and *Ie no hikari* in different locales, supporting the popularity of both, also makes clear the disparity between rural and urban preferences (ibid., 216, 218–19).

9 Smith and Wiswell, *The Women of Suye Mura*, 11.

10 Notably, elsewhere in the book Partner mentions that "newspapers (which most Kosugi families had to beg or borrow to get a look at)" were less available (*Toshié*, 74, 81).

Over the 1920s and 1930s, a growing number of individuals were living lives quite apart from their families and hometowns. Nagamine explains why this was significant in reference to magazines:

Workers in the cities were largely disconnected from traditional culture, atomized and alienated, and among the urban popular culture there was a growing feeling of unease and isolation. Those workers, separated far away from their families and villages, integrated themselves through print media into a collective awareness created by *Kingu*. Within the false guise of this pseudo-community that *Kingu* supplied, these folks remembered a bit of transient peace. While this kind of quiet personal realm found while reading may be completely commonplace to us today, before *Kingu* no such kind of general phenomenon existed.[11]

Workers in Osaka, Tokyo, and other larger industrial centres were among the more avid consumers of publications like *King*. However, scholars who depict the advent of mass print media as comprising *only* these independent lonely readers, living their atomized existences and poring over their magazines and novels, do not fully reflect the lived realities of Japan. The collective reception of magazines – like the reader groups and rallies – was at the heart of their success and actually served to promote social interaction and a sense of belonging throughout the twentieth century.

In addition, reading magazines in the presence of their families, or other social configurations, was quite popular in these years. Among alumni associations, school groups, and military units, at factories, companies, government offices, and banks, there is evidence of the existence of fan clubs and reading groups. Those at Kōdansha, through *Kingu*, were at the forefront of promoting these groups and expanding, even helping to systematize, their popularization. There was a kind of meta-conversation happening about *Kingu* fan clubs and reading groups within the publication itself (serving as its own kind of publicity). For example:

In the military and schools, the [only] unconditionally permitted reading is *Kingu*. Well, not to the degree that it was overtly promoted, rather a step at a time a reading fan base progressively grew. Thus, mayors and

---

11 永嶺, 雑誌と読者の近代 (*Modern Magazines and Readers*), 222.

village heads looked to the example set by *Kingu* fans, so within towns you constantly see significant number of folks continuing along this path. The factory and company managers see five hundred to a thousand issues delivered monthly among the workers and a great number of them greet each new issue month after month enthusiastically. It's such a remarkable development that [*Kingu*] is used as auxiliary reading in all manner of supplementary schools as well.[12]

The pattern that emerges from these sources is that *Kingu* made inroads among the general populace, ingratiated itself within officially recognized institutions, and thereby became respectable and commonplace: an engine for common sense.

In addition, fan groups helped to increase the communal acceptance of these publications. Some of these fan groups were spontaneously established, as was the case with the Hokkaidō *Kingu* Club, according to their president in September of 1925; there are also records from a Sapporo *Kingu* Club established independently by residents of the city.[13] But some were organized by figures of influence, such as school principals, company presidents, and the like. In those contexts, as the above statement observes, a large number of copies would be obtained for the clubs to be distributed among members:

When speaking of the "microcosm" of workplaces, groups of young men, and schools, there was a class of leaders like educators, school principals, mayors, military, and young officers who held a kind of paternalistic authority over their realm, but they were playing the role of a kind of *Kingu* popularization agent. In fact, this class of authorities was the recipient of the hundreds of issues of *Kingu* delivered by direct mail and they satisfied the expectations well.[14]

---

12 Cited in 永嶺, 雑誌と読者の近代 (*Modern Magazines and Readers*), 220, 226.
13 松本剛, 広告の日本史, 192.
14 Nagamine continues: "This popular magazine, more specifically as the only acknowledged magazine among the military, alternatively used as supplementary reading in schools, or as the recommended magazine among workers in factories and offices, or as reading materials for youth leaders, from the top down by use of various social apparatus of the nation-state ... *Kingu* was used as a medium of ideological guidance." 永嶺, 雑誌と読者の近代 (*Modern Magazines and Readers*), 225–6.

Kōdansha quickly learned from readers writing in to the magazine that in places like schools, barracks, factories, offices, and hospitals, *Kingu* was rapidly and happily becoming the preferred public reading staple of the urban populace. Kōdansha capitalized on this by offering free or discounted copies for the managerial staff to distribute, thus boosting exposure and the number of eventual purchasers through power structures already in place.

The collective reading experience in workplaces and schools repeated itself within family units. As an example of how the magazines' popularity was reinforced through familial *ondoku* practices, there is a reader letter from October of 1925:

> Without fail, after dinner on Sundays, we have a family recreational get-together that centres on *Kingu*. We read some short articles, a bit of the fiction, and do the puzzles, play some of the games, even as far as trying out the tips for conjuring tricks. Just once, I'd like the writers to see the complete uproar when the eight of us in the household get together, rolling around laughing because of *Kingu*.[15]

This playful and evocative admission hints at the appreciation readers had for the role the magazine could play within the family (of eight people, in this case). The family was having fun together, as many families surely must have done before, but at the centre of this fun was a magazine. This was what made the practice truly a new feature of the Japanese cultural landscape.

This is also another example of why the circulation and subscription numbers, even when they number in the millions, are underestimates of magazines' impact. Children, for example, frequently did not subscribe to these kinds of publications, but their parents very commonly did. Only one of the eight members of the household mentioned above would have been calculated in the numbers commonly cited for *Kingu* and *Ie no hikari* readership, but obviously all eight people were exposed to the content. We must keep the social reading practices in mind when talking about circulation numbers if we are to understand the actual social impact of this kind of media. Kōdansha's slogan of "one issue per household" or the plans to make *Ie no hikari* the "one copy per house, all-purpose magazine" necessitate a connection to this larger picture of

---

15 Ibid., 222–3.

the way the magazines were consumed and the socialization process it included.

Where families gathered, those who had better reading abilities aided the others in a collective enjoyment of magazines as leisure entertainment. One scholar familiar with the history of *Kingu*, Satō Takumi, describes the magazines in terms that highlight the conversational and vocalized nature of the publication, calling it a "radio-like magazine."[16] Nagamine, as well, goes as far as to say that *Kingu* was at root a performative medium because it was most often read aloud. Magazine readers themselves would make the same claim, saying things like:

> It's always so interesting! Since becoming a huge fan of *Kingu*, I wait for the new issue to come out every month and it's not just me, but also mother and the kids who enjoy my reading aloud to them. Thanks to *Kingu*, quiet evenings on the farm have become a lot more enjoyable. (January 1930)
>
> *Kingu*! *Kingu*! I read "Filial Seiichirō" to my little sister. It was a lovely little piece of writing. Mother, sitting by my side, was also touched. (April 1925)[17]

As these statements suggest, many readers perused their copies not in isolation but collectively, with family members, friends, or coworkers. Rural families who regularly pooled resources and shared even bath water surely shared their leisure reading as well.[18]

Moreover, the inclusion of all family members in this process was also significant in terms of shifting practices of information acquisition within the family structure. Okuhara, the chronicler of *Ie no hikari* noted earlier, explains that, where "previously the spread of the Kumiai ideals was dispersed through the husbands into households, with *Ie no hikari*, other family members were allowed to learn of the ideals themselves directly through magazine content."[19] The leisure practices of families throughout Japan transformed in these years, and magazines were crucial to the changes that were occurring.

---

16 ラジオ的雑誌 in the original: 佐藤, 「キング」の時代 (*The Era of "King"*), 234, 199–322.

17 永嶺, 雑誌と読者の近代 (*Modern Magazines and Readers*), 224.

18 The detailed recounting of hosting the weekly bath for community members is a memorable aspect of Toshié's childhood, and *Ie no hikari* is specifically mentioned as the family's "only regular reading." See Partner, *Toshié*, 15–17, 64.

19 奥原, 家の光の二十五年 (*Twenty-Five Years of "Light of the Home"*), 20.

The cultural currency that reading this magazine provided was impetus enough for many to jump on the bandwagon. If the content of *Kingu* was known to be the general topic of conversation in the workplace, and *Ie no hikari* came to be regularly referenced among one's peers in the village, the "benefits" of the magazines (so often and explicitly promoted by their publishers) would have been all too clear to the Japanese audience. Considering that Noma's purpose was to teach the masses through his publications and that the Cooperative sought similar effects, this development was indeed a boon. Combine this tendency towards the promotion of communal participation with a kind of baseline ideological guidance and you have a profoundly influential medium by the early 1930s.

The importance and influence of magazines was not observed solely by their own publishers. European observers of Japanese society in these years were also taking note of the expanding world of magazines in Japan because of the impact they were coming to have. Included in several issues of *Kingu* were advertisements that reported comments about *Kingu* that had appeared in European publications. The texts and images of the originals were reproduced (in part or whole) alongside a translation of the content into Japanese.

As early as August of 1925, Albert de Bassompierre (the Belgian ambassador to Japan, 1920–39) noted *Kingu* as being the most widespread magazine in a short statement that was otherwise concerned with comparing Belgium to Japan. The brief piece, as an interesting side note, claims that Belgium and Japan have much in common, including, according to Bassompierre, abiding loyalty to the empire ("le loyalisme envers la Dynastie") among the populace, absolute devotion to upholding justice ("le dévouement absolu a la cause de la justice"), a veneration for the land of their forefathers, and the ability to succeed in their sacred tasks of protecting their respective nations for their descendants. He goes on to note that, while Belgium was decimated after the First World War (he states numbers of sixty-five thousand dead and more than seventy thousand crippled) and Japan likewise devastated after the Great Kantō Earthquake, both countries in a short span of only a few years had managed to return to a peaceful continuance of productivity, of which the success of *Kingu* was evidence.

In the January edition from 1931 there is a copy of an excerpt from an Italian publication with a suitably imposing portrait of Noma below a representative spread of his magazine covers. It compliments *Kingu* on "making the greatest efforts to reach all of Japan" and touts the publication as truly aimed at the masses under the moral direction of Noma.[20] These kinds of references in foreign publications and from European emissaries are indicative of the obvious and widespread presence and influence of these magazines. For the editors, these reports additionally provided independent confirmation of Japan's justified participation in global affairs and of Japanese society's positive qualities that both publications so strongly supported.

Reports from readers themselves most frequently cited enjoyment, interest, or fun as being the primary reason for reading magazines like *Kingu*, but there was also a secondary reason behind the publication's popularity. The readers described magazines as being useful for cultivating common sense and discipline; their discourses had been absorbed. The evidence presented, specifically in the surveys already mentioned as well as the overwhelming popularity of these magazines in general, shows that the editors of *King* and *Light of the Home* had managed to find a winning mixture of "utility and enjoyment."[21]

Useful can mean a variety of things. On a mundane level, these magazines were apparently appreciated for simple tips to make life a bit easier or more pleasant. One description of common bathing practices included reference to knowledge gained from reading one of these periodicals. Wiswell reports that the women she observed quite commonly washed themselves communally and, after bathing, "next, as recommended by *Ie no hikari*, they wash[ed] their face with cold water to prevent wrinkles. (Magazine instructions are much followed.)"[22] The articles pertaining to household management also regularly included these kinds of cosmetic and health ideas, thus contributing to gender norms related to beauty and hygiene standards. (Contemporary magazines the world over still use this tactic.)

Another measure of usefulness can be calculated in the wider social world, as with the ability to more easily converse with colleagues and coworkers that aids in a sense of belonging and social cohesion. The fact that *King* articles regularly made appearances in school entrance examinations and on job applications should indicate the relative cultural weight of that publication. This widespread institutional entrenchment only contributed to the further success of these

20 "Advertisement," キング (*King*), 1 January 1931, front matter.
21 永嶺, 雑誌と読者の近代 (*Modern Magazines and Readers*), 232–3.
22 Smith and Wiswell, *The Women of Suye Mura*, 9.

publications and lends weight to their importance as meaning makers within Japanese society.

Entrance exams for a range of schools throughout Japan, from high schools to technical colleges, included questions pertaining to popular media meant to gauge common sense, and prior to the late 1920s such questions had excerpted publications like *Chūō kōron*. By 1928, exams regularly reproduced content from *Kingu* instead.[23] When the editors selected items "worth knowing" for common sense, the resulting social capital gained (or exams passed) confirmed for the audience that the magazines were trustworthy. Institutions actively chose to respect, and thus contributed to the perceived value of, these publications in ways increasingly obvious to average people in Japan.

Also, the entertainments available in rural areas in particular were somewhat scarce, and these magazines were genuinely fun to consume. Those left behind in the rural areas learned from their children, who had moved to cities, what kinds of pleasure were available in urban areas. Youths in cities could go to cafés and dance halls, window shop on commercial avenues, see the technological marvels modern society was integrating in Japan. Accordingly, cultural practices like the *O-bon* dancing, festivals, folk ditties sung on holidays, and similar historically common hometown diversions seemed to pale in comparison to what was becoming available as modernization efforts were shifting lifestyles more rapidly in cities.

In the global economic depression and deepening deprivation of farming communities in the late Taishō and early Shōwa years, people wanted leisure and socially acceptable forms of entertainment. Farming communities enjoyed an interim status of entertainment, such that old recreational practices ceased to deliver entertainment satisfaction, but movies and other urban delights were rare at best in the countryside. By 1925, an urban resident might see upwards of seven movies a year, but someone in a village would, if lucky, see one. "When asked 'what kind of things do you do for fun?' young, old, man, and woman alike replied, 'there's nothing fun to do.'"[24] Until radio and movies managed to make their way fully into rural regions of Japan in the postwar years, reading magazines as a form of leisure was an obvious and accessible outlet for most of the population.

---

23 永嶺, 雑誌と読者の近代 (*Modern Magazines and Readers*), 237–8.
24 Quoted from ibid., 233.

What the producers of these magazines were hoping to accomplish was, in part, to reach the widest audience they possibly could, and, by the middle of the 1930s, they had succeeded in that aspect of their mission.

The Participating Audience

How these magazines reached these levels of popularity is critically important – it is a central motor for the creation of the Japanese masses. Indeed, the producers of these magazines expended great efforts and resources to increase their reach. These processes manifested on a number of levels, including some detail-oriented adjustments to methods of editing, on one end of the spectrum, and huge campaigns and spectacular events, on the other.

Mundane policies regarding the distribution plans of *Ie no hikari*, for example, were periodically tweaked and finessed. One such plan read:

Distribution Services:
1. In villages, counties, and cities nationwide (and all administrative districts in Japan), the ... distribution committee members will contact one another about figures and the progress of distribution activities;
2. Create special subscription contracts with the cooperatives nationwide;
3. Create the special subscription contracts with various locales nationwide for union members as the principal organizers of ... *Ie no hikari* clubs and autonomous *Ie no hikari* activities;
4. Deploy correspondents in areas of national importance in order to collect materials for rural areas;
5. Complete the task of creating a bulletin for the editors (*Ie no hikari Monthly Report*) and aim for the constant improvement of the content and format ...[25]

The diligent implementation of these plans helped *Ie no hikari* succeed and is evidenced by the steadily increasing subscription rates through the 1920s and 1930s. After all, by 1935, the Cooperative's "Million Issue

---

25 奥原, 家の光の二十五年 (*Twenty-Five Years of "Light of the Home"*), 40.

Plan" for *Ie no hikari* had been achieved in roughly half the time estimated to reach that number of subscriptions.[26]

This expansion was supported by the larger efforts to expand the Cooperative, based, at least in part, on the Cooperative Societies Law (revised September 1932). For example, according to a 1937 Department of Agriculture and Forestry Report, at the end of 1936 there were 15,460 Co-ops – an increase of 1,108 over the 14,352 documented at the end of 1932. Such growth was part of the more general effort of the state to better integrate agrarian communities into the cooperative movement for the purpose of economic revival through debt reduction (read: utilization of credit services provided by the Co-ops), if not directly through price regulation or increased production, on which policies had focused in the past.[27]

On a broader level, though, *King* and *Light of the Home* were strikingly successful in creating and capturing a mass audience through techniques of audience inclusion. The magazine not only spoke to the readers but also sought their active participation. This was done, in the case of *Ie no hikari*, though the solicitation of reader contributions and reader rallies. Rallies were large public events with a variety of entertainments that also served to focus on the publication. With *Kingu*, evidence of fan clubs suggests the importance of social practices surrounding reading magazines and their expansion into a mass phenomenon.

Magazine readers in the United States circumvented the cost of subscriptions by circulating used magazines among several families, rural families especially, and participated in fan clubs and reading groups. That audience saw themselves, in Ellen Gruber Garvey's words, as participating in "a community of magazine readers," and the targets of the American publications she discusses, thus, were similar to those of *Kingu* and *Ie no hikari* in that the numbers given for circulation were smaller than the numbers of people actually exposed to the materials because of the way magazines circulated socially.[28] American magazines also attempted to make their materials accessible to the whole family through the inclusion of a variety of sections and content, showing how massification can have common mechanisms in many contexts.

---

26 Ibid., 42.
27 Yagi, "The Second Three-Year Expansion Plan of the Co-Operative Movement," 24, 19, 22–3.
28 Garvey, *The Adman in the Parlor*, 6, 188–9, 211–12.

In the case of *Kingu* it was not reader submissions as much as contests and prizes that allowed a reader to contribute and be acknowledged as a participant in the community. *King* held regular contests and competitions seeking poetry, songs, and various other forms of writing; the results of these contests were included in the table of contents of most issues throughout the 1920s and 1930s and prominently advertised within the issues of *Kingu*, often filling a two-page spread with images and text. Readers could feel connected to other readers and able to gain recognition and affirmation by giving to their favourite publications, in what amounted to both publicity and free content for the publishers.

An example of the postings in *Ie no hikari* common to every issue announced, "Looking for accurate accounts of actual household finances for a month or entire year … In what specific ways does your wife endeavor to continue being prudent? Manuscripts of 80 lines or less"; and "Your cooking specialty. Every house has its own special dishes, write them up so they are easy to understand."[29] Another example of a similar request reads,

[Requesting] Correspondence: This column will be for the benefit of all readers and we ask that you contact us with your various opinions. Furthermore, in order to endeavor on behalf of the cooperative, together with our leadership, we ask for you to volunteer your correspondence.[30]

These explicit announcements invite the participation of readers in the production of their magazine as a portal onto involvement in the broader activities of the Cooperative. They also provided a sense of acknowledgment and importance for the audience, reinforcing the avowals of these publications that their readers possessed valuable characteristics. It would have been affirming to readers that their ideas, opinions, and habits could be interesting and beneficial to others "who were just like them" and boosted feelings of being in it together with others.

Ie no hikari had sections like "our self-sufficient home": there were articles about homemade soy milk for infants, easy to make insecticides, economical concrete baths, along with new instructions on how to make or tips on how best to use a variety of rural daily household items in each issue. "Our household experiments" looks surprisingly

---

29 "Announcement," 25.
30 "読者講談室 (Reader's Lecture Room)," 88.

similar to the modern-day *Cook's Illustrated*'s "Quick Tips"; it provided helpful tips submitted by the magazine's readers, like the tip offered by Masuda Shizuko from Shizuoka on what to do with egg shells. She explains:

> Whenever I want to transfer oil, soy sauce, and the like into a small-mouthed bottle, I divide an eggshell in half and make a small hole in the bottom in order to make a perfectly good funnel.[31]

Such material was endless and complimentary from the readers themselves. How to make a variety of bento lunches, dried taro, and drying baskets, how to store *mizumochi* to prevent mould, clues for sturdy *getta* (sandals), the list covered literally hundreds upon thousands of pages over the course of *Ie no hikari*'s publication.

This technique was common to other Japanese publications of the day as well. Barbara Sato relates that "confessional articles" (*kokuhaku kiji*) were used regularly in many women's magazines like *Fujin sekai*, *Fujokai*, *Fujin no tomo*, and *Fujin kurabu*.[32] Aside from these actual contributions from readers to their favourite publications, the very style of the magazines suggested a kind of mutual relationship where the audience was also drawn into the confidence of the magazine through its conversational style.

There was a related precedent for this in early newspapers. Yamada Shunji explains how this relationship worked: "acting as an emblem and agent for the affairs of the day, newspapers transcended tangible human relationships based on blood and region [i.e., common hometown] and were a vision of social relations in a symbolic world where images of the nation and society were supplied on a daily basis."[33]

---

31 "我家の実験 (Our Household Experiments)."

32 For instance, "From 1918, *Shufu no tomo* regularly solicited contributions from readers about their personal problems. Murakami Nobuhiko calls this a two-sided policy. Although he believes it originated as a way for the magazine to lower its editorial expenses, he also considers it a means for Ishikawa [Takemi] to make contact with the readers" (Sato, *The New Japanese Woman*, 197).

33 Yamada focuses on the move to *ōshinbun* (so-called large newspapers) from the older *kōshinbun* (small newspaper) format, spearheaded by *Yomiuri Shinbun*. In his analysis of this mode of presentation, he argues that the transition from older formats and styles to a new kind of publication had larger implications for print media more generally. 山田, 大衆新聞がつくる明治の〈日本〉 (*The Creation of "Japan" by Popular Meiji Newspapers*), 258–9.

Periodicals thus became, in some ways, a new friend and neighbour happily welcomed into the community by people in Japan and easily fitted within their daily conversations. Such publishing trends are certainly supported by the evidence from publications like *Kingu* and *Ie no hikari* and reports about them.

This process unearths a genealogy for periodicals and illuminates the shifting social role they played in Japanese society. The antecedents of mass magazines were, to some extent, newspapers, but not because of the commonalities they had as print media. Rather, newspapers had been part of the culture of *ondoku* since the turn of the twentieth century; reading rooms, for example, had been present in Japan since the Meiji era for at least urban residents to collectively discuss print media.[34] Thus, magazines embedded themselves in a pre-existing practice as part of an expanding world of media, but also thereby transformed that culture into something on a much larger scale and of a significantly altered content. Whole families and communities (small and large – rural and urban) were now participating in the consumption of a common commodity, a commodity that reinforced particular ideas about the collective in which the audience was participating.

This participation, moreover, was not simply a benign leisure activity, but had political implications as well. Among Japanese historians, Adachi Ikitsune has written on *Ie no hikari*'s particular flavour of agrarianism and the role it had to play in bolstering mass participation in media that allowed for, in his estimation, the greater dissemination of fascist governmental ideology.[35] Adachi provides additional evidence for *Ie no hikari*'s ideologically driven mission, present from the outset of the project, and ties this mission directly to the choices made about the content and promotional methods of the magazine. He quotes a spectator of one of the initial rallies as being overwhelmed by the "magic and spectacle" of seeing one thousand women stand in unison simply at the behest of the Kumiai representative who was speaking and had asked them to do so.[36] Those at the Cooperative with the desire for mass participation and the determination to execute their plans for the

---

34 Kornicki, "The Publisher's Go-Between," 333.
35 安達, "『家の光』の歴史 – ある農本主義とその媒体 (The History of 'Ie No Hikari' – The Media of Agricultural Fundamentalism)."
36 Ibid., 62.

promotion of *Ie no hikari*, like Shimura, Arimoto, and Umeyama, succeeded in previously unanticipated and frightening ways.

The flavour of ideology present in the editorial position of magazines like *Ie no hikari*, particularly with its emphasis on leaving high politics up to the "experts" and keeping women obediently focused on the domestic, is what marks it out for Adachi as being easily manipulated by fascist forces. Most importantly though, the mechanisms of these rallies, according to him, provided the "prototypes" that became supremely useful to the government and its extra-official organizations and that developed into huge institutions integral to home-front wartime support in the late 1930s and early 1940s and then to recovery in the transwar years, such as the much-discussed Women's Associations.[37]

Since *Ie no hikari* was among the first, if not in fact the first, to have rallies of this scale, its influence is all the more significant. If we can assume that mechanisms of extra-governmental organizations propelled the rise of militarism and nationalism in Japan beginning in the 1930s, and if these mechanisms have roots in the *Ie no hikari* rallies, then there is a clear line tying those larger social phenomena in the 1930s and 1940s to the ideological visions of the producers of these magazines in the 1920s. These magazines, therefore, must be included among the influences for those developments.

Kingu and *Ie no hikari*, especially, expanded their circulation numbers and influence by tapping into the communal nature of people's interactions with their magazines. In addition to the group discussions and phenomena of reading magazines aloud, the Cooperative decided to promote their publication and ideals at *Ie no hikari* rallies. These events were quite popular and drew surprising numbers of attendees. The rallies were advertised in the publication itself and seem to have been communicated through heads of the local branches to other members of farming communities.

An example of an announcement for such an event was included in the first issue of the magazine, supposedly penned by a Mrs Imai, and ran:

Bringing *Ie no hikari* rallies to the countryside … *Ie no hikari* readers together have organized *Ie no hikari* rallies in various places and I think

---

37 For two such treatment of the women's organizations, see Garon, "Women's Groups and the Japanese State"; 鞠谷, 戦争を生きた女たち (*Women Who Lived the War*).

you'll see the announcements [for them]. Being rural women, I think we can certainly do beneficial work by laboring together. Just as the Central Committee has led this request, I too ask for the support of all of you.[38]

Such statements make it clear that the impetus for the rallies came from the Cooperative Committee members, but it also illuminates the ways in which average women were incorporated into the promotional process. In these early stages of the spread of *Ie no hikari*, it would be irresponsible to say that the women were coopted or manipulated in a systematic way for these ends, but the editors were certainly aware of the convenient potential women had to influence each other and spread excitement and interest in Kumiai events.

There were also calls for smaller group activities involving the magazine. Listed alongside the above announcement was also this one:

A Call for Family Leisure Clubs: We rural residents are starved for entertainment. Or, perhaps, our optimistic kind of society shouldn't seek amusement, but working straight through is beyond human efficiency and can't continue. A fitting relaxation or recreation is indispensable. The significance of this is that I ask you to become a supporter of *Ie no hikari* and open a leisure club … for the education and industry of your region.[39]

The Cooperative actively and explicitly sought out each segment of the population in order to blanket rural communities with opportunities for engagement with their magazine and with union efforts more generally. The move, therefore, to large rallies in support of the magazine was a natural outgrowth of the attitudes and expectations of Kumiai leaders.

What was a rally? Towards the end of the 1920s, distribution efforts ramped upward, and in March of 1928 the first of the *Ie no hikari* rallies was held. Local branches in a number of villages sponsored these events through the district, village, or prefectural unit. Local union leaders and invited speakers would promote the goals of the Cooperative by focusing on the current goals of the union while also explicitly promoting *Ie no hikari*. There would be a variety of talks, entertainments, even films which lent an air of celebration and excitement to what might have

---

38 "読者講談室 (Reader's Lecture Room)," 88.
39 Ibid.

otherwise been perceived as boring pronouncements from the men of the Kumiai. Without these rallies, it is unlikely that the impact of *Ie no hikari*, and by extension the Industrial Cooperative itself, would have been so pronounced.[40] With the striking uptick in circulation numbers after their inception in 1928, this becomes all the more obvious.

Thirteen prefectures were selected at first to host these rallies and were chosen from among all prefectures that had sought direct assistance from the Cooperative. This move was understood as both an attempt to spread the spirit of the Sangyō Kumiai and an opportunity to inform those who had not yet subscribed of *Ie no hikari*'s existence.[41] The events were photographed and extensive records made about attendance and reception. Almost immediately after the first rallies were held in the selected locations, these photographs and reports were in turn used to further promote the rallies and the magazine (see figure 4.1).

There was consistent cooperation with local newspapers and businesses to publicize and promote the events, which included plays, dances, *naniwabushi* (recitation of stories accompanied by samisen, also called *ryōkyoku*), and movies, along with, naturally, lectures from Kumiai representatives. In the September 1928 issue of *Ie no hikari*, readers were presented with a lively description of some of the initial rallies. The report from Nagano stated that the event was held on 10 July, opening at nine in the morning, though people began gathering as early as six. There were so many participants, furthermore, that the rally required more than one building; the total number of attendees, all women, equalled sixteen hundred people, where the first building held twelve hundred and the second about four hundred. The chapter head, Mr Yamada, spoke as the first location filled to capacity. Then several other named members gave "moving" orations. The audience returned at one o'clock after a break for lunch at noon. The second location was a similar scene, and the whole event ended at four o'clock in the afternoon.

One gets the impression from these large events – sometimes overflowing from local buildings into parks and other spaces nearby – that, since women were rarely, if ever, allowed to congregate publicly in such numbers, they found the day-long communal activities a welcome change from their daily routines. Rallies became an opportunity

---

40 奥原, 家の光の二十五年 (*Twenty-Five Years of "Light of the Home"*), 24.
41 北村, 家の光の四十年 (*Forty Years of "Light of the Home"*), 16.

Figure 4.1. Photographs of rallies, *Ie no hikari* 4, no. 9 (September 1928)

to congregate in a way that was, in other contexts, unacceptable and potentially even illegal. The Cooperative was, thus, able to capitalize on rural women's enthusiasm for participation as a means to promote their publication. Once one member was interested and committed to the publication, that opened the door to the rest of the household. *Ie no hikari*'s success came to flow in large part from the activities and campaigns at the core of these rallies.

Similar accounts are given about the events held in Kagoshima and Niigata on 9 August and 14 July, respectively.[42] Of the two thousand attendees in Kagoshima, most were wives of members of the Cooperative who were "hopeful for the continued dissemination of *Ie no hikari*" in their prefecture (Kagoshima lagged behind the two prefectures with the greatest subscription rates, namely Nagano and Yamaguchi).[43] The next month's issue described the rallies held in August 1928 in Kagoshima and Chiba.[44] At each event there were representatives from the Central Committee present to oversee the proceedings, and large numbers of participants. One chronicler of the Cooperative's history ventured that "people were having more interest in leisure," and this apparent desire for leisure in rural communities was convenient for the Cooperative and its hopes for an expanding audience for its publication and practices.[45] The fact that Kumiai representatives noticed this need and were able to see how connecting their magazine to that craving would help achieve multiple goals also united the audience in innovative and truly voluntary ways.

These rallies were introduced to the readers of the magazine as a twenty-fifth anniversary commemorative event for the Cooperative upon the successful completion of the publication of *Ie no hikari*. The mission of making the values of the Cooperative the complete foundation for the home was always unabashedly at the forefront. Descriptions of the events were offered as an invitation for others to attend future rallies; the rallies were in fact successful wherever they were held and frequently attracted attendees that numbered around one thousand even in the most remote locales.[46]

---

42 "家の光読者大会 (*Light of the Home* Reader Rallies)," 1 September 1928, 54–5.
43 北村, 家の光の四十年 (*Forty Years of "Light of the Home"*), 18.
44 "家の光読者大会 (*Light of the Home* Reader Rallies)," 1 October 1928, 27.
45 北村, 家の光の四十年 (*Forty Years of "Light of the Home"*), 18.
46 "家の光読者大会 (*Light of the Home* Reader Rallies)," 1 September 1928, 54.

And while the publication was explicitly not a women's magazine, it was readily apparent to any observer that women were the driving force behind both the success of the rallies and the gaining of individual rural households' subscriptions to *Ie no hikari*. The role ascribed to women anecdotally, if not in fact, as keepers of household economies and the mainspring behind household consumption decisions clearly played a part in the decision to focus rallies around women's interests and participation. Ideas about gender that played out in the pages of *Ie no hikari* and in the social practices surrounding its consumption are thus all the more significant for our understanding of mass media's influence on gender norms in these years.

Media Interactions

Though it seems second nature in most countries today, cross-marketing products – with integrated placement in multiple media – was only just becoming a common phenomenon in the interwar years. Consequently, having newspapers, songs, magazines, films, and other media coordinating in the promotion of certain commodities was an exciting development for publishers, producers, and advertisers alike. These activities ranged over not just product placement and cross-pollination but also a variety of contests (beauty pageants, for example) and brand-focused clubs with all the attendant swag and prizes.[47]

Kingu Records (officially a recording label in 1931) entered a market already highly active with foreign participants: Victor, Columbia, and Polydor, for example. Attempting to compete directly with those companies seemed counterproductive to the actual aims of the enterprise, so Kōdansha sought collaboration with one of them, in no small part in order to avoid the capital outlay of having to produce and distribute the gramophone records themselves. It was the Polydor logo that was pressed onto the discs manufactured under the name of *Kingu* Records. These records and advertisements for them became highly visible in a number of public domains.

Noma was dismayed by popular songs in the early years of Shōwa because of their increasingly self-indulgent and melancholy themes, with

---

47 Kim Brandt addresses beauty contests in a forthcoming essay and monograph, but in Japanese, see 井上, 美人コンテスト百年史 (*One Hundred Year History of Beauty Contests*). For Shiseidō's Camellia Club, see Weisenfeld, "Selling Shiseido."

such titles as "The Withering Pampas," "A Caged Bird," and "*Saké*, a Tear or a Sigh." He reasoned that if he could influence people visually with his magazines, then the same ideological guidance might be possible with music. And so, for several months beginning in 1930, *Kingu* announced a competition for readers to write their own lyrics and submit them under the theme of "a wholesome song," one the publisher hoped could "purify popular music and brighten Japan." The first enthusiastic round of contest entries numbered well over 190,000 submissions; Kōdansha's robust ability to incorporate readers through participation in its mission, consequently, found a new channel when *Kingu* Records was born.[48]

The astoundingly high levels of participation – nearly two hundred thousand entries requiring voluntary creative effort – shows just how successful these publications were at getting the audience involved with their activities. Moreover, as in the case of this particular contest, the audience was participating in an explicitly moral endeavour directly in line with the values promoted by Kōdansha's prized periodical. The methods succeeded and were adaptable; in many ways, they served as a model for reader, thus consumer, involvement in the coming decades.

Normalizing commodities (magazines, records, etc.) in multiple formats, through a variety of techniques, therefore, served to familiarize the Japanese masses with viewing, discussing, purchasing, and owning those products in a way that would not have been possible in years before these media interactions. When a Japanese factory worker, say, went to a film in which certain products and music were seamlessly integrated into the viewing experience, those things would seem familiar, and yet the advertiser would not have been hampered by any negative feelings that same worker might have had towards more conventional forms of advertising. Further, the mention of films, records, and products within the pages of *Kingu* and *Ie no hikari* would have served as mental reinforcements for the other experiences as magazines increasingly integrated into collective social practices. Cross-marketing fitted effortlessly within the world of fan clubs and rallies as well.

---

48 For a thorough and thoughtful discussion of "vulgarity" and its relationship to
   popular music and censorship, as well as of the planning and execution of *Kingu*
   Records, see, respectively, Nagahara, "Unpopular Music"; 佐藤,「キング」の時代
   (*The Era of "King"*). Original Japanese song titles are 枯れすすき, 籠の鳥, and 酒
   は涙か溜息か. 社史編纂委員会 (Committee for the Compilation of the Company
   History), 講談社の歩んだ五十年 (*The Path of Kōdansha's First Fifty Years*), 186–8. For
   the postwar years, see also Dorsey, "Breaking Records."

Aside from the rallies and reader groups, eventually those at *Ie no hikari*, in the same way Kōdansha did with *Kingu*, created extra editions of the magazine itself. These supplements (*furoku*) varied in size and type, but all served to bolster the popularity of the original publications. They were different in various ways from standard issues of the magazines, depending on what kind of supplements they were.

The first of these publications from the Cooperative came in 1930 and included a prefatory statement from Shimura. It also included articles on farming families and ideals for Cooperative activities that would have been recognizable as quite similar to what was present in the magazine itself.[49] In 1931, the original plan to print fifty thousand copies of "The Strength of the Cooperative" to be sold at five sen apiece was a grossly pessimistic estimate of the demand. The publication was thirty-two pages long and, like many of the extra editions, printed in the (no longer used) *kiku* size.[50] Eventually an astounding 1,450,000 copies of this supplement were sold. These *furoku* were released in addition to the regular full monthly editions of *Ie no hikari* itself, and a partial list of other extra editions runs thus:

in 1931, "Business Conditions from the Cooperative" in *kiku* edition 48 pages, price 5 sen, 1,541,308 copies; in 1932, "Our Wish for an Ideal State" in *kiku* edition 48 pages, price 5 sen, 431,000 copies; the same year, "Now is the Time for the Rebirth of the Cooperative" 1,400,000 copies, 5 sen; in 1933, "To the Front Lines of the Cooperative" 310,000 copies, 5 sen; "Household Reader for the Time of Crisis" 1,510,000 copies, 5 sen; in 1934, "Protect the Homeland" 1,500,000 copies, 5 sen; in 1935, "Brightening Japan" 5 sen, 1,630,000 copies; in 1936, "*Ie no hikari*'s Medical Almanac" 1,850,000 copies at 5 sen.[51]

The reports indicate that there were no returned or remaindered copies of any of these publications, since these circulation numbers were based on advance orders before the presses were run. In addition, from

---

49 産業組合中央会家の光編輯部 (Editors of *Light of the Home*, Industrial Cooperative Central Committee), 家の光: 人の一生と産業組合 (*Light of the Home: The Industrial Cooperative and the Span of Your Life*).
50 *Kiku* editions used a common size of paper before the contemporary standardized sizes, such as A5, appeared. The whole sheet measured 636 millimetres (2尺1寸) wide by 939 millimetres tall (3尺1寸) and was folded in sixteen before being bound.
51 奥原, 家の光の二十五年 (*Twenty-Five Years of "Light of the Home"*), 35.

the titles alone, one can discern that the moralizing and pedagogical mode present in the magazines was also in full force in the supplements. After many years of success, around 1947, the Sangyō Kumiai began the publication of companion magazines in the hopes of mirroring the success of Kōdansha's variety of offerings. Some of these titles included *The Soil*, *The Collected Light of the Home*, *Light of the Home Youth Library*, and *Light of the Home Picture Book*.[52]

By 1927, Noma was also making supplements to *Kingu*. The *furoku* to the magazine proper were sometimes elaborate and followed the usual flair often deployed by Kōdansha. These publications could be considered as loss leaders that were not expected to make profits individually, but meant mostly to stimulate interest in the magazine in the hopes of procuring more loyal readers.[53] *Kingu's* supplements ranged from maps to poetry collections, from dictionaries of "common sense" to compendia of quotations, and from pithy comedic compendiums to assemblages of editorials written by Noma.[54] The maps were ornate and stylish, but since they were supplements they could be had for the same regular issue price of fifty sen. The maps in particular became associated with the *Kingu* name and were envied by other publishers as the industry standard they must follow.[55]

One of these *Kingu* supplements, *The Illustrated Meiji Taishō Shōwa*, was beautifully printed in full colour as a large two-sided, foldout, accordion-style book of roughly two hundred pages.[56] It was sold at a price of seventy sen, though frequently the *furoku* were given out free along with the purchase of the regular monthly issues of the publication. This particular supplement was produced at great expense and did not make a significant profit by itself, as it was sold together with "The Cornerstone of Success" collection containing an assortment of Noma's writings.

---

52 Ibid., 4.
53 Akimoto, *Seiji Noma "Magazine King" of Japan*, 25.
54 佐佐木, 古今名歌集; キング, 繪ばなし古間學; 淵田, 支那事變忠勇談・感激談: 附支那事變誌; キング, 繪ばなし古間學; 淵田, 偉人は斯く教へる (*The Teachings of Great Men*); 武者小路, 名言名訓集 (*Collected Quotations and Sayings*); 長谷川, 明治大帝 (*Emperor Meiji*); 鳩山, 新語新知識: 附常識辭典 (*Neologisms and New Knowledge: Dictionary of Common Sense*).
55 社史編纂委員会 (Committee for the Compilation of the Company History), 講談社の歩んだ五十年 (*The Path of Kōdansha's First Fifty Years*), 272–3.
56 Wonderfully preserved in Waseda University's collection. 淵田, 明治大正昭和大絵巻 (*The Illustrated Meiji Taishō Shōwa*).

The Illustrated Meiji Taishō Shōwa is organized chronologically and has articles to accompany the images on each page (sometimes several of each per page, depending on the year). The content is varied in terms of topics, as one might expect from the Kōdansha style that was in full swing by 1931 when the supplement was released. Consistently throughout this publication, there are repeated images and text in support of the imperial institution and its aspirations abroad, notable social paragons, patriotism more generally, and a distaste for social disorder. The images of the Meiji, Taishō, and Shōwa emperors grace the first page alongside an illustration of the Imperial Palace, and there are representations of the promulgation of the Meiji Constitution and other such officially promoted and commemorated dates of import.

Gender and its representation are less straightforward in this publication. Women are rarely depicted at all in the "important events" of the illustrated history, but when they do appear they are represented as subservient or domestically focused, in socially acceptable modes of feminine behaviour; these include placing sandals at the ready for a spouse, tending to children, or dancing at a festival, for example.

A notable exception is an image for 1911 (see figure 4.2). One of the significant events that year was the establishment of the *Seitō* (Bluestockings) group and its resultant journal by Hiratsuka Raichō, among others. The text is neutral in its description of the *Seitō* call for women's emancipation and its explanation that this movement was prompted by ideas imported from the West. But the impression given by the image is not particularly positive, especially with the inclusion of one woman (with her back turned to the viewer) rattling a sabre labelled "women's rights." In the illustration, moreover, several women are shown drinking wine and holding a placard reading "Blue Stomping" instead of "Bluestockings," in what might be taken as derision of the prominent feminist publication and its creators. Notably, the name of the group is given accurately within the text.[57]

Another striking choice for the representation of women is on the 1910 page (see figure 4.3). The "Annexation of Korea" article is presented with an image of a Korean woman dressed in a long, high-waisted skirt (*hanbok*), holding a baby and looking down at what are taken to be her two other children, who are holding Japanese flags in the foreground. In this bucolic scene of a coastal Korean town, there are

---

57 "青踏" instead of the correct "青鞜" Ibid., 1911 (Meiji 44).

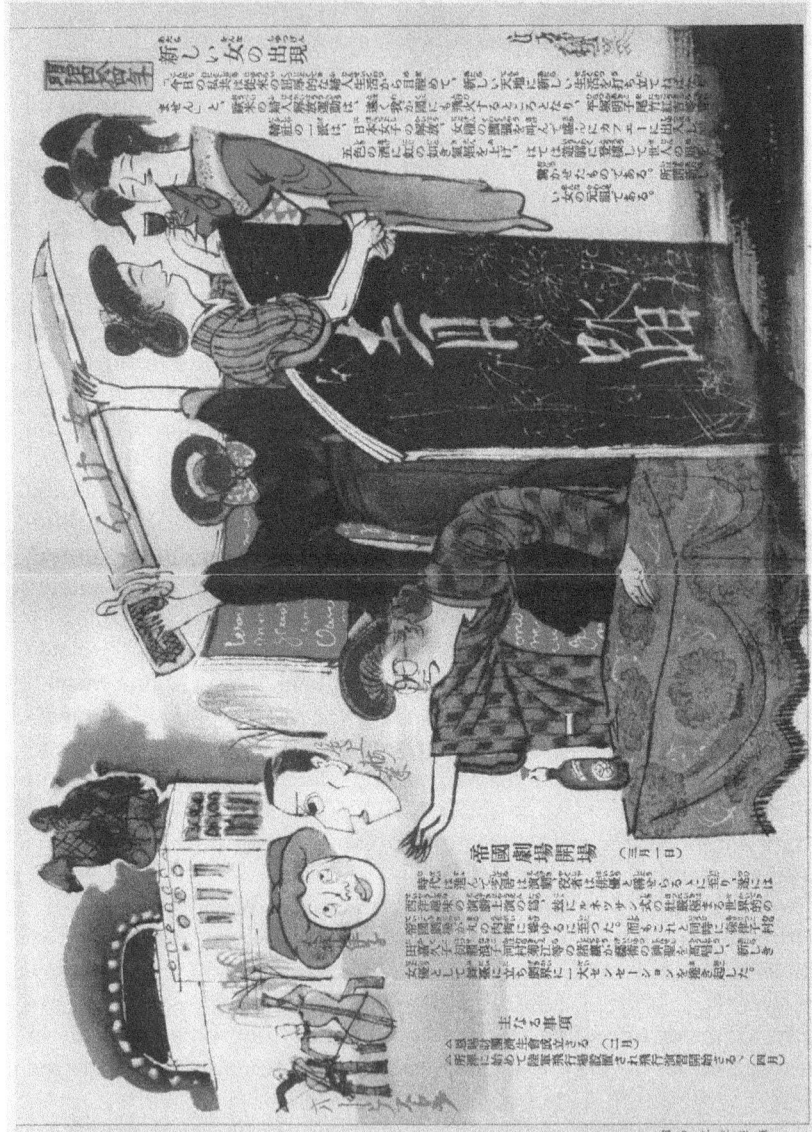

Figure 4.2. "Events of 1911," *The Illustrated Meiji Taishō Shōwa*, January 1931

Figure 4.3. "Annexation of Korea," *The Illustrated Meiji Taishō Shōwa,* January 1931

Japanese flags flying amidst the houses in the background and people carrying baskets atop their heads (holding what looks like rice) walking along the path towards the female figure and facing the viewer. The text fits comfortably within the then popular discourse supporting imperialistic Japan as benefactor of East Asia. It reads: "After the Russo-Japanese War, Korea was placed under our protection for the eternal peace of the Orient, and in addition to increasing Korea's welfare it has been elevated as one alongside our countrymen to share entirely in our [collective] happiness for many years."[58] The choice to depict a woman with children as a stand-in for the imperial relationship to one of Japan's colonies is a loaded one, to say the very least.

The supplements for both *Kingu* and *Ie no hikari* consistently focused on communal support of the Japanese imperium, dutiful devotion to national causes, and the actions of individuals committed to raising themselves and Japan in the world. The times of crisis which beset Japan made their impact on these publications over the course of the 1930s, but from their inception, *Kingu* and *Ie no hikari* and their *furoku* sought to instil a sense of participation in the community of Japan.

Concluding Thoughts

The importance of massification lies in the normalization of a mechanism for participation in, and communication with, a *mass* audience. Other important collective large-scale events also existed during these years. Sporting events and labour union rallies (quite distinct from the rallies discussed above) were sometimes similar in scale to the events surrounding and supporting these publications, but those events were overwhelmingly local or regional in nature. In addition, such events that had a political basis (election speeches, etc.) would likely not have included women, at least not legally. But the rallies, contests, fan clubs, and other promotional events that served to promote and spread the magazines did not create mass culture; rather, the magazines themselves provided the mechanism.

Reading groups and fan clubs for American magazines around the turn of the twentieth century also sought to draw in reader participation at the same time as they created a loyal customer base. Ellen Gruber Garvey argues that "within new models of fluid, shifting identity,

---

58 Ibid., 1910 (Meiji 43).

nostalgia for the possibility of making a permanent mark, an assertion of stability, was grounded in the child, someone on whose mind the preference for a brand could be 'impressed' or 'engraved,'" and this happened such that "childhood became a repository of a commercial unconscious" and comprised a precious demographic.[59] Contests and clubs, specifically ones aimed at children, helped to bring American reading audiences into a kind of community in which they enthusiastically participated; this kind of community building among the magazines' audience (also unambiguously consumers) served to foster loyalty not only to the magazines themselves but also to those who advertised within them.

These American magazines also attempted to make their materials accessible to the whole family through the inclusion of a variety of sections and content. Magazine readers in the United States circumvented the cost of subscriptions by circulating used magazines among several families, rural families especially, and participated in fan clubs and reading groups. The targets of the American publications Garvey discusses were similar to those of *Kingu* and *Ie no hikari* in that the numbers given for circulation were smaller than the numbers of people actually exposed to the materials because of the way magazines circulated socially. Moreover, the conception of magazines as being a family affair parallels the features of the more important publications in Japan, even if the advertising in Japanese publications was not so child-directed as was the case in American periodicals like *St. Nicholas*, *Booklovers*, *McClure's*, and *Women's World*, to name a few examples.[60]

The historical story of public engagement with magazines has to include the fact that some people deliberately chose to purchase these commodities. The publishers knew this quite well:

> *Ie no hikari* was created with a goal of the education of the masses of union members in mind; however ... Magazines that were well read were limited to those that charged. In order to get large numbers of readers, magazines had to be free of the smell of publicity; you had to have editing that made the reader feel there was value in taking out money to pay for a general family magazine.[61]

---

59 Garvey, *The Adman in the Parlor*, 53.
60 Ibid., 6, 51–79, 188–9, 211–12.
61 奥原, 家の光の二十五年 (*Twenty-Five Years of "Light of the Home"*), 13, 16.

People invested value in the things that they chose to purchase. Magazines were increasingly among those commodities, as readers in enormous numbers would ante up their twenty or fifty sen per issue each month in order to have access to their contents. Even in dire economic times, *Kingu* and *Ie no hikari* gained in popularity. One explanation was that

> ... because one [*Ie no hikari*] issue's price was a mere 20 sen, in each house that subscribed, family members could leisurely read the magazine and at the same time keep the magazine preserved as it was, and it was among the first circulating magazines to transition to household paid subscriptions.[62]

The inexpensive price of *Kingu* and *Ie no hikari*, combined with social reading practices involving one's family, school groups, military cadres, or workplace cohorts, meant that all members of a household or group were entertained and enriched, resulting in an inextricably integrated form of Japanese media. This kind of assimilation meant that these commercially produced publications became embedded within state-supported institutions – schools, hospitals, etc. – resulting in a tacit, if not explicit, official approval of their existence and content.

Something else that cannot be separated from all the images and text of these publications has not yet been discussed: the advertisements in *Ie no hikari* and *Kingu*. Regularly comprising up to 20 per cent of the magazines' pages, these advertisements had effects that were not anticipated by those at the Kumiai or Kōdansha. Most significantly, collective practices naturalized collective and participatory consumption for the audience of magazines. While these magazines offered one educational conduit through the content of the articles proper, the images and messages in the advertisements scattered throughout their pages also provided instruction of a different stripe. The most fundamental impact of these magazines in the postwar years is found in the education the readers received about *consumption*, not just ideology or participation; the next chapter addresses this dual nature of mass magazines and the tutoring that *Kingu* and *Ie no hikari* fans gained about participating in the economy.

---

62 Ibid., 21.

Chapter Five

Learning to Consume: How Magazines Politicized Advertising

What *Kingu* and *Ie no hikari* helped to create was the foundation for a mass Japanese consumer culture that exploited growing mercantile trends. These shifts were the direct result of the fact that Japanese were consuming not only the magazine itself (a commodity for sale) but also the advertising intermingled within the pages of each issue. This explains why the postwar figure of a mass Japanese *consumer* was already ingrained in the mass Japanese *audience* of these magazines – the "top of the bottom" that the publishers so avidly hunted. The Japanese mass was unavoidably and necessarily *not* middle-class only; it was far bigger and more inclusive.

It was this *mass* and their perceived, and yet uncreated, desires that publishers wished to mould, and advertising was an essential part of this story. Though this is not a comparative study, British and American perspectives help to gauge the uniqueness or commonality of the Japanese case. Comparisons such as these are useful especially since both the Japanese and American cases are frequently depicted as exceptional, when both were enmeshed in common global trends that deserve greater recognition.[1]

---

1 Most scholarship that attempts to answer questions on how the content of magazines reflected and shaped nationalist ideology focuses on the Allied countries during the Second World War, although there is some work being done to address advertising within Axis countries. One article shows the complexities one encounters, when dealing with advertising within national contexts, because of the international nature of companies that advertised during the war years. The author explains that "Instead of joining in this attempt to encompass both Auschwitz and ice-cold Cokes within a new and improved concept of modernization, this essay takes the term 'Coca-Colonization'

Historical Background

Department stores first became a sight in Tokyo and then other cities in Japan around the turn of the twentieth century. Former dry goods stores, like Mitsukoshi, transformed into more "modern" displays of middle-class affluence, even as that class was still a minority in the early decades of the century.[2] This was partly because some of the population had enough disposable income to use for non-essential products and activities, but it was also because these habits and practices were modelled for those who could not themselves partake.

The impact of British government policies and propaganda in support of war was as great on ads as it was on the content of articles. Advertising from the mid-1940s in the United Kingdom, where even cosmetics were connected to the wartime rhetoric, however, blatantly and in a wholesale fashion accepted its role as mobilizer of the home front for the war effort. Ads in the British context for fingernail polish regularly asked women to "keep up appearances" despite the war effort, for example. In the UK, once the war began, advertising for a wide range of products, including toothpaste, fingernail polish, stockings, sewing machines, and medical treatments, immediately reflected the war effort. English women's magazines especially showed an immediate and drastic change in advertising as soon as war was declared on 3 September 1939.[3] This perhaps reflects the assumptions about how quickly and directly British civilians might be pulled into the conflict, in contrast to the Japanese situation, where fear of foreigners invading the home islands was not on the minds of many political and military leaders even in the late 1930s. Japanese ads from the 1930s generally did *not* become drastically altered by the war effort, and when they

---

literally when analyzing Coca-Cola's marketing in Nazi Germany. In examining the actual dynamics involved in the internationalization of Coca-Cola (company, beverage, and icon), this approach reveals that Coke's success under Hitler demonstrates the process of cultural 'creolization' – a narrative of Coca-Cola's 'Germanization' as much as Germany's 'Americanization' or 'modernization' ... Indeed ... Coca-Cola could appear 'indigenous' wherever it was bottled" (Schutts, "'Die Erfrischende Pause,'" 152–3).

2   Sand, *House and Home in Modern Japan*.
3   Jane Waller and Michael Vaughan-Rees have detailed how British women's magazines were drastically altered by the war effort in the UK (*Women in Wartime*, 6–7, 94–109, passim).

did begin to reflect the "time of crisis" it was only relatively late in the 1930s.

Tracking American advertising through the Great Depression and into the Second World War, it seems that advertisers managed to keep afloat and ingratiated themselves with the government in new ways that proved invaluable in the postwar years.[4] And while some find that advertisers were uncertain how best to incorporate the reality of war in advertising, others find the relationship straightforward. Approaching the Second World War from the American side, the US government chose to motivate women specifically to work for the war effort by influencing the media, including magazines, to incorporate government propaganda. Maureen Honey argues that "war had an immediate and dramatic impact on advertising," as it did in the UK.[5] One gendered outcome of this process was that American advertising created a dualistic image of the ideal woman that combined the role of mother and worker in singular devotion to the national cause.[6]

This dualistic image in the American case is very similar to the ideal of women in Japan.[7] Images of women, in both the American and Japanese versions, combined productive and reproductive responsibilities of women into a newly mobilized woman-worker role articulated in government ideology and popular media. The feminine ideal also created expectations for women that damaged self-worth and personal fulfilment for many, not only because they were unrealistic to achieve with the limited time and resources most of them had, but also because they were an unattainable contradiction in their very essence.

In the business world of America during the late 1930s and early 1940s, advertising was also depicted as causing fears about the collapse of the industry itself until the relationship ads could have to war was reimagined by inventive men on Madison Avenue. Advertisers were initially wary of including any mention of war in their advertising; this was the case not only because "war often meant no goods to sell and valid reasons for not buying" but also because "war's inherent

---

4 Lears, *Fables of Abundance.*
5 Honey, *Creating Rosie the Riveter,* 28–9, 109–37.
6 Ibid., 109–37.
7 Miyake, "Doubling Expectations."

violation of the pleasant association rule (whereby advertised products are displayed in pleasurable surroundings)" made industry figures fear the onset of total war.[8] Clever advertisers, however, learned to take the war effort to heart and reengineered what advertising was, the language it used, and the ends to which it could be put, all for the sake of saving themselves and helping the government to present "a coherent view of what the war was all about, why the United States was involved in it, and what the significance of an American victory would be."[9] There is little evidence to suggest such a reimagining of the nature of advertising in Japan in the 1930s, however; that would have to wait until later.

Magazines and their content – the advertising, illustrations, text, and graphic design – are a total package. When one looks through a magazine, the eye views everything on the page. One might momentarily focus on one part, reading the text, or seeing what products are advertised, noticing the snippets of fiction interspersed with the articles, or glancing over the pictures included among the pages. However, the reader's experience of interacting with this type of media results in exposure to all of these elements collectively. While we have little record of the editorial process behind the typesetting and formatting decisions of such publications, what we are left with nonetheless is the resulting mixture of words and images. But, this is what the audience had as well; they saw the completed aggregate. Magazines are a mixed visual medium or a unified visual experience. This mélange developed within an expanding and adapting environment of commercial activity, one that was not restricted to Japan domestically either.

Because most text passages were situated among illustrations and advertisements, the experience of reading magazines was not simply one of reading the articles and fiction. The exploration of the formal integration of advertising in these magazines is the primary focus of this chapter, but a consideration of the substance of the advertising also makes a secondary point. The placement and things offered for sale within these magazines exemplified the advertisements that so many people absorbed through their interactions with these periodicals. It

8 Fox, *Madison Avenue Goes to War*, 10.
9 Ibid., 11.

was the normalization of the advertisements' implicit and explicit ideas and language that conditioned mass Japanese consumer culture.[10]

Generally speaking, people did not look upon advertising itself kindly in Japan in the 1920s. There have been documented periods in the United States, Britain, Europe, and elsewhere when the general population looked upon advertisers as liars, cheats, and scoundrels; this was the case in Japan as well. Noma himself had publicly bemoaned his compatriots' scorn and disapproval of advertising. He saw this negativity, though, as an opportunity for change and was convinced that, via education and exposure to the right kind of advertisements, people could grow to welcome advertising's usefulness because it allowed them to see a thing and simultaneously made them understand what importance or value it had.[11] Others in the advertising and publishing industries also saw possibilities for improving the standing of advertising and propaganda by glossing their combined output as "media," with a high degree of success – and with much continuity with the present day.[12]

It is not the point of this chapter, it should be noted, to create an exhaustive picture of all of the memes that were present in the decades' worth of ads contained in *Kingu* and *Ie no hikari* (numbering in the hundreds of thousands); as Michael Schudson puts it, "I will perform no

---

10 As Schudson explains: "In the case of advertising, people do not need to 'believe' in the values advertisements present. Nor need they believe for a market economy to survive and prosper. People need simply [to] get used to, or get used to not getting used to, the institutional structures that govern their lives. Advertising does not make people believe in capitalist institutions or even in consumer values, but so long as alternative articulations of values are relatively hard to locate in the culture, capitalist realist art [advertising] will have some power" (*Advertising, the Uneasy Persuasion*, 232). And the point is reinforced by Marchand when he explains that "In the process of selling specific products, advertisers also communicated broader assumptions about social values. Implicit value statements, passed along unconsciously as givens, usually carried an ideological bias toward 'system reinforcement.' Manufacturers and ad agency leaders recognized their stake in the contemporary configuration of economic and social institutions, and thus found little reason to portray realities that might bring the system into question. Advertisements therefore promulgated what Jacques Ellul has characterized as 'integration propaganda' – that is, ideas and images that reinforce and intensify existing patterns and conceptions" (*Advertising the American Dream*, xviii).
11 社史編纂委員会 (Committee for the Compilation of the Company History), 講談社の歩んだ五十年 (*The Path of Kōdansha's First Fifty Years*), 613.
12 Hanes, "Media Culture in Taishō Osaka," 285; Kushner, *The Thought War*, 64, 68.

high-wire acts of semiotic analysis, no magic tricks to draw out of a hat of commercials a rainbow of cultural messages."[13] Neither is this my chosen methodology, because advertising essentially warps the realities of culture rather than accurately reflecting them.[14] Instead, I have elected to track one particular issue, nationalism – since it was so central to the editorial content and the mission of the magazines' creators – in order to see what kind of impact it had on the advertising. *Nationalism is marked here by those images and text that make direct and supportive reference to the nation and imperialistic military activities.*

The editorial stance of *Kingu* and *Ie no hikari* in no way hindered the habits of advertisers within their pages or the seeming propensity of their audience for being consumers; however, *King's* and *Light of the Home's* advertising did not display the nationalistic and explicitly ideological perspective of the producers of these magazines. It is only in the late 1930s, when the nation was gearing up for total war, that the advertising became overtly nationalistic.

What does this disconnect between the editorial and advertising aspects of the magazine suggest? It may be that, prior to the creation of a mass consumer culture, such public and political ideologies had not fully penetrated into the private sphere of personal consumption, and

---

13 Schudson, *Advertising, the Uneasy Persuasion*, 5. Barak Kushner does provide one possible reading of themes for advertising in the war years; see *The Thought War*, chapter 3.

14 Marchand elucidates this conundrum in the US: "I cannot conclusively say that the American people absorbed the values and ideas of the ads, nor that consumers wielded the power to ensure that the ads would mirror their lives. In fact, as advertisers quickly perceived, people did not usually want ads to reflect themselves, their immediate social relationships, or their broader society exactly. They wanted not a true mirror but a *Zerrspiegel*, a distorting mirror that would enhance certain images. Even the term *Zerrspiegel*, denoting a fun-house mirror, fails to suggest fully the scope of advertising distortions of reality. Such a mirror distorts the shapes of the object it reflects, but it nevertheless provides some image of everything within its field of vision. Advertising's mirror not only distorted, it also selected. Some social realities hardly appeared at all. One has to search diligently in the ads of the 1920s and 1930s to find even fleeting glimpses of such common scenes as religious services, factory workers on the job, sports fans enjoying a boxing match or baseball game, or working-class families at home. The angle of refraction, and hence the degree of distortion of these advertising images, was determined not only by the efforts of advertisers to respond to consumers' desires for fantasy and wish-fulfillment but also by a variety of other factors" (*Advertising the American Dream*, xvi–xvii).

that, only in the late 1930s, did they manage to do so. More significantly, though, the relative consistency of the type and amount of advertising throughout the 1920s and 1930s, as well as the continued spread of the publications themselves, demonstrates that they implicitly – if not overtly – encouraged mass consumerism.

In creating a mass audience that desired magazines to read, these media also created a conduit for communicating other aspirations to that audience. This is the lasting impact of greatest significance, the contribution of magazines to Japanese mass culture; once magazines established an atmosphere in which they were accepted as trusted sources for entertainment and cultural capital, the advertisements contained in magazine pages served as new intermediaries to a mass audience.

There was complete harmony between, on the one hand, the lessons readers learned about how to be dutiful participants in society and in the empire they saw in the articles, and, on the other, the instructions that advertisements delivered on how they could consume *things*, in addition to ideas, in order to make themselves happy and productive. Advertising tells the audience "implicitly or explicitly that freedom, fulfillment, and personal transformation lie in the world of goods."[15] The naturalization of exposure to actual advertising and the imagined acts of self-definition that ads spur contributed to transwar Japanese massification.

One further thing the investigation of advertising in these magazines helps to highlight is that many Japanese bought toothpaste, collectively read their magazines, and generally got on with life at the same time as horrible offences were being committed against Japanese foes across Asia and the Pacific.[16] Wartime Japan is clearly not the only place, nor the only time, where life carried on "normally" as atrocities were being committed abroad. This happened at the hands of the Japanese military in the years prior to 1945, but it also happened via the indirect support of American military forces in the alliances of the Cold War years that followed the Second World War.

---

15 Schudson, *Advertising, the Uneasy Persuasion*, xix.
16 In Ruoff's moving articulation, "the goal here, far from minimizing Japan's rapacious side, is to inform us that even as individuals in areas under Japanese control suffered the full brunt of the violent, repressive force that the modern Japanese state could bring to bear, life went on surprisingly normally for many Japanese" (*Imperial Japan at Its Zenith*, 146).

Advertising in *Ie no hikari* and *Kingu*

So, what did the ads in these publications look like and how many of them were there? As soon as one opens the magazine, there are advertisements. Each issue had advertising integrated throughout the magazine, beginning with the inside of the front cover and interspersed throughout until the back cover, which itself was usually an advertisement.

One example from *Ie no hikari* in September 1933 had a cover image of a seated woman in a kimono holding a fan, with a waving, similarly dressed, little girl. On the inside of the cover were two facing pages of advertisements: one for a cosmetic face cream, Hakubieki (lit. "whitening beauty water"), and one for a topical lotion featuring the image of a Western beauty with dark hair and lipstick baring her arm, right shoulder, and upper back in a tight-fitting silken strappy gown.[17]

Turn the page again to find one more advertisement; this time for a Kidani sleep aid that "is always a good medicine to take to prevent insomnia and the horrible feminine ailments that can destroy your body," offering a "promise for a sound sleep and a healthy tomorrow" and featuring an illustrated female face in profile facing upward with eyes closed and hair streaming behind her. On the facing page is the first non-advertising content of the issue, a short piece accompanied by a photo of farmers wearing hats and bent in the midst of working in a field.

A few more examples should provide a general feel for what the audience would have encountered in terms of format. The 1931 November issue has a photo section showing the "Urban Expansion of the Industrial Cooperative" on page 10 with a lecture advertisement opposite

---

17 It should be noted as well that art historian Gennifer Weisenfeld has done stellar work in decoding the images from certain Japanese magazines, especially their advertising. By focusing on the Shiseidō brand, Weisenfeld shows advertisements "reflecting the changing ideals of feminine beauty, the emergence of a vibrant consumer culture, cutting-edge trends in advertising and packaging, and the persistence of cosmopolitan ideals even in the midst of the rise of militarism in the 1930s." Her work, in addition to supporting claims about the persistence of consumer culture throughout the 1930s, is an example of how much information can be unpacked from the images, text, and design of advertisements ("Selling Shiseido: Japanese Cosmetics Advertising and Design in the Early 20th-Century" and "'From Baby's First Bath'").

it, two unnumbered pages of intervening advertising (for things like Fuji cameras, other lectures, sewing lessons), and one more ad opposite a "Woman's Devotional *Bidan*" on numbered page 11. The December 1937 issue had a special foldout photo depicting women in Niigata Prefecture bowing to each other while wearing sashes from the Volunteer Labour organization against a backdrop of a field, over which the Japanese flag waves (see figure 5.1). Opposite this evocative image is an advertisement for Club Brand toothpaste. Politics and product placement, thus, all neatly presented together.

In the editorial stance already seen, the 1933 volume 9, number 10 issue has an "Era of Greater Asianism" feature running from pages 42 to 54, including articles such as "Japan as Asia's Heart"; "East Is East, West Is West"; "Advanced Nations of World Culture – Asia"; "The Light from Asia"; "The Arrival of an Age of World Fascism"; "Why Has Fascism Gained Power?"; "The Truth behind the German Denunciation of the Jewish Race"; "The Objective of the Jewish Conspiracy"; "An Analysis of the Underlying Anxiety to the Anglo-Japanese Relationship"; and "What Will Be the Role of the United States?" This feature section concludes on the same page as an "Utena Lemon Cream" advertisement. One must have smooth and supple skin while pondering the rise of fascism or the egregious and paranoid mistreatment of the Jews.

Over time the format changed so that you had to go physically through the ads before you could even read the table of contents. As both *Kingu*'s and *Ie no hikari*'s page lengths increased, the contents came to be printed on gatefold pages with flaps tucked into each issue; once these flaps were folded open out of the way, you could then see the entirety of the table of contents for the month over the elongated pages. On the outside of these flaps (when viewed closed) were printed advertisements. By the late 1930s, none of the table of contents of *Ie no hikari* was visible through the ads in most issues. The advertising could not be detached from the other content of these Japanese magazines; it would have been physically impossible to remove it and still keep the magazine readable. It was formally embedded throughout the pages and mingled with the articles, comics, and fiction in a way that was inseparable (see figure 5.2).

These periodicals were notably *unlike* their American magazine counterparts in this early integration of the advertising; American magazine publishers historically pasted the advertising in a separate (and removable) section on the outside of the content underneath the cover. Ads were sandwiched between the cover and the content. Thus, with many

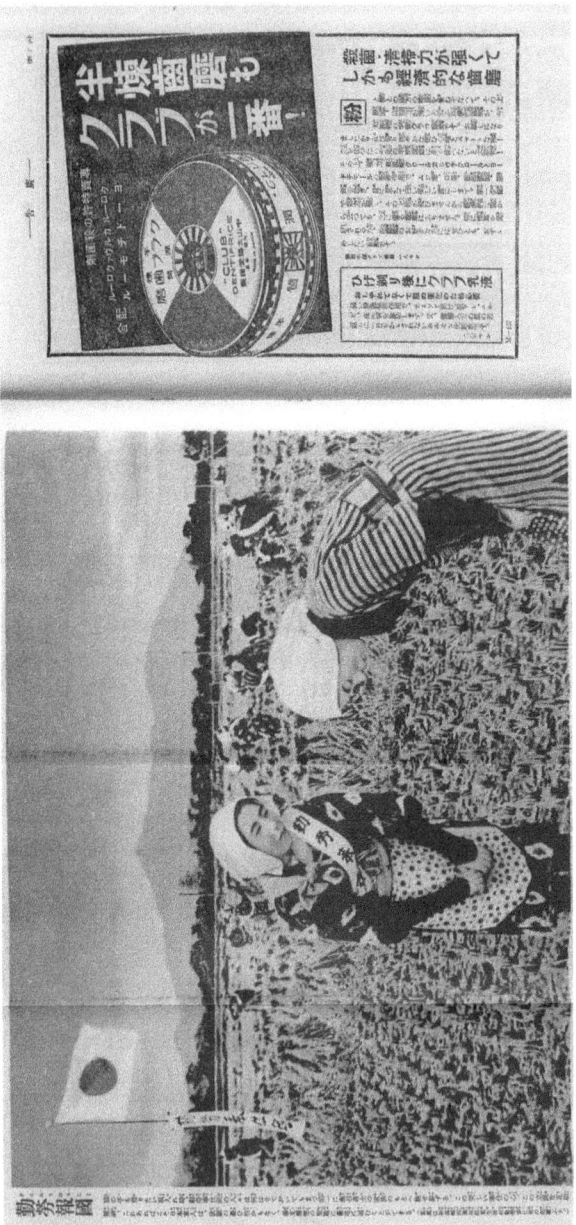

Figure 5.1. Niigata Volunteer Labour Group photo/Club toothpaste ad, *Ie no hikari*, December 1937

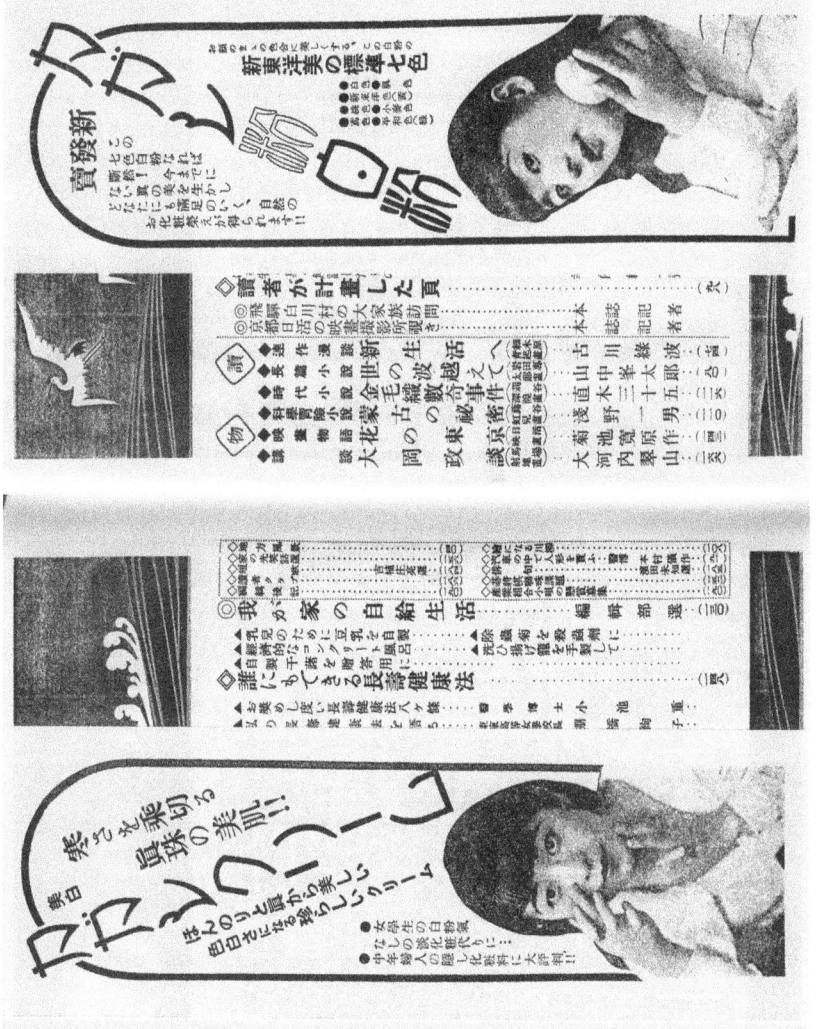

Figure 5.2. Gatefold table of contents, *Ie no hikari*, September 1933

magazines in the United States, one could simply rip the advertising out of an issue and be left with the remaining content.[18] This would have been materially unachievable with *Kingu* or *Ie no hikari*.

Anyone who encountered these magazines, even if only to flip through the pages, would have immediately noticed that advertising was a significant portion of each issue. It ranged from 10 to 16 per cent of the content of *Ie no hikari* throughout the 1930s, for example. The number of pages of advertisements as a percentage of the total content of each monthly issue, from 1930 until the end of the decade, fluctuates only slightly.[19] The low appeared for 1933–5, bottoming out at 9.4 per cent of total content, while the highs peaked later at 16.2 per cent for late 1937 and early 1938. Overall there were, however, notable amounts of advertising in each issue throughout the whole decade. In addition, if we look at the ads in terms of numbers of advertising pages, a similar progression emerges. The number of ad pages increased by the end of the decade, if it did so in a slightly uneven fashion (see table 5.1). Here too, though, we see that advertising was a consistent portion of the content included in the periodical.

The small lull in advertising in the first half of the 1930s is mentioned by those writing in the advertising trade journals of the day and explained at least in part by corporate desire to economize advertising expenses during a period of a loss of industry confidence and competition with no-name products that did not advertise. Various brand-named companies, to give one example, moved towards so-called tie-in advertising in popular films in order to economize advertising expenditures during this period.[20]

It seems that the amount of advertising fluctuated slightly over the decade of the 1930s in a way that mirrors some of the larger instabilities

---

18 Scholes and Wulfman, *Modernism in the Magazines*, 196–7; "Modernist Journals Project."

19 This count is for full-page advertisements, done by the author. There are inset ads in *Ie no hikari* that do not take up a full page, but I have not included them in this tally. Since there was no simple way to include them in percentages without having to arbitrarily decide the manner in which to include them (i.e., do they count as 0.25 of a page, or 0.5, etc.), I have chosen to use only the full-page ads in the count. However, after checking a sampling of issues for the amount of the inset ads using first 0.25 and then 0.5 values, it is clear that they have a similar pattern to the full-page ads, and thus their exclusion would not affect my tallies in any significant way.

20 The phrases used by the author are "広告費の節約" and "産業精神の喪失である。" 大久保, "『廣告非常時 (Advertising in the Time of Emergency)," 33.

Table 5.1. *Ie no hikari* of the 1930s

Mo./yr.	Vol.	Non-ad pages	Full-page ads	Total pages	% of ads
May 31	25	180	33	213	15.5
Jun 31	25	181	30	211	14.2
Sep 31	27	192	33	225	14.7
Oct 31	27	194	28	222	12.6
Jan 32	29	208	30	238	12.6
Feb 32	29	206	26	232	11.2
May 32	31	228	31	259	12.0
Jun 32	31	226	30	256	11.7
Sep 32	33	222	33	255	12.9
Oct 32	33	222	34	256	13.3
Jan 33	35	222	34	256	13.3
Feb 33	35	224	33	257	12.8
May 33	37	222	33	255	12.9
Jun 33	37	222	35	257	13.6
Sep 33	39	222	28	250	11.2
Oct 33	39	222	29	251	11.6
Jan 34	41	222	23	245	9.4
Feb 34	41	222	23	245	9.4
May 34	43	222	24	246	9.8
Jun 34	43	222	23	245	9.4
Sep 34	45	222	23	245	9.4
Oct 34	45	222	27	249	10.8
Jan 35	47	222	26	248	10.5
Feb 35	47	222	23	245	9.4
May 35	49	222	30	252	11.9
Jun 35	49	222	36	258	14.0
Sep 35	51	222	32	254	12.6
Oct 35	51	222	30	252	11.9
Jan 36	53	226	37	263	14.1
Feb 36	53	226	36	262	13.7
May 36	55	226	36	262	13.7
Jun 36	55	226	36	262	13.7
Sep 36	57	226	37	263	14.1
Oct 36	57	226	39	265	14.7
Jan 37	59	230	43	273	15.8
Feb 37	59	230	40	270	14.8
Mar 37	60	230	41	271	15.1
Apr 37	60	228	42	270	15.6
May 37	61	230	41	271	15.1
Jun 37	61	228	43	271	15.9
Sep 37	63	228	41	269	15.2
Oct 37	63	228	44	272	16.2
Jan 38	65	221	41	262	15.6
Feb 38	65	222	43	265	16.2
May 38	67	228	43	271	15.9
Jun 38	67	228	43	271	15.9
Sep 38	69	232	43	275	15.6
Oct 38	69	232	44	276	15.9

Chart 5.1. Number of advertising pages in *Ie no hikari*

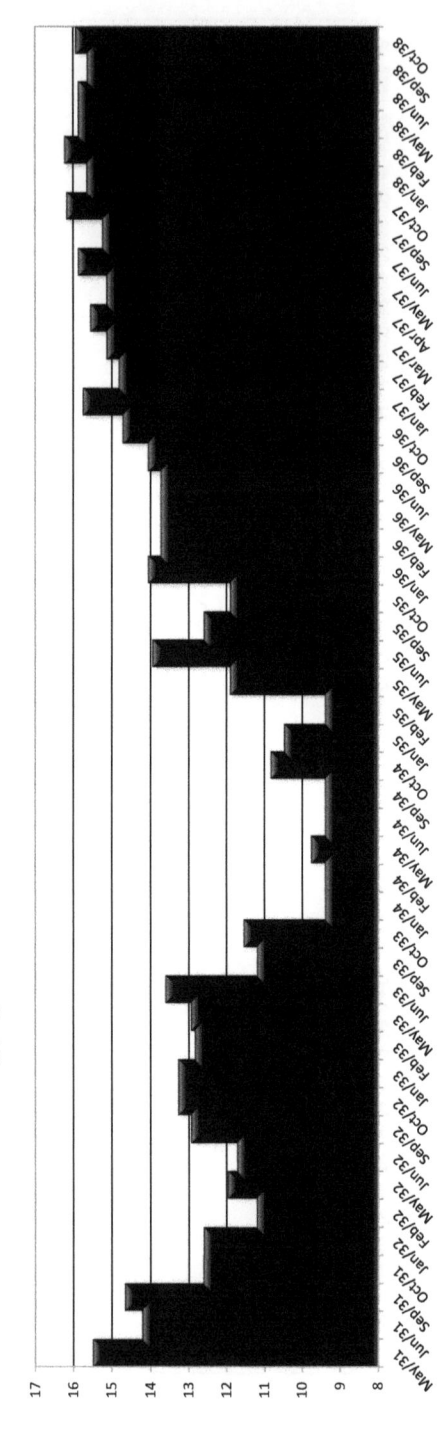

of the national economic situation. During a period of economic downturn from 1931 to 1936, the percentage of ads was lower than in the period of relative economic growth that occurred from 1936 forward, when the percentage of ads was slightly higher. The lack of consistency in the advertising might also be partly explained by the uneven development of these years, when the agricultural sectors saw fewer benefits from the national economic upturn than industrial producers did.[21]

Just as with the number of advertisements, the type and content of advertisements changed little over the span of the 1930s. Even after 1937, when in other contexts propaganda and moral suasion campaigns were reaching new levels of infiltration into the daily lives of average Japanese, the level of militaristic and nationalistic rhetoric and imagery is limited in the advertising content of *Ie no hikari*. Most features in *Ie no hikari* or *Kingu*, including the ads, remained constant. For example, for all of the 1930s there was always an advertisement on the inside front cover of each issue of both publications. Advertisements for Kikkoman soy sauce regularly graced the outside flaps of the gatefold table of contents for *Kingu*, for example. And most issues of both magazines, though with greater repetition in *Kingu* than in *Ie no hikari*, had advertisements for the other publications – magazines or otherwise – from the publisher.

Further, ads from the same company or for the same product often ran for sequential periods of time in roughly the same place in each issue. Some ads would run for a few months in the same location and then never be seen again. Other ads popped up in almost every issue for the whole decade. Hakubieki ran one of the longest campaigns and was particularly consistent within *Ie no hikari* in both its placement and content (see figure 5.3). This ad campaign conveniently shows that the impact on advertising occurred only after Japan had committed fully to the military actions in China and was fortifying for Total War more generally.

---

21 Allen explains, "the index of industrial production rose steeply after re-inflation was introduced ... the greater part of the increased industrial production was not in the form of goods available for consumption, but consisted of munitions and capital equipment for industry at home and in Manchuria ... the boom did not communicate itself to agriculture ... So a very large part of the economy remained depressed in spite of the boom in manufacturing industry" (*A Short Economic History of Modern Japan*, 139).

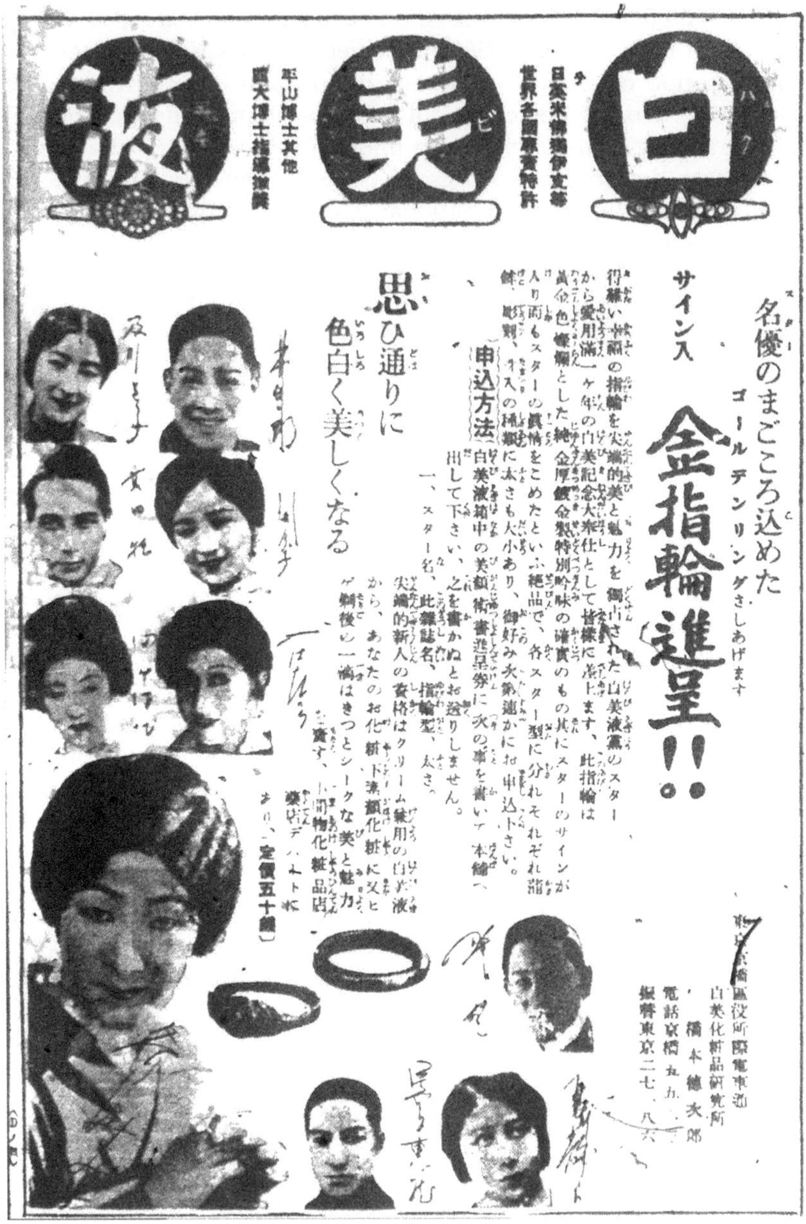

Figure 5.3. Hakubieki advertisement, *Kingu*, May 1931

Most of the Hakubieki ads of the 1930s featured smiling faces of women, who had supposedly received the benefits of using the product, with occasional special offers for promotional items such as rings. Whereas previous ads and campaigns featured imagery of Western women and abstract and stylized symbols such as stars, the January 1938 issue showed an apparent awareness of the war situation (see figure 5.4). This particular promotion for Hakubieki offers to help provide ladies with a "patriotic mark." In that advertisement, the promotional item changes to a ring with the *Hi no Maru* flag of Japan. These ads suggested that there was no real need to change one's purchasing habits – "Ladies, please continue buying your cosmetics," the advertisers insinuated – but in this case those purchases were framed to be acceptable within the growing demands for patriotic mobilization. This kind of patriotism, as we have seen, had been overtly advocated by the overwhelming majority of the editorial content of the magazines since they began in 1925, but simply had not been present in the advertisements in the same publications.

It is interesting to note that there were variations in advertising between *Kingu* and *Ie no hikari* even in the cases where the same company was placing the ads. Where ads for Hakubieki in *Ie no hikari* ran along the lines described above, in *Kingu* the copy and images were different. In one example from May of 1931, famous figures from the stage were deemed to be more fitting for the advertisements directed at the more urban-focused audience of *Kingu*, even though the promotional item mentioned is a ring similar to those in the advertisements from *Ie no hikari* already mentioned. This variance marks what advertisers must have seen as either the expectations of the different audiences or the preferences of the editors of those periodicals.

Generally, a wide range of products and services was represented in the ads of the 1930s, and this diversity continued throughout the decade, showing the readers how many "choices" were available to them. Many of these ads make references to "Japan" or to being first/ best in the nation, but all provide opportunities for participation in mass culture through the consumption of goods. Many of them made promises about more beautiful faces, less tired bodies, healthier lives, easier lives, happier lives, and all the other kinds of idealized realities we have come to recognize from advertising copy. There were slightly more ads in the early period for things resembling luxury goods, but this by no means suggests that ads for luxury items did not appear in the latter half of the decade.

Figure 5.4. Hakubieki advertisement, *Ie no hikari*, January 1938

To get a rough idea of the variety in the kinds of product and imagery used in the advertising, consider these examples. There were clutter-free ads for work shoes, as well as text-heavy descriptive ones for musical instruments. There were also ads for sewing machines, penmanship lessons, dictionary sets, face cream, and a girls' school. The style often reflected the type of product being advertised, and many different categories of ads dotted the pages of *Ie no hikari* for all of the 1930s. Throughout the early to mid-1930s, almost no patriotic, nationalistic, or militaristic imagery could be seen in them; it was as if the advertisers had no inkling as yet of the war efforts which so occupied the minds of the editors of the same publications.

The trends explored in the advertisements of *Ie no hikari* hold true for *Kingu* as well. There is a consistent amount of advertising (in terms of both pages and percentage of content) over the course of the 1930s. There is also only a minimal intrusion of militaristic and nationalistic imagery and text into the adverts. The reader saw a mixture of products and advertisers, as was the case in *Ie no hikari*. Kikkoman soy sauce ads were present in almost every issue of *Kingu*, and major brands of the day like Kao (for soap) and Utena (for cosmetics) appeared frequently. Watches, clothing, and toothpaste figured often as well. More frequently in *Kingu* than in *Ie no hikari*, one also finds advertisements for other Kōdansha publications. The few ads that do appear to have any kind of connection to the military or war situation in the issues from the late 1930s come in the form of announcements about lectures and appeals for youth participation, although a series of ads promoting Hitler's writings also appeared.

Based on the advertisements, one would have no idea that life in Japan was much different in mid-1937 than it was in 1931. At the beginning of 1937, the content and imagery of ads in *Ie no hikari* continued along the lines of the preceding six years. Thus, there is no drastic or dramatic change in what kind of things are being advertised.

However, beginning in late 1937, a small number of advertisements began including images and text connected to Japan's war effort. Kurabu (Club) brand began running toothpaste ads that included an inset textbox imploring customers to include the "travel-sized" (*kogata*) tube of Club toothpaste in comfort bags for soldiers and featuring an image of a solider. The main text of the ad touted the scientific benefits of the toothpaste and was almost verbatim in Club adverts from the whole decade. Similarly, another ad placed in the same issue for a *kendō* (Japanese fencing) lecture includes a picture of a Japanese flag and soldier and text evoking Japanese forces fighting the enemy wearing headbands bearing the naval Flag of the Rising Sun. Many issues of *Ie no hikari* had ads for *kendō* lessons or lectures before this one, but most frequently those ads, if they contained any images, showed pictures of boys in *kendō* practice gear or a picture of the master who would be providing the lessons. The Sakata Company, as well, began including soldiers in their advertisements for seed catalogues with text that mentions a "breakthrough in the time of emergency."

These companies had placed ads in earlier *Ie no hikari* issues, but none of the previous ads used such imagery or referred to a national crisis or war effort. These examples are *not* representative of other encroachments of propaganda or militaristic imagery into the advertising of *Ie no hikari* or *Kingu*; they are, rather, the only cases where this phenomenon did occur. The vast majority of the advertising in these publications gave little indication that the life of a consumer in Japan in the late 1930s was very much changed from the late 1920s. Certainly, new products had been developed or old ones "improved," but by and large one would have a difficult time tracking any major social or political shifts if advertisements to the Japanese masses were the only sources being used. Thus, what is interesting to note is exactly how *few* ads in late 1937 and early 1938 incorporated such imagery – three or four ads, and not even full-page ones, out of more than forty pages of advertising per issue. This is quite different from the progression of the non-advertising content of *Ie no hikari*, which was ideologically charged and nationalistic from the outset.

Concluding Thoughts

The magazine producers of *Kingu* and *Ie no hikari* adopted an explicitly pedagogical and ideological editorial stance in their missions to create a mass audience. These magazines achieved incredible success in creating that mass audience; indeed, the publications became central features of Japanese society and embedded themselves in the leisure of tens of millions of people. Nonetheless, the advertisements in these publications did not adopt an explicitly ideological position, replete with the nationalist values to be found throughout the other content of these magazines, at least not until total war had beset Japan. Whereas the editors attempted from the beginning to instil certain values in their readers, and these values quickly became militaristic in the early 1930s, the advertising remained silent on such matters until the late 1930s and, even then, referred to them only to a small degree.

In trade journals like *Printing and Advertising*, *The Japanese Printer*, and *Publishing and Printing*, advertisers and publishers were discussing the "period of emergency" by 1936, and some of them viewed the Manchurian Incident positively as the foundation for the rapid development of modern advertising.[22] Explicit discussions of the "crisis" and "emergency" and their relationship to advertising and printing were, however, not present in the opening years of the 1930s, despite the significance of the Manchurian Incident and common references to "crisis" in other media, including film and text. And while publishers, and indeed the public, seemed comfortable with the advance to war, advertisers seemed more uncertain about how to make the connection between their products and the (inter)national emergencies Japan faced. Or, at the very least, they saw no impetus to do so until late into the 1930s. This stands in stark contrast to the immediate and unabashed support of empire from the editors of *Kingu* and *Ie no hikari* or advertisers in, for example, the British context. After all, it was not until the late 1930s that the Japanese government bothered to take up formal regularized interaction with publishing companies.[23]

This gap suggests a separation between consumer capitalism and the state on one side and the intimate practices of consumption and the masses on the other. Put another way, perhaps one thing marking the late 1930s as different from what comes before and after is in fact this breaking down of the barrier between consumption as a private, state-neutral act and its use by the state towards its own aims.

By 1940, there was a noticeable and more complete integration of commercial enterprises with ideologically charged governmental and military agendas in Japan. This breaking down is what Ruoff describes in his work on the collaboration of commercial publishers, travel agents, and others with the government-sponsored celebrations

---

22 Just one such example is 大久保, "「廣告非常時 (Advertising in the Time of Emergency)."

23 As Kushner explains, "On October 15, 1937, fifty-four major publishing houses, including Iwanami Shoten, Kaizōsha, Chūō Kōronsha, Bungei Shunjū, and Kōdansha, formed the Publishers' Symposium. While the group was a voluntary, private organization, it held its monthly meeting in Home Ministry offices to discuss issues relating to the war and publishing. The Home Ministry also began to exert more direct pressure on magazine editorial policy and writing ... The government differentiated its rules for newspapers and magazines, but similar measures applied" (*The Thought War*, 62).

surrounding the 2,600th anniversary of the Japanese empire. Kushner argues that "advertising executives and the industry in general recognized they had a window of opportunity to join with the government, jump on the war bandwagon, and raise their professional prestige," because "opportunism and the desire to increase profits merged nicely with patriotic fever."[24] More work would have to be done to parse these varying interpretations about what advertisers were saying to each other into the 1940s and to fully assess what impact these transformations had throughout the transwar years or how they compare to other global contexts.

We can, however, draw some provisional conclusions here. For one thing, the disparate nature of the organizations, companies, and individuals that comprised the advertising sector of society (better referred to as a media complex) meant it did not have a unified mission like the one that the Kumiai or Kōdansha quite clearly possessed, whereas in the American case, there was a more unified clique producing pro-war advertising material out of Madison Avenue and thereby a more consistent vision for the advertising of that era.

In the United States at the turn of the twentieth century, overproduction due to increases in manufacturing may have caused a surplus of commodities which in turn led manufacturers to push for greater consumption of those products (which they could newly produce in great quantities) and gave birth to modern American advertising.[25] But the two cases under study here challenge such a causal explanation. *Ie no hikari* lacked the heavy dependence on advertising that was present in, for example, Japanese newspapers by the 1920s. *Kingu* certainly gained a good deal of revenue from advertising, but Noma was willing to balance his losses on certain business ventures in exchange for the promotion of others. An example of this is the supplements that were published with little to no profit in order to attract more attention to the magazine proper.

King may have been profitable overall, but it was something that Noma supported on an ideological level. He pushed Kōdansha to make it possible for that specific publication to flourish, even, one gets the impression, if it had not made the company a single yen. Arimoto, similarly, was willing to support *Ie no hikari* out of his

---

24 Ibid., chapter 3; Ruoff, *Imperial Japan at Its Zenith*.
25 Ohmann, *Selling Culture*.

personal funds should the need arise because he wholeheartedly believed in the publication's potential importance. Thus, it seems that the missions of these magazine producers in Japan stemmed not from any particular pressure from the advertising or manufacturing industries but from an inborn desire to reach the masses for their own purposes.

These missions produced consumers nonetheless. The consistent placement and volume of advertisements within the pages of *Light of the Home* and *King* showed readers a variety of options for consumables that could make everyday life "new" or "better." Just as readers could learn about how to most efficiently use the products in their homes, they could see how modern electrical appliances were slowly making their way into the countryside. Clocks, heated pillows, electric rice heaters (not a true rice cooker), *kotatsu*, fans, clothes wringers, indoor lights were displayed for readers to marvel over, even as they suffered to make ends meet during the deepest years of the depression.[26] The socialization that occurred via the non-advertising content was more explicitly ideological in its pedagogy, but the advertisements nevertheless helped to educate the audience on how to participate in the growing mass national culture. Products – Kikkoman, Kurabu, Kao, etc. – presented submerged ideals and values layered behind the explicit ones. Advertisements in magazines helped to normalize the presence of consumer culture and consumption in practice, and offered fallacious meanings for the Japanese masses.

But, advertising is fundamentally unrelated to actual principles – buying certain things does not make you different from who you are, despite how desperately the companies selling products would like to make you think so. As Jason Stanley suggests, "commercial advertising is an attempt to attach possession of the product advertised to an attractive ideal, when possessing that product is in the normal case irrelevant to achieving that ideal."[27] At the very least, mass culture participated in the advancement of discourses related to consumerism and (militaristic) imperialism in Japan.

26　家の光 (*Light of the Home*), 1 February 1932, 16–17.

27　Stanley defines advertising as "a contribution to public discourse that is presented as an embodiment of certain ideals, but in the service of a goal that is irrelevant to those very ideals … Effective advertisement exploits flawed ideology that connects, for example, material possessions to aesthetic worth" (*How Propaganda Works*, 60).

This intimate relationship is remarkable because magazines mediated on behalf of editors and advertisers in a combination that galvanized their audience for mass culture.[28] Alternatives to the status quo were missing – disparity, injustice, and violence were unseen as well. Consequently, a Japan without consumer culture was becoming less and less possible as reality was constrained and lived existences altered irreparably.

---

28 "Mediating consumption makes it have signifying capabilities; once that is established it only remains for audiences to negotiate the specific meanings in various contexts" (Horning, "Media and Consumer Desire").

Conclusion

Where magazines are read, they seem to have robustly influential powers. The recent "Arab Spring" was deemed the source of a rebirth for magazines: there were "150 new journals and magazines in Benghazi alone."[1] One study done in today's United States claims that "Magazines provide superior reach compared to TV programs for major target audiences, including adults 18–49, women 18–49, African Americans 18–49 and teens 12–17, when Carat's cross-media research compared the top 25 prime-time TV programs and top 25 magazines." And, moreover, "Magazines and magazine ads garner the most attention: When consumers read magazines they are much less likely to engage with other media or to take part in non-media activities compared to the users of TV, radio or the internet."[2] There is still a lot of money and energy spent trying to get people to read magazines the world over, as is evidenced by organizations like the Association of Magazine Media. Likewise, magazines are more popular in Japan than almost anywhere else in the world even in recent times: 2,200 magazines about advertising alone were published in the 1990s in Japan.[3]

Taking magazines as sources can broaden our understanding of societal trends in the first half of the twentieth century and show how mass media adapted their relationship with the populace by educating them to be citizens *and* consumers – which are categories not so discrete.

---

1 "MPA – The Association of Magazine Media (Formerly Magazine Publishers of America)"; Lapeska, "Hisham Matar on Libya's Awakening."
2 "Reach" in this usage means audience (Link, "Magazine Handbook," 10, 25).
3 Moeran, *A Japanese Advertising Agency*, 202.

Another reason for the significance of publications like *Kingu* and *Ie no hikari*, particularly the ways in which they created and sustained mass culture, lies in the political realm. The practice of consuming magazines was, in fact, political.

Commercial producers, in Japan and elsewhere, regularly reinforced state-sponsored forms of mass mobilization and participation in imperialist and illiberal projects in a way that simply cannot be dubbed apolitical.[4] Arguments divorcing an exceptional citizen role from a distinct and lesser consumer role are problematic, since the realm of consumption and the world of the political are not so far removed from one another. This connection exists because "the contrast between citizen and consumer stands not outside our civic life but is a constitutive element of it."[5] In other words, what one buys and how one chooses to spend time are inextricably coupled to one's political existence.

The complicated relationship between individuals' perceptions of politics and their patterns of product consumption characterizes this connection. Jean-Christophe Agnew provides a concrete example of an American soldier:

> As one wartime GI was reported to have said, "I am in this damn mess [the Second World War] as much to help keep the custom of drinking Cokes as I am to preserve the million other benefits our country blesses its citizens with." ... this redefinition of rights and obligations articulated itself in the seemingly innocuous language of soft drinks, cars, and household appliances, and ... it therefore occurred, as Colin Campbell might put it, privately, imaginatively, and inconspicuously – in short, without

---

4 As has been mentioned, the discussions in Ruoff's *Imperial Japan at Its Zenith* serve to support this line of thought. For comparative purposes, the German case is instructive as well. As Victoria de Grazia mentions, "No doubt about it: the Nazi regime well understood that yet one other means to enhance its totalitarian grip lay in reestablishing political power over the slippery terrain of the commercial public sphere ... Advertising has a central role to play in a market that pretended to modify the class-divisive nature of cultural goods and distribute scarce resources by rewarding and depriving consumers according to their place in the *Volksgemeinschaft*'s hierarchy of utility and race" ("Foreword," xvi).

5 Schudson states, "On the whole, I think it [this connection] may have made it marginally more difficult for ordinary people to become politically engaged and it certainly has made it more difficult for journalists, critics, and scholars to understand everyday political life" ("The Troubling Equivalence of Citizen and Consumer," 193, 198).

discussion … it is precisely because the meanings of commodities are so fluid and recontextualizable that questions of responsibility and account-ability remain submerged within them … As the GI's invocation of Coke suggests, commodities can be used – ironically, nostalgically, militantly – to put the state in its place; but they are next to useless when deciding what to put in place of the state.[6]

The vague sense of being able to buy things or services one wants and to participate in certain habits and lifestyles became political over the middle of the twentieth century. This sense developed partly because people's conceptions about their consumption had shifted. The state protected individual's "rights," and, thus, people supported state activities and policies that were newly intertwined with the reinforce-ment of certain kinds of "common sense" and safeguards for lifestyles.

The state was able to harness side effects of this association and continue advancing its own aims. Just as, in the Euro-American con-text, "the razzle-dazzle of commodity culture is at home with dismal inequality, and the champagne bubbles of advertising creatively fizzle away amid the sledgehammer destructiveness of capitalist progress," Japan manifested this archetype as well.[7] Mass Japanese culture com-fortably supported growing consumerism *and* participation in wartime empire, just as it tolerated economic recovery *and* postwar occupation. Consumption became tied to nationalist cultures around the globe because of the prominence of the modern nation-state during these years, but could have taken other forms had the nation not been the prevailing model.

Put another way, these magazines helped to channel individual Japa-nese experiences into collective participation in national mass culture. Even in the case of rural *Ie no hikari*, one resulting contribution to the postwar era was an embedded preference for an urban consolidation of culture. Magazines' participation in consumer culture and the mass audience's inclusion in the larger national context favoured those places where commodities were produced and most readily available, namely urban areas. Thus, even as *Ie no hikari* and *Kingu* promoted harmonious families and support of small communities throughout Japan (and the empire), massification and growing exposure to the advertising these

---

6 Agnew, "Coming Up for Air," 31–4.
7 de Grazia, "Foreword," xvii.

magazines contained allowed for a naturalizing of commodity culture. This culture, moreover, prefigured many economic and cultural developments: deteriorating rural communities, specifically heightened urbanization, and the resultant political changes of the postwar years.

The Death of *Kingu*

In October of 1938, Noma Seiji died of heart failure. With his passing, the dynamism of Kōdansha's magazine editing waned, and other changes took place as well. Kōdansha continued to be successful, however, and still is one of the largest publishers in Japan to the present day.

During the height of the war years, governmental proscriptions required the use of Japanese vocabulary rather than foreign loan words (*gairaigo*), as a part of intensifying anti-foreign, nationalistic campaigns. The renaming of baseball (*bāsu bāru*, from the English) to *yakyū*, among the best-known public revisions, was far from the only change made. *Kingu*, too, was forced to find a suitable new title. Several options were discussed at a meeting in late 1942, with suggestions including *Hikari* (light), *Sakura* (cherry blossom), *Fuji* (for Mount Fuji), and *Kuni no hikari* (Light of the Nation), though *Fuji* was ultimately chosen. Kōdansha distributed a letter to shop owners and included a notice in the February issue of *Kingu* that explained the name change.

The revision of the title would not change the fundamental characteristics of the publication or the spirit behind the editorial mission, readers were told. However, fiction expanded to fill a larger part of each issue, because it was viewed as being less controversial during heightening government censorship, resulting in a deterioration of *King's* distinct appeal. Many readers came to view *Fuji* as simply another leisure or entertainment magazine (*goraku zasshi*) rather than a true family magazine with the specific winning combination of features subscribers had come to recognize over the course of the 1930s.[8] Unfortunately for Kōdansha, exactly because of these changes to its character, *Fuji's* circulation numbers declined after about a year or two, despite initial carryover success from *Kingu*.

During the years of the American Occupation, those members of the Supreme Command for the Allied Powers (SCAP) tasked with assessing

---

8   社史編纂委員会 (Committee for the Compilation of the Company History), 講談社の歩んだ五十年 (*The Path of Kōdansha's First Fifty Years*), 271–1, 509–11.

the state of popular media (like the Information Division's Press and Publication Branch Chief, Robert H. Berkov) initially categorized *Kingu* not as a "war magazine" (*sensō zasshi*) but as a "farmer's magazine" (*nōmin zasshi*) in what initially might seem a misguided evaluation.[9] The appraisal of *King*, however, was rooted in an approval of the populist thrust of the publication. Because of its mass consumer focus, SCAP members appreciated what they viewed as a democratic, anti-elitist impulse in *Kingu*. Thus, they deemed that it sought to raise the average Japanese's social awareness of the world and provided social capital to even the lowliest farmers, just as Noma had claimed it did. The Americans also noted that the magazine had achieved a peak in circulation numbers in the years preceding the attack on Pearl Harbor and was no longer top dog in the competitive media world.[10]

Rapid growth years followed on the heels of the slump and hardships of the immediate postwar period. The stock market opened under new auspices in 1949. Large conglomerates, like Mitsui and Mitsubishi, had all been privately held, so corporate ownership was opened to the public. By 1960, thirteen million people owned stock, a sixfold increase over 1950. The Occupation government also tried to break up what were seen as monopolies (former *zaibatsu*), aggressively at first, but then pulled back as one part of the reverse course on the "Democratization, Demilitarization and Decentralization" policies more generally.

The hugely ambitious Land Reform policy implemented during the Occupation sought fundamental social change and succeeded in massively altering rural lives across Japan. To avoid a repeat of the supposed evils of the wartime system, SCAP's general logic explained that wealth had been too concentrated and land needed to be more evenly distributed. First, much of the land in Japan was consolidated so that it could be redistributed mostly to those who were actually farming it, as opposed to the often absentee landlords who supported inequitable tenant farming practices during the war years. One-third of all the land in Japan changed hands during these reforms, affecting nearly 40 per

---

9 Takemae, *The Allied Occupation of Japan*, 184.

10 A more thorough detailing of SCAP's announcements about what was and wasn't acceptable in the postwar regime is discussed in both 社史編纂委員会 (Committee for the Compilation of the Company History), 講談社の歩んだ五十年 (*The Path of Kōdansha's First Fifty Years*), 599–605, and in 佐藤, 「キング」の時代 (*The Era of "King"*), 397–403.

cent of the population. The landlords were compensated based on 1945 prices, but received (because of inflation) very little in return. SCAP wanted the money given to the landlords to offset their losses, but this exchange did not allow for the support of their previous lifestyles.

The Land Reform had large and lasting impacts socially, especially because of the huge increases in land values in the postwar period. From 1950 to 1975, land in many regions of Japan became 350 times more valuable. The former tenant farmer families (if they managed to maintain ownership of their land over that time) made substantial profits in the postwar decades and enjoyed a significantly raised standard of living.

The audience for *Kingu*, even after the September 1945 reversion to its original title, continued to dwindle over the later years of the 1940s and early 1950s. Despite this fact, *Kingu* was chosen as one among the "best three" mass magazines (*taishū zasshi*) in 1950 at a national publishing industry fair. Based on actual numbers, though, it is clear that *Ie no hikari* had already surpassed Kōdansha's pet publication by a large margin. As Kōdansha expanded into publishing more titles (nearly twice as many as its wartime production), the influence of each of those individual titles waned as they melted into the larger media complex that became increasingly available in the postwar years.[11] By the 1960s, *Kingu* was defunct, while the Industrial Cooperative was still dependably selling its flagship magazine in over a million copies, devotedly continuing in its mission to improve the everyday lives of rural Japanese. Kōdansha had moved on to other entrepreneurial projects that maintained its profitability in other ways, even into the twenty-first century.

These facts reflect an intensification of shifts that were happening throughout the twentieth century and help us approach transwar trends from new angles.[12] First, *Ie no hikari* adapted to the postwar realities of rural life, and, in so doing, continued to dominate in that market. More

---

11 佐藤,「キング」の時代 (*The Era of "King"*), 412; 社史編纂委員会 (Committee for the Compilation of the Company History), 講談社の歩んだ五十年 (*The Path of Kōdansha's First Fifty Years*), 744–6.

12 The useful and detailed scholarship of the postwar period is too voluminous to mention in full, but see Allinson, *Japan's Postwar History*; Gordon, *Postwar Japan as History*; Gordon, *The Wages of Affluence*; Milly, *Poverty, Equality, and Growth*; Waswo, *Housing in Postwar Japan*; Hein, Diefendorf, and Ishida, *Rebuilding Urban Japan after 1945*.

effectively than *Kingu*, *Ie no hikari* was still able to provide entertainment, advice, and a sense of belonging to rural households in the many places where the lifeways of farming were shifting in the reorganized and "democratized" towns and hamlets of postwar Japan. At the same time that farmlands were redistributed, "agricultural commodities" were increasingly emphasized, and part-time farm work progressively became the norm.[13] *Ie no hikari* through the 1960s, 1970s, and 1980s provides an interesting window onto the social and cultural transformations in such shrinking rural communities that deserve further study.

But what is more, the media complex exploded in the postwar years, especially in urban areas, with the upsurge of radio and TV as the most common form of entertainment. As these media expanded to fill leisure spaces in the lives of millions of Japanese, the social and cultural role of magazines like *Kingu* became less central. This is not to say that magazines had disappeared, but they were integrated into a more diverse media setting that has continued to expand in depth and variety until the present day.

What remained, however, across all of these interacting and cross-pollinating forms of leisure was the integration of consumer culture. Leisure habits surrounding periodicals combined easily with, if they were not supplanted by, radio and then television, at least in part because of their novel yet familiar qualities. As families had once gathered together to collectively read their magazines, after the war most Japanese gathered while happily being warmed by the glow of their TV screens – twenty-seven million sets by 1979.[14] Noma himself would have been satisfied by how fully normalized and accepted the integrated advertising within the televised worlds on view had become.

The Afterlife of *Ie no hikari*

In the 1960s, one in three rural households subscribed to *Ie no hikari*, ranking it between radio and newspapers as the most consumed media.

---

13 For a varied treatment of the continuities and change in Japanese farming life, see Waswo and Nishida, eds., *Farmers and Village Life in Twentieth-Century Japan*. The quoted phrase is on page 204. There is also much good work done on the agricultural communities post-1945 and their transforming relationship with the state. See Mulgan, *Japan's Agricultural Policy Regime*; Mulgan, *The Politics of Agriculture in Japan*; Maclachlan, *Consumer Politics in Postwar Japan*.

14 Tsurumi, *A Cultural History of Postwar Japan, 1945–1980*, 46.

It is still published even today. *Ie no hikari* has continued to be marketed as a "Family Magazine" and regularly includes contemporary versions of the types of articles present from the outset of its publication. The January 2010 issue, to provide a representative example, has articles on cooking, happy farming families, caring for the kimono, and *ikebana* (flower arrangement) (see figure 6.1). There are humorous comics, fiction, tips and tricks for improving health, and puzzles for general entertainment. The advertisements range from products by large farming equipment companies like Kubota and Yanmar to purses from Kitamura, cosmetics, and herbal remedies from a variety of companies.

It is interesting to observe that products are not solely presented in separate advertisements located sporadically throughout the magazine as they were in the early years of its publication. One example in this particular issue, in the section called "Manufacturing Products: A Story," discusses a Myōshun brand salad dressing (see figure 6.2). The article details the labour of farmers who grow the onions and the factory employees involved in the making of the product. Farmers and workers alike are mainly women, we are told. The piece goes on to provide a brief history of the company and this particular product recipe, makes some suggestions about how to use the dressing in common dishes one can easily make at home, and gives information on how to purchase it, with details about the average price (450 yen for a 200mL bottle).[15] This is not the lone example, either. Products are frequently integrated into the articles proper with a higher degree of blending of advertising and content than was present in the interwar and immediate postwar issues; this is a logical progression for the amalgamation of consumption within magazines prefigured by the developments discussed at length in the preceding chapters.

This January issue also contains a short piece written by a fourth-grade elementary student from Shimane Prefecture about the end of winter holiday. A poem of sorts, it was the winner of a contest seeking reader submissions, and the page on which it appears includes a note that new submissions are still being sought.[16] There is also a lengthy article on the different kimono styles of Empress Michiko over the decades of her graceful public appearances, including a number of photos of her

---

15 "ひらめきから生まれた下仁田ねぎの生ドレッシング (An Onion Dressing Born from the Inspiration of Shimonita)."
16 安達, "子どもの目 (Child's View"), 187.

人·JA·地域が元気 Family Magazine

大正14年9月29日第三種郵便物認可　平成22年1月1日発行（毎月1回1日発行）第86巻第1号

JANUARY 2010

家の光

1

新春の
花あしらい
年越しからお正月のしきたりとマナー
よい年の迎え方

〈特集〉
日日に新たに
うちの
家訓

畑の情報便
直売名人に聞く
畑のプランニング
夫婦で初めてのライフプラン
人生味わった者勝ち
寺島しのぶさん
随想／おせちと前世
角田光代さん

Figure 6.1. Cover, *Ie no hikari* 86, no. 1 (January 2010)

上／作業は毎回、ネギの皮むきから始まる。そういう意味でも地味だがだいじな作業
下／ラベルはりも手作業で。ボトルに詰めたあとの仕上げに、一枚一枚ていねいにはっていく

市場出荷前の10月に使用するネギは、山田さんの農場で作っている

かないだろうかと、佐藤さんは考えていました。そんなとき、ネギのない夏場に、みょうぎ物産センターを訪れた観光客から、「下仁田ネギはないんですか？」と聞かれたことから、「下仁田ネギの加工品を作れば売れるのでは」と思いました。地元の人が感じている以上に下仁田ネギが知れ渡っていたのです。

それまで、下仁田ネギの加工品はほとんどありませんでした。まず、頭に浮かんだのは、おやきの生地に青ジソやネギなどを練り込むこと。群馬のおやきは生地に青ジソやネギなど、季節の食材を練り込む方法があります。しかし、それはすでにその日に食べてもらうことになります。そこで賞味期限が一定期間あって売れるものを作らなければと思いました。

平成十四年二月のある日、JAのATMでお金を下ろそうとしたさい、そこにあった料理カードの文字に目が留まりました。「タマネギのドレッシング」です。
「次の瞬間、「そうだ！下仁田ネギのドレッシング」と思ったんです」
佐藤さんはかつて、テレビ番組で下仁田町を訪れたアナウンサーがすりおろした下仁田ネギに「辛い！」と絶句したことを思い出しました。ネギをすりおろすことへの興味から自分でもやってみたこと。そのときにできた、ネギの泡が、卵の泡に

とがあります。

似ていたことを思い出しました。マヨネーズは、酢と油を混ぜる乳化剤の役割として卵黄が使われます。卵の代わりにネギの軟白部を使えば、乳化するのではないかと確信したといいます。料理カードを見た瞬間に、これまでの知識や経験が一本の糸としてつながりました。

同じ年の十一月、妙義町の農業祭の産物加工品コンクールに出品。まず、頭にあったドレッシングを初めてかたちにしました。その結果、最高賞に当たる町長賞を受賞。
「町長賞を受賞する自信はありましたが、ドレッシングはイメージ以上のできで感激しました」
と、佐藤さんは振り返ります。

翌十五年三月、メンバーの神宮恵里子(58)さんから、「あのドレッシング、おいしいから商品化しようよ」と提案がありました。

佐藤さんは、個人で商品化するかグループで商品化するか決めかねていましたが、地域の活性化には、グループで起業するほうがいいと考え、神宮さんと三人で、ほかのメンバーに呼びかけました。そして、農業改良普及センターや町の協力を得て、商品化のための準備を進めました。

十五年十一月、こうしてできあがったのが、乳化液状タイプの「妙旬・下仁田ねぎの生ドレッシング」でした。

Figure 6.2. "An Onion Dressing Born from the Inspiration of Shimonita," *Ie no hikari* 86, no 1 (January 2010)

highness in kimono with (the reader is told) tasteful accord in various settings and seasons.[17] Many of the photographs depict the Empress with her Emperor husband and their children as well, presenting her as a bivalent figure, honoured and apart from normal folk but also recognizable as "mother" and "wife."

Notably as well, the "Korean Boom" most prominent among interested middle-aged Japanese women (though not limited in popularity to them) is evidenced by ads retailing posters, DVDs, CDs, and books from and about several Korean or "K-Pop" stars like Bae Yong Joon and Kwon Sang Woo. And, finally, the issue comes with a supplement (*furoku*) to the magazine proper that comprises a year's worth of recipes in a "Cooking Calendar."[18] This calendar was included as a gift along with the magazine itself, which could be purchased easily, via a simple request form on the internet, for 880 yen (roughly ten dollars US at the time).

The detailing of these features most familiar to the early issues of *Light of the Home* is not meant to suggest that nothing has changed in the magazine world of Japan since 1925; far from it. While magazines still sell quite well in Japan, the audiences have become highly segmented in the way they were when these periodical publications first appeared. Whereas the early magazine publishers had not conceived of audiences which included multiple categories of readers, contemporary magazines have narrowed their focus for marketing purposes. Magazine publishers of today have "tended to address smaller, more select audiences and so to permit more precise targeting by would-be advertisers."[19] In this highly varied selection of magazine titles, publishers "try to create loyalty to the *publishers* themselves by introducing a series of magazines, whose contents will attract young men and women and take them on from one title to the next as they become older, outgrowing some interests and growing into others."[20] The interconnection of the world of advertising and the use of magazines as vehicles for consumerism has, thus, taken on different methods and meanings in the postwar and more recent years. The Japanese masses of the transwar era have remained, however.

---

17 渡辺, "美智子さまとお着物 (Michiko-Sama and Her Kimono)."
18 家の光協会, 2010年お料理カレンダー365日 (*The 2010 365-Day Cooking Calendar*).
19 Moeran, *A Japanese Advertising Agency*, 203.
20 Ibid., 203–4.

After an interlude of intense American influence in the immediate postwar period, 1960s Japan showed a return to the homegrown. Those who were children in the interwar years, now adults in the decades following the American Occupation, would have found the nationalistic focus of electronics advertising, film and television programming proudly produced in Japan, and the installation of the professional housewife in her bright new life to be wistfully linked to an era less colonized by American supervision. Postwar Japan was once again attempting to make its mark on a global scale through the recruitment of average Japanese; this time not for the pursuit of empire but as peaceful and industrious members of the world community. It matters less that Japanese in the interwar years were not yet buying on the scale of the 1960s, when mass *consumption* became a sociological reality for so many, because the mass *audience* had already been created. This audience knew how to parse the menu of items on offer and how to participate among the multitudes because they had been primed through their interactions with family magazines.

In the same way that this project could have looked backwards to a more thorough treatment of what came before these publications, in small and large newspapers and other early modern publications, many pages could be spent discussing the developments of the postwar years. But I have chosen to focus on the pivotal period of massification because it encapsulates the birth of mass culture. Consequently, the focus of this study has been the role of magazines in the massification of Japan and the origins of mass culture, since these publications provide a rich source for understanding that process. They are less useful, however, for helping to uncover causal motors after roughly 1960. This is partly because of the rise of other media, notably television, and social and cultural meaning makers that overtook magazines in importance at that point in Japan.

Why the Audience Remains

The mass culture born from the mechanisms of magazines is highly significant for our understanding of Japan's social and cultural development more generally. This snapshot in time illuminates that culture in order to examine the relationship of media and culture, people and the products they consume. What magazines like *Ie no hikari* and *Kingu* constructed, in part, was individual Japanese consumers, but the outcome of this media's naturalization, measured in the shifts in social and cultural practices, was far broader than that.

Consumption was integrated into the very core of the magazines – in order to be among the mass audience, one had to be consuming some aspect of these media – at the very least, the magazines themselves, and more often other attendant products habitually advertised within the media. The inclusive community that was created among the audience of publications like *Kingu* and *Ie no hikari*, moreover, helped to reinforce participation in the Japanese nation and nurtured a collective culture which naturalized the consumption of mass media and normalized social interactions related to that media. The establishment of these mechanisms was a foundation for the rise of consumer culture during the transwar years.

Perhaps consumption in the context of the modern nation-state is necessarily intertwined with all that imperialism encompasses, unpleasant as that may seem in its implications for collective accountability or complicity in the actions of the states of which we are all a part. This is not to say that all consumption leads to participation in fascism (or nationalism or militarism). Rather, since, as the Japanese imperium was tending towards fascist ideologies and practices, the interwar participation of the Japanese in their mass culture provided a means for participation in the specific empire of which they were members. Different kinds of imperialism are, after all, possible.

At the simplest level, though, the creation of a mass Japanese audience advanced consumerism, which facilitated easy participation in a fascist wartime empire. It also enabled, just as comfortably, participation in the illiberal SCAP-run "democracy" that followed the end of the Second World War. One need only look at the voluminous scholarship on the acceptance of the Treaty of Mutual Cooperation and Security between the United States and Japan, SCAP censorship and their "reverse course," or the career of Nobusuke Kishi for evidence of the failure of democratic ideals in Japan after 1945.

Without the imagination and efforts of people who envisioned a national audience and created the means and infrastructure to distribute products and information to that audience, there would not be mass culture. Japan is key to our understanding of how nationalism can play a role in the development of media industries, and vice versa. Since this process of massification was happening at slightly different speeds in many places around the world, Japan is but one example of the ways in which this process can unfold.

Bibliography

Adorno, Theodor W. *The Culture Industry: Selected Essays on Mass Culture.* London and New York: Routledge, 2001.

"Advertisement." キング (*King*), 1 January 1931.

"Advertisement:" キング (*King*), 1 February 1931.

Agnew, Jean-Christophe. "Coming Up for Air: Consumer Culture in Historical Perspective." In *Consumption and the World of Goods*, edited by John Brewer and Roy Porter. London and New York: Routledge, 1993.

Akimoto, Shunkichi. *Seiji Noma "Magazine King" of Japan – A Sketch of His Life, Character, and Enterprises.* Tokyo: Dai NIhon Yūbenkai Kōdansha, 1927.

Allen, G.C. *A Short Economic History of Modern Japan.* New York: St Martin's Press, 1981.

Allinson, Gary D. *Japan's Postwar History.* Ithaca: Cornell University Press, 2004.

Anderson, Benedict R. *Imagined Communities: Reflections on the Origin and Spread of Nationalism.* London and New York: Verso, 1991.

"Announcement." 家の光 (*Light of the Home*), 1 May 1925.

Ariga, Chieko. "The Playful Gloss: Rubi in Japanese Literature." *Monumenta Nipponica* 44, no. 3 (Autumn 1989): 309–35.

Ariyama, Teruo. "「民衆」の時代から「大衆」の時代へ: 明治末期から大正期のメディア (From the Era of 'the People' to the Age of 'the Masses': Media from the Late Meiji to to the Taishō Period)." In メディア史を学ぶ人のために (*For Those Learning Media History*), edited by Akiko Takeyama. Kyoto-shi: Sekai Shisosha, 2004.

Berry, Mary Elizabeth. *Japan in Print: Information and Nation in the Early Modern Period.* Berkeley: University of California Press, 2006.

Burke, Timothy. *Lifebuoy Men, Lux Women: Commodification, Consumption, and Cleanliness in Modern Zimbabwe.* Durham, NC: Duke University Press, 1996.

Carey, James W. *Communication as Culture: Essays on Media and Society*. New York: Routledge, 2009.

Cohen, Anthony. *Self Consciousness: An Alternative Anthropology of Identity*. London: Routledge, 1994.

Cook, James W., Lawrence B. Glickman, and Michael O'Malley, eds. *The Cultural Turn in U.S. History: Past, Present, and Future*. Chicago: University of Chicago Press, 2009.

Curaj, Adrian, Peter Scott, Lazr Vlasceanu, and Lesley Wilson, eds. *European Higher Education at the Crossroads between the Bologna Process and National Reforms*. Dordrecht: Springer Verlag, 2012.

Davidann, Jon Thares. *Cultural Diplomacy in U.S.–Japanese Relations, 1919–1941*. New York: Palgrave Macmillan, 2007.

De Bary, William Theodore. *Sources of East Asian Tradition: The Modern Period*. Vol. 2. New York: Columbia University Press, 2008.

de Certeau, Michel. *The Practice of Everyday Life*. Berkeley: University of California Press, 1984.

de Grazia, Victoria. "Foreword." In *Selling Modernity: Advertising in Twentieth-Century Germany*, xiii–xviii. Durham, NC: Duke University Press, 2007.

Doctorow, Cory. "Old Toy for Teaching Children to Accurately Drop Atom Bombs – Boing Boing." *Boing Boing*, 29 February 2012. https://boingboing.net/2012/02/29/old-toy-for-teaching-children.html.

Dorsey, James. "Breaking Records: Media, Censorship, and the Folk Song Movement of Japan's 1960s." In *Asian Popular Culture: New, Hybrid, and Alternate Media*, edited by John A. Lent and Lorna Fitzsimmons, 79–108. Lanham, MD: Lexington Books, 2013.

Dower, John W. *War without Mercy: Race and Power in the Pacific War*. New York: Pantheon Books, 1986.

Dower, John W., and Harvard University Council on East Asian Studies. *Empire and Aftermath: Yoshida Shigeru and the Japanese Experience, 1878–1954*. Cambridge, MA: Council on East Asian Studies, Harvard University, distributed by Harvard University Press, 1979.

Driscoll, Mark. *Absolute Erotic, Absolute Grotesque: The Living, Dead, and Undead in Japan's Imperialism, 1895–1945*. Durham, NC: Duke University Press, 2010.

Embree, John F. *Suye Mura, A Japanese Village*. Chicago: University of Chicago Press, 1939.

Foucault, Michel. *Discipline and Punish: The Birth of the Prison*. New York: Pantheon Books, 1977.

Fox, Frank W. *Madison Avenue Goes to War: The Strange Military Career of American Advertising, 1941–45*. Provo, UT: Brigham Young University Press, 1975.

Frederick, Sarah. *Turning Pages: Reading and Writing Women's Magazines in Interwar Japan*. Honolulu: University of Hawai'i Press, 2006.

Fujitani, Takashi. *Splendid Monarchy: Power and Pageantry in Modern Japan*. Berkeley: University of California Press, 1996.

Garon, Sheldon. *Molding Japanese Minds: The State in Everyday Life*. Princeton: Princeton University Press, 1997.

– "Women's Groups and the Japanese State: Contending Approaches to Political Integration, 1890–1945." *Journal of Japanese Studies* 19, no. 1 (Winter 1993): 5–41.

Garon, Sheldon, and Patricia L. Maclachlan, eds. *The Ambivalent Consumer: Questioning Consumption in East Asia and the West*. Ithaca: Cornell University Press, 2006.

Garvey, Ellen Gruber. *The Adman in the Parlor: Magazines and the Gendering of Consumer Culture, 1880s to 1910s*. New York: Oxford University Press, 1996.

Geertz, Clifford. *The Interpretation of Cultures: Selected Essays*. New York: Basic Books, 1973.

Gerow, Aaron Andrew. *Visions of Japanese Modernity: Articulations of Cinema, Nation, and Spectatorship, 1895–1925*. Berkeley: University of California Press, 2010.

Gerteis, Christopher. "Political Protest in Interwar Japan." *Visualizing Cultures Website, Massachusetts Institute of Technology*, n.d. https://ocw.mit.edu/ans7870/21f/21f.027/protest_interwar_japan/pij1_essay01.html.

Gibbons, Michael. *The New Production of Knowledge: The Dynamics of Science and Research in Contemporary Societies*. London: Sage Publishing, 1995.

Gluck, Carol. "After the Shipwreck: New Horizons for History-Writing." Lecture, Brown University, 6 October 2006.

– *Japan's Modern Myths: Ideology in the Late Meiji Period*. Princeton: Princeton University Press, 1985.

– *Two Lectures by Carol Gluck : The Maruyama Lecture and Seminar 2004*. Berkeley: Center for Japanese Studies, University of California, Berkeley, 2004.

Gordon, Andrew. "Consumption, Leisure and the Middle Class in Transwar Japan." *Social Science Japan Journal* 10, no. 1 (2007): 1–21.

– "From Singer to Shinpan: Consumer Credit in Modern Japan." In *The Ambivalent Consumer: Questioning Consumption in East Asia and the West*, edited by Sheldon Garon and Patricia L. Maclachlan, 135–62. Ithaca: Cornell University Press, 2006.

– *Labor and Imperial Democracy in Prewar Japan*. Berkeley: University of California Press, 1991.

– "Social Protest in Imperial Japan: The Hibiya Riot of 1905." *Visualizing Cultures Website, Massachusetts Institute of Technology*, n.d. https://ocw.mit.edu/ans7870/21f/21f.027/social_protest_japan/index.html.

– *The Wages of Affluence: Labor and Management in Postwar Japan*. Cambridge, MA: Harvard University Press, 1998.

Gordon, Andrew, ed. *Postwar Japan as History*. Berkeley: University of California Press, 1993.

Gramsci, Antonio. *Prison Notebooks*. Edited by Joseph A. Buttigieg. New York: Columbia University Press, 1992.

Hanes, Jeffrey E. "Media Culture in Taishō Osaka." In *Japan's Competing Modernities: Issues in Culture and Democracy, 1900–1930*, edited by Sharon Minichiello, 267–87. Honolulu: University of Hawai'i Press, 1998.

Harootunian, Harry D. *Overcome by Modernity: History, Culture, and Community in Interwar Japan*. Princeton: Princeton University Press, 2000.

Havens, Thomas R.H. *Farm and Nation in Modern Japan: Agrarian Nationalism, 1870–1940*. Princeton: Princeton University Press, 1974.

– *Parkscapes: Green Spaces in Modern Japan*. Honolulu: University of Hawai'i Press, 2011.

Hein, C., J.M. Diefendorf, and Y. Ishida. *Rebuilding Urban Japan after 1945*. New York: Palgrave Macmillan, 2003.

Herman, Edward S., and Noam Chomsky. *Manufacturing Consent: The Political Economy of the Mass Media*. New York: Pantheon Books, 2003.

Hershatter, Gail. *The Gender of Memory: Rural Women and China's Collective Past*. Asia Pacific Modern. Berkeley: University of California Press, 2011.

Highmore, Ben. *Everyday Life and Cultural Theory: An Introduction*. London and New York: Routledge, 2002.

Honey, Maureen. *Creating Rosie the Riveter: Class, Gender, and Propaganda during World War II*. Amherst: University of Massachusetts Press, 1984.

Horkheimer, Max, and Theodor W. Adorno. "The Culture Industry: Enlightenment as Mass Deception." In *The Consumer Society Reader*, edited by Juliet B. Schor and Douglas B. Holt, 3–19. New York: New Press, 2006.

Horning, Rob. "Media and Consumer Desire." *New Inquiry*, 1 May 2015. https://thenewinquiry.com/blog/media-and-consumer-desire/.

Huffman, James L. *Creating a Public: People and Press in Meiji Japan*. Honolulu: University of Hawai'i Press, 1997.

Ishida, Takeshi. *Japanese Society*. New York: Random House, 1971.

Ivy, Marilyn. *Discourses of the Vanishing: Modernity, Phantasm, Japan*. Chicago: University of Chicago Press, 1995.

– "Formations of Mass Culture." In *Postwar Japan As History*, ed. Gordon, 239–58. Berkeley: University of California Press, 1993.

Jones, Mark A. *Children as Treasures: Childhood and the Middle Class in Early Twentieth Century Japan*. Cambridge, MA: Harvard University Asia Center, distributed by Harvard University Press, 2010.

Jung, Carl G., H.G. Baynes, and Cary F. Baynes. *Contributions to Analytical Psychology*. London: Routledge and Kegan Paul, 1948.

Kammen, Michael G. *American Culture, American Tastes: Social Change and the 20th Century*. New York: Knopf, 1999.

Kasza, Gregory James. *The State and the Mass Media in Japan, 1918–1945*. Berkeley: University of California Press, 1988.

Kitamura, Hiroshi. *Screening Enlightenment: Hollywood and the Cultural Reconstruction of Defeated Japan*. Ithaca: Cornell University Press, 2010.

Kōdansha. *Kodansha Encyclopedia of Japan*. Vol. 6. 1st ed. 9 vols. Tokyo and New York: Kodansha, 1983.

Kogawa, Tetsuo. "New Trends in Japanese Popular Culture." *Telos*, 20 June 1985, 147–52.

Kornicki, Peter. "The Publisher's Go-Between: Kashihon'ya in the Meiji Period." *Modern Asian Studies* 14, no. 2 (1980): 331–44.

Kushner, Barak. *The Thought War: Japanese Imperial Propaganda*. Honolulu: University of Hawai'i Press, 2006.

Lapeska, David. "Hisham Matar on Libya's Awakening." *National*, 28 October 2011. https://www.thenational.ae/arts-culture/books/hisham-matar-on-libyas-awakening?pageCount=0.

Lears, T.J. Jackson. *Fables of Abundance: A Cultural History of Advertising in America*. New York: HarperCollins, 1994.

Levine, Lawrence W. *Highbrow/Lowbrow: The Emergence of Cultural Hierarchy in America*. Cambridge, MA: Harvard University Press, 1988.

Lincicome, Mark E. *Imperial Subjects as Global Citizens: Nationalism, Internationalism, and Education in Japan*. AsiaWorld. Lanham, MD: Lexington Books, 2009.

Link, Nina, ed. "Magazine Handbook: Engagement to Action (A Comprehensive Guide and Factbook)." Magazine Publishers of America, November 2010.

Lipsitz, George. *Time Passages: Collective Memory and American Popular Culture*. Minneapolis: University of Minnesota Press, 1990.

Maclachlan, Patricia L. *Consumer Politics in Postwar Japan: The Institutional Boundaries of Citizen Activism*. New York: Columbia University Press, 2002.

Marchand, Roland. *Advertising the American Dream: Making Way for Modernity, 1920–1940*. Berkeley: University of California Press, 1985.

Marshall, Bryon K. *Capitalism and Nationalism in Prewar Japan: The Ideology of the Business Elite, 1868–1941*. Stanford: Stanford University Press, 1967.

Matsusaka, Yoshihisa Tak. "Nationalist Journalism and Foreign Policy Crises in Meiji and Early Taisho Japan." Presented at the 2011 New England Association for Asian Studies Conference, Wellesley College, 22 October 2011.

McLuhan, Marshall. *Understanding Media: The Extensions of Man*. New York: McGraw-Hill, 1964.

Milly, Deborah J. *Poverty, Equality, and Growth: The Politics of Economic Need in Postwar Japan*. Cambridge, MA: Harvard University Asia Center, distributed by Harvard University Press, 1999.

Minichiello, Sharon. *Japan's Competing Modernities: Issues in Culture and Democracy, 1900–1930*. Honolulu: University of Hawai'i Press, 1998.

Miyake, Yoshiko. "Doubling Expectations: Motherhood and Women's Factory Work under State Management in Japan in the 1930s and 1940s." In *Recreating Japanese Women, 1600–1945*, edited by Gail Bernstein, 267–95. Berkeley and Los Angeles: University of California Press, 1991.

"Modernist Journals Project." A joint project of Brown University and the University of Tulsa. *The Modernist Journals Project*, 10 May 2011. http://www.modjourn.org/.

Moeran, Brian. *A Japanese Advertising Agency: An Anthropology of Media and Markets*. ConsumAsianN. Honolulu: University of Hawai'i Press, 1996.

"MPA – The Association of Magazine Media (Formerly Magazine Publishers of America) – The Definitive Resource for the Magazine Industry." 8 March 2012. http://www.magazine.org/.

Mulgan, Aurelia George. *Japan's Agricultural Policy Regime*. London: Routledge, 2006.

– *The Politics of Agriculture in Japan*. London and New York: Routledge, 2000.

Nagahara, Hiromu. "Unpopular Music: The Politics of Mass Culture in Modern Japan." Dissertation, Harvard University, 2011.

Ohmann, Richard. *Selling Culture: Magazines, Markets, and Class at the Turn of the Century*. Haymarket Series. London and New York: Verso, 1998.

Partner, Simon. *Assembled in Japan: Electrical Goods and the Making of the Japanese Consumer*. Berkeley: University of California Press, 1999.

– *Toshié: A Story of Village Life in Twentieth-Century Japan*. Berkeley: University of California Press, 2004.

Pratt, Mary Louise. *Imperial Eyes: Travel Writing and Transculturation*. London and New York: Routledge, 1992.

Quinn, Aragorn. "Political Theatre: *The Rise and Fall of Rome* and *The Sword of Freedom*, Two Translations of *Julius Caesar* in Meiji Japan by Kawashima Keizō and Tsubouchi Shōyō." *Asian Theatre Journal* 28, no. 1 (Spring 2011): 168–83.

Richards, Grant. *Guarding Childish Feet*. 1904. https://library.uoregon.edu/ec/e-asia/imagesa/imperial.htm.

Robertson, Jennifer. "Sexy Rice: Plant Gender, Farm Manuals, and Grass-Roots Nativism." *Monumenta Nipponica* 39, no. 3 (1984): 233–60.

Robertson, Jennifer Ellen. *Takarazuka: Sexual Politics and Popular Culture in Modern Japan*. Berkeley: University of California Press, 1998.

Rogers, Everett M. *Communication Technology: The New Media in Society.* Series in Communication Technology and Society. New York: Free Press, 1986.

Ross, Kristin. *Fast Cars, Clean Bodies: Decolonization and the Reordering of French Culture.* Cambridge, MA: MIT Press, 1996.

Rubinger, Richard. *Popular Literacy in Early Modern Japan.* Honolulu: University of Hawai'i Press, 2007.

Ruoff, Kenneth J. *Imperial Japan at Its Zenith: The Wartime Celebration of the Empire's 2,600th Anniversary.* Ithaca and London: Cornell University Press, 2010.

Sand, Jordan. *House and Home in Modern Japan: Architecture, Domestic Space, and Bourgeois Culture, 1880–1930.* Cambridge, MA: Harvard University Asia Center, distributed by Harvard University Press, 2003.

Sato, Barbara Hamill. "An Alternate Informant: Middle-Class Women and Mass Magazines in 1920s Japan." In *Being Modern in Japan: Culture and Society from the 1910s to the 1930s*, edited by Elise K. Tipton and John Clark, 137–53. Honolulu: University of Hawai'i Press, 2000.

– *The New Japanese Woman: Modernity, Media, and Women in Interwar Japan.* Durham, NC: Duke University Press, 2003.

Schäfer, Fabian. *Public Opinion, Propaganda, Ideology: Theories on the Press and Its Social Function in Interwar Japan, 1918–1937.* Leiden and Boston: Brill, 2012.

Schivelbusch, Wolfgang. *The Railway Journey: The Industrialization of Time and Space in the 19th Century.* Berkeley: University of California Press, 1986.

Scholes, Robert, and Clifford Wulfman. *Modernism in the Magazines: An Introduction.* New Haven: Yale University Press, 2010.

Schudson, Michael. *Advertising, the Uneasy Persuasion: Its Dubious Impact on American Society.* New York: Basic Books, 1984.

– "The Troubling Equivalence of Citizen and Consumer." *The ANNALS of the American Academy of Political and Social Science* 608 (November 2006): 193–204.

Schutts, Jeff. "'Die Erfrischende Pause': Marketing Coca-Cola in Hitler's Germany." In *Selling Modernity: Advertising in Twentieth-Century Germany*, edited by Pamela E. Swett, 151–81. Durham, NC: Duke University Press, 2007.

Shillony, Ben-Ami. Review of *The Age of Hirohito: In Search of Modern Japan*, by Daikichi Irokawa, Mikiso Hane, and John K. Urda. *Journal of Japanese Studies* 23, no. 2 (1997): 450–4.

Silberman, Bernard S., Harry D. Harootunian, and Gail Lee Bernstein. *Japan in Crisis: Essays on Taisho Democracy.* Center for Japanese Studies, the University of Michigan, 1999.

Silverberg, Miriam Rom. *Erotic Grotesque Nonsense: The Mass Culture of Japanese Modern Times.* Berkeley: University of California Press, 2009.

Smith, Henry D. "The History of the Book in Edo and Paris." In *Edo and Paris: Urban Life and the State in the Early Modern Era*, edited by James L. McClain, John M. Merriman, and Ugawa Kaoru, 332–52. Ithaca: Cornell University Press, 1994.

Smith, Kerry Douglas. *A Time of Crisis: Japan, the Great Depression, and Rural Revitalization*. Cambridge, MA: Harvard University Asia Center, distributed by Harvard University Press, 2001.

Smith, Robert John, and Ella Lury Wiswell. *The Women of Suye Mura*. Chicago: University of Chicago Press, 1982.

Stanley, Jason. *How Propaganda Works*. Princeton: Princeton University Press, 2015.

Suarez-Villa, Luis. *Invention and the Rise of Technocapitalism*. Lanham: Rowman and Littlefield, 2000.

Takemae, Eiji, ed. *The Allied Occupation of Japan*. Translated by Robert Ricketts. New York: Continuum, 2003.

Tansman, Alan. "Introduction: The Culture of Japanese Fascism." In *The Culture of Japanese Fascism*, edited by Alan Tansman, 1–28. Durham, NC: Duke University Press, 2009.

Thompson, John B. *Ideology and Modern Culture: Critical Social Theory in the Era of Mass Communication*. Stanford: Stanford University Press, 1990.

Tsurumi, Shunsuke. *A Cultural History of Postwar Japan, 1945–1980*. London and New York: KPI, distributed by Methuen, 1987.

Untitled item. キング (*King*), 1 March 1939, 49.

Wada-Marciano, Mitsuyo. *Nippon Modern: Japanese Cinema of the 1920s and 1930s*. Honolulu: University of Hawai'i Press, 2008.

Waller, Jane, and Michael Vaughan-Rees. *Women in Wartime: The Role of Women's Magazines 1939–1945*. London: Macdonald Optima, 1987.

Washburn, Dennis C., and Carole Cavanaugh, eds. *Word and Image in Japanese Cinema*. Cambridge and New York: Cambridge University Press, 2001.

Waswo, Ann. *Housing in Postwar Japan: A Social History*. London: RoutledgeCurzon, 2002.

Waswo, Ann, and Yoshiaki Nishida, eds. *Farmers and Village Life in Twentieth-Century Japan*. New York: Routledge, 2003.

Weber, Eugen. *Peasants into Frenchmen: The Modernization of Rural France, 1870–1914*. Stanford: Stanford University Press, 1976.

Weisenfeld, Gennifer S. "'From Baby's First Bath': Kao Soap and Modern Japanese Commercial Design." *Art Bulletin* 86, no. 3 (September 2004): 573–98.

– "Japanese Typographic Design and the Art of Letterforms." In *Bridges to Heaven: Essays on East Asian Art in Honor of Professor Wen C. Fong*, edited by

Jerome Silbergeld, Dora C.Y. Ching, Judith G. Smith, and Alfreda Murck, 1:827–48. Princeton: Princeton University Press, 2011.
– "Selling Shiseido: Japanese Cosmetics Advertising and Design in the Early 20th-Century." *Visualizing Cultures Website, Massachusetts Institute of Technology*, 2008. https://ocw.mit.edu/ans7870/21f/21f.027/shiseido_01/index.html.
Westney, D. Eleanor. *Imitation and Innovation: The Transfer of Western Organizational Patterns in Meiji Japan*. Cambridge, MA: Iuniverse, 2000.
Wilson, Sandra. "Bureaucrats and Villagers in Japan: Shimin and the Crisis of the Early 1930s." *Social Science Japan Journal* 1, no. 1 (1998): 121–40.
Yagi, Yoshinosuke. "The Second Three-Year Expansion Plan of the Co-Operative Movement." *Kyoto University Economic Review* 12, no. 2 (December 1937): 19–41.
Young, Louise. *Beyond the Metropolis: Second Cities and Modern Life in Interwar Japan*. Berkeley: University of California Press, 2013.
– *Japan's Total Empire: Manchuria and the Culture of Wartime Imperialism*. Berkeley: University of California Press, 1999.
"いろいろの兵器 (Various Armaments)." 家の光 (*Light of the Home*), 1 February 1938.
キング. 繪ばなし㘴間學 (Worldly Learning Illustrated Picturebook). 東京 (Tokyo): 大日本雄弁会講談社 (Dai Nihon Yūbenkai Kōdansha), 1935.
"キング十徳 (Ten Virtues of *King*)." キング (*King*), 1 March 1925.
"キング新年号予告 (Advance Notice for the New Year's Issue of *King*)." 読売新聞 (*Yomiuri Shinbun*). 1 December 1926, morning edition.
「キング」編輯局同人(From the Editors of *King*). "『キング』が世に出るまでの苦心 (The Agony Until *King* Appeared)." キング, 1 January 1925.
"ひらめきから生まれた下仁田ねぎの生ドレッシング (An Onion Dressing Born from the Inspiration of Shimonita)." 家の光 (*Light of the Home*), 1 January 2010.
丸山真男. 現代政治の思想と行動 (*Thought and Behaviour in Modern Japanese Politics*). Tokyo: Miraisha, 1964.
井上哲次郎. "幸福なる生活の基礎 (Foundations for a Blessed Life)." 家の光 (*Light of the Home*), 1 May 1927.
井上章一. 美人コンテスト百年史: 芸妓の時代から美少女まで (*One Hundred Year History of Beauty Contests: From the Age of Geisha to the Beautiful Girl*). Tokyo: Shinchosha, 1992.
佐佐木信綱, ed. 古今名歌集. キング第12巻第1号付録 (*Famous Songs, Old and New. King* 12, no. 1, supplement). 東京 (Tokyo): 大日本雄弁会講談社 (Dai Nihon Yūbenkai Kōdansha), 1936.
佐藤卓己. 「キング」の時代: 国民大衆雑誌の公共性 (*The Era of "King": The Public Nature of a National Popular Magazine*). Tokyo: Iwanami Shoten, 2002.

八條隆正. "組合の家庭化と家庭に組合化 (Making the Cooperative into a Family and Making the Family a Cooperative)." 家の光 (*Light of the Home*), 1 March 1929.

前田愛. "音読から黙読へ: 近代読者の成立 (From Reading Aloud to Silent Reading: The Establishment of the Modern Reader)." In 近代読者の成立 (*The Establishment of the Modern Reader*) (February): 16, 132–67. 東京 (Tokyo): 岩波書店 (Iwanami Shōten), 2001.

勝田主計. "農村振興と教育第一 (The Encouragement of Farming Villages and Putting Education First)." 家の光 (*Light of the Home*), 1 February 1929.

北村宗之助. 家の光の四十年 (*Forty Years of "Light of the Home"*). 東京 (Tokyo): 家の光協会 (Ie no Hikari Association), 1968.

– 家の光六十年史 (*The Sixty-Year History of "Ie no hikari"*). 東京 (Tokyo): 家の光協会 (Ie no Hikari Association), 1986.

千葉胤明. "明治天皇御聖徳の一斑 (Sightings of the Imperial Virtues of Emperor Meiji)." 家の光 (*Light of the Home*), 1 August 1927.

南博, and 社会心理研究所. 昭和文化: 1925–1945 (*Showa Culture: 1925–1945*). 10 April. 東京 (Tokyo): 勁草書房 (Keisō Shobō), 1987.

四方田犬彦. 日本映画史 100年 (*100 Years of Japanese Film History*). Tokyo: 集英社 (Shūeisha), 2000.

大久保武. "『廣告非常時─一九三五年の新聞廣告を回顧する』(Advertising in the Time of Emergency – Recollections on Newspaper Advertising of 1935)." 印刷と広告 (*Insatsu to Koukoku*) 3, no. 1 (1936): 32–3.

大倉邦彦. "母の横顔とうしろ姿: 私の希望する家庭教育 (Mother's Profile and the Figure Behind: The Home Education I Hope For)." 家の光 (*Light of the Home*), 1 November 1937.

奥原潔, ed. 家の光の二十五年 (*Twenty-Five Years of "Light of the Home"*). 東京 (Tokyo): 家の光協会 (Ie no Hikari Kyokai), 1949.

安達安恒. "『家の光』の歴史-ある農本主義とその媒体 (The History of *Ie no hikari* – The Media of Agricultural Fundamentalism)." 思想の科学 (*Shiso No Kagaku*) 18, no. 6 (1960): 59–76.

安達浩二. "子どもの目: 休みももう終わり (Child's View: Winter Break Is Already Over)." 家の光 (*Light of the Home*), 1 January 2010.

家の光協会. 2010年お料理カレンダー365日: 野菜たっぷりのやさしい食卓 (*The 2010 365-Day Cooking Calendar: Vegetable-Filled Easy Cuisine*). 1月号付録 (Supplement to the January issue). キング (*King*). 東京 (Tokyo): 大日本雄弁会講談社 (Dai Nihon Yūbenkai Kōdansha), 2010.

家の光協会 (Ie no Hikari Kyōkai). 家の光五十年の人と動きと (*Fifty Years of the People and Developments of "Light of the Home"*). 東京 (Tokyo): 家の光協会 (Ie no Hikari Kyokai), 1976.

"家の光読者大会 (*Light of the Home* Reader Rallies)." 家の光 (*Light of the Home*), 1 September 1928.

"家の光読者大会 (*Light of the Home* Reader Rallies)." 家の光 (*Light of the Home*), 1 October 1928.

山本武利. 近代日本の新聞読者層 (*Newspaper Readers of Modern Japan*). Tokyo: 法政大学出版局 (Hōsei University Publishers), 1981.

山田俊治. 大衆新聞がつくる明治の〈日本〉(*The Creation of "Japan" by Popular Meiji Newspapers*). 東京 (Tokyo): 日本放送出版協会 (Nihon Hoso Shuppan Kyokai), 2002.

– "文字文化としての音読と黙読—歴史の重層的な把握をめざして (Print Culture for Reading Aloud and Silent Reading – Towards a Multi-Layered Understanding of History)." In 音声と書くこと (*Writing and the Voice*), edited by 河添房江, 221–43. 叢書想像する平安文学 10. Tokyo: 勉誠出版 (Bensei Shuppan), 2001.

岡實. "家の光、国の光 (Light of the Home, Light of the Nation)." 家の光 (*Light of the Home*), 1 May 1925.

志村源源太郎. "共同心の泉 (The Spring of the Spirit of Cooperation)." 家の光 (*Light of the Home*), 1 May 1925.

– "産業組合の大衆化 (The Massification of the Industrial Cooperative)." 家の光 (*Light of the Home*) 6, no. 4 (1930): 17.

"我家の実験 (Our Household Experiments)." 家の光 (*Light of the Home*), 1 January 1932.

新田義之. 澤柳政太郎: 随時随所楽シマザルナシ. ミネルヴァ日本評伝選 (Sawayanagi Masatarō: Times and Places of Never-Ending Fun). Kyoto: ミネルヴァ書房 (Mineruva Shobō), 2006.

"日支事変第二報: 守れ生命線 (Second Report on the Conflict with China: Protect Our Lifeline)." 家の光 (*Light of the Home*), 1 November 1937.

松本剛. 広告の日本史 (History of Japanese Advertising). 東京 (Tokyo): 新人物往来社 (Shin Jinbutsu Oraisha), 1973.

板垣邦子. 昭和戦前・戦中期の農村生活: 雑誌「家の光」にみる (*Rural Life in Showa during and after the War: Viewed through the Magazine "Light of the Home"*). 東京 (Tokyo): 三嶺書房 (Mitsumine Shobo), 1992.

森本厚吉. "家の光は自己にあり (The Light of the Home Is in the Self)." 家の光 (*Light of the Home*), 1 July 1925.

森武麿. "戦時経済体制下における産業組合: 群馬県西横野村を例 として (Industrial Cooperatives within the Wartime Economy: The Example of Gunma Prefecture's Nishiyoko Village." 一橋論叢 (*Hitotsubashi Review*) 70, no. 4 (April 1973): 361–80.

武者小路實篤. 名言名訓集 (*Collected Quotations and Sayings*). キング新年號附録 (*King* New Year's supplement). 東京 (Tokyo): 講談社 (Kōdansha), 1936.

永嶺重敏. 雑誌と読者の近代 (*Modern Magazines and Readers*). 東京 (Tokyo): 日本エディタースクール出版部 (Nihon Edita Sukuru Shuppanbu), 1997.

河原撫子. "異様な輝き (The Strange Glow)." 家の光 (*Light of the Home*), 1 May 1925.

"油が無くなると国が滅びる (The Disappearance of Oil and the Ruin of Our Country)." キング (King), 1 February 1925.

淵田忠良, ed. 偉人は斯く教へる (The Teachings of Great Men). キング新年號第九巻第一號附録 (King 9, no. 1, New Year's supplement). 東京 (Tokyo): 講談社 (Kōdansha), 1933.

– ed. 支那事變忠勇談・感激談: 附支那事變誌 (Loyalty and Gratitude in the China Incident: The China Incident Collection). キング第十四巻第三號附録 (King 14, no. 35, supplement). 東京 (Tokyo): 大日本雄辯會講談社 (Dai Nihon Yūbenkai Kōdansha), 1938.

– ed. 明治大正昭和大絵巻 (The Illustrated Meiji Taishō Shōwa). キング新年号第7巻第1号附録 (King 7, no. 1, New Year's supplement). 東京 (Tokyo): 講談社 (Kōdansha), 1931.

渡辺みどり. "美智子さまとお着物 (Michiko-Sama and Her Kimono)." 家の光 (Light of the Home), 1 January 2010.

澤柳政太郎. "名家一説 (A Notable Opinion)." キング (King), 1 January 1925.

– "母性尊重と家庭教育 (Home Education and Respect for Motherhood)." 家の光 (Light of the Home), 1 May 1925.

"燦たりキングの出現 (King's Brilliant Arrival)." キング (King), 1 January 1925.

産業組合中央会家の光編輯部 (Editors of Light of the Home, Industrial Cooperative Central Committee). 家の光: 人の一生と産業組合 (Light of the Home: The Industrial Cooperative and the Span of Your Life). Tōkyō (東京): 家の光協会 (Ie no Hikari Association), 1930.

"皇軍奮起の目標 (The Goals of Our Inspiring Imperial Army)." 家の光 (Light of the Home), 1 November 1937.

社史編纂委員会 (Committee for the Compilation of the Company History). 講談社の歩んだ五十年 (The Path of Kōdansha's First Fifty Years). Tokyo: Kōdansha, 1959.

笛木悌治. 私の見た野間清治: 講談社創始者・その人と語録 (The Noma Seiji I Saw: The Founder of Kōdansha, The Sayings of That Man). Fujisawa: 富士見書房 (Fujimi Shobō), 1979.

糀谷美規子. 戦争を生きた女たち: 証言・国防婦人会 (Women Who Lived the War: Testimony of the Women's National Defence Association). 京都市 (Kyōto-shi): ミネルヴァ書房 (Mineruva Shobō), 1985.

"編輯部より (From the Editors)." 家の光 (Light of the Home), 1 May 1925.

荒木貞夫. "全国に燃え上がる日本精神 (The Japanese Spirit Burning through the Entire Nation)." 家の光 (Light of the Home), 1 April 1935.

"読者講談室 (Reader's Lecture Room)." 家の光 (Light of the Home), 1 May 1925.

講談社 (Kodansha Ltd.). "Home Page." Kodansha International, 18 August 2011. http://www.kodansha.co.jp/english/.

"講談社「おもしろくて、ためになる」出版を" ("Kōdansha – Publishing 'to Edify and Entertain'"), 18 August 2011. http://www.kodansha.co.jp/.

貴司山治. "「キング」論 (Discourse on *King*)." In 綜合ヂャーナリズム講座 (*Comprehensive Journalism Lectures*), 3:163–79. 東京 (Tokyo): 內外社 (Naigaisha), 1930.

"農村と婦人雑誌 (Farming Villages and Women's Magazines)." 家の光 (*Light of the Home*), 1 June 1925.

"遂に日支事変へ (Finally towards the Conflict in China!)." 家の光 (*Light of the Home*), 1 November 1937.

"都市の防空 (City Air Defences)." 家の光 (*Light of the Home*), 1 February 1938.

野間清治. 出世の礎 (*The Cornerstone of Success*). キング付録. 東京 (Tōkyō): 大日本雄弁会講談社 (Dai Nihon Yūbenkai Kōdansha), 1931.

– "如何にして希望を達すべき呼: 道は邇きに在り (How You Should Reach Your Dreams: The Path Is Near)." キング (*King*), 1 January 1925.

– 私の半生 (*My Early Life*). 東京 (Tokyo): 千倉書房 (Chikura Shobo), 1936.

長谷川卓郎, ed. 明治大帝 (*Emperor Meiji*). キング十一月號(第3巻第11號)附録 (*King* 3, no. 11, supplement). 東京 (Tokyo): 講談社 (Kōdansha), 1927.

馬場由雄. "大和民族性と青年覚悟 (Japanese Ethnicity and Youth Preparedness)." 家の光 (*Light of the Home*), 1 June 1925.

鳩山一郎, ed. 新語新知識: 附常識辭典 (*Neologisms and New Knowledge: Dictionary of Common Sense*). 東京 (Tokyo): 講談社 (Kōdansha), 1934.

キング (*King*), 1 February 1927.

Index

Note: To avoid multiple cross-references, information is organized in this index favouring the Japanese terminology with English glosses provided. Japanese names are provided in the Family Name Given Name convention, unless the individual has published in English under anglicized naming conventions, which are then listed under Family Name, Given Name.

Adachi Ikitsune, 147

Adorno, Theodore, 15, 31

advertising: contemporary integration in *Ie no hikari*, 194; differences between Japanese and American, 171–4; disconnection from principles, 185; examples of products offered, 181–2; as fun-house mirror, 168n14; integrated format of, 170, 194, 199; negative attitudes towards, 167; as percentage of magazine content, 174; variance between *Ie no hikari* and *Kingu*, 179

Agnew, Jean-Christophe, 188

agrarianism, 105

agriculture: percentage of interwar population engaged in, 51, 73, 108

Albert de Bassompierre, 140

Allen, G.C., 177n21

Ariga, Chieko, 30n11, 84n14

Arimoto Hideo, 32, 38, 52, 55, 148, 184

Ariyama Teruo, 9n13

Association of Magazine Media, 187

audience, 7–8, 11, 24–5; limitations of earlier magazines, 23, 54; motivations, 35; participation, 100, 144–5, 147, 154, 160, 189; resisting mass culture, 12; of Taishō novels, 45; in the Tokugawa era, 44. *See also* mass national audience

Berkov, Robert H., 191

Berry, Mary Elizabeth, 39n27, 44

bicycles, 48

bidan (beautiful stories), 73, 104, 111, 171

Booklovers, 161

British Empire, 21–2

Bungei kurabu (Literature Club), 80

Bungeishunjū, 132

Burke, Timothy, 35n19

capitalists: serving the nation, 61

Carey, James: culture as communication, 6–7

censorship, 47, 78–80, 190; Hiromu
  Nagahara on, 154n48; SCAP
  (Supreme Command for the Allied
  Powers), 199
Chiba Taneaki, 118
Chūō kōron (Central Review), 47, 64,
  132–3, 142, 183n23
cinema. *See* film
circulation, 23, 40, 61–2, 66, 75, 150,
  155–6; problems with reported
  statistics, 40, 138, 144, 161
citizen vs consumer, 187–8
citizens: process of creating, 11, 37–8
collective identity, 25, 46, 109
colonies, 7, 16, 22, 37, 85, 148;
  gendered representation of, 160
"common sense," 11, 28, 38, 98, 112,
  114, 117, 127, 137, 141–2, 156, 189
communal reading, 26, 39, 137,
  141, 148
cooperation: as an ideal, 54, 61,
  97, 101–3
culture: definition, 6–8; flow between
  rural and urban areas, 72; sense of
  shared, 36–9

de Grazia, Victoria, 188n4, 189
department stores, 164
discourse, 15, 34, 34n19
Dower, John, 32, 35, 120
Driscoll, Mark, 66n48

editor(s): acceptable critiques, 113;
  awareness of influence, 31; con-
  cealing selection principles, 89;
  duplicity of, 66; principles of, 104;
  separate from audience, 38. *See
  also* Aritomo Hideo; Noma Seiji;
  Shimura Gentarō
editorial cartoons, 120–2

Edogawa Ranpō, 94
educational outreach, 54
educational system, 21, 26
Embree, John, 46, 50, 74; on film and
  radio, 48
empire, 7, 11, 13–16, 22, 79,
  111, 199; as compatible with
  consumption, 189
Empress Michiko, 194
entertainments: lack of, in
  rural areas, 142
ethnic minorities, 37

family magazines. See *katei zasshi*
fan clubs, 39, 131, 136–7, 160–1;
  American magazine, 144
fascism, 6, 15, 36n22, 130, 171, 199
film, 42, 47–8, 73, 131, 142, 153–4, 174
Fordism, 31
Foucault, Michel, 15n24, 34n19
Frederick, Sarah, 85n16
freedom of the press, 77
Fuji (changed name of *Kingu*), 46,
  86–7, 190
Fuji Paper Manufacturing, 81
Fujin Kurabu (Women's Club), 135
Fujin sekai (Women's World), 47
Fujo shinbun (Women's
  Newspaper), 47
Fukuzawa Yukichi, 86
furigana. See rubi
furoku (supplements), 116, 160,
  184; more recent, 197; sample
  of titles, 155–6
Furuse Denzō, 74

games, 94–6
Garvey, Ellen Gruber, 144, 160–1
gas lighting, 20
gasoline, 113–14

Geertz, Clifford: definition
of culture, 6
gendai shōsetsu (contemporary
novels), 94
gender: norms and roles, 14, 31,
115, 141, 153, 165; representations
of, 157
Gondō Seikyō, 105
goraku zasshi (entertainment
magazine), 190
Gordon, Andrew, 46n4, 48, 130, 192
Gotō Shinpei, 66, 79n5
Gregorian Calendar, 21

Haiyu (Actors and Actresses), 135
Hakubieki, 170, 177, 178–80, 191
Hakubunkan, 80
Havens, Thomas, 50n15, 51n20,
hegemony, 15
Hershatter, Gail, 13
Hinomaru Tarō, 126
Hirata Tōsuke, 105
Hiratsuka Raichō, 157
Hokuetsu Kishu Paper Company, 81
Honey, Maureen, 165
Huffman, James, 46

ideology, 6, 15, 32, 35n21, 78, 107,
147–8, 162, 163n1; flawed, 109n62,
185n27
Ie no hikari (Light of the Home): advertising choices, 71–3; after 1960,
193–4; children's section, 123–6;
discount system, 75; distribution
plans, 143; early opposition to, 52,
55; emphasis on youth, 107; first
cover, 57, 58; first issue, 97–110;
first proposal, 53; page length,
97, 171; pricing, 31, 103; purchase
of seen as investment, 75; stated

editorial principles, 104;
subscription rates, 76
imperialism, 14–16, 21–3, 127, 130,
199; lack of opposition to, 54
Industrial Cooperative. *See*
Sangyō Kumiai
Information Division: of SCAP, 191
Inoue Tetsujirō, 117
Ishida Takeshi, 66
Ivy, Marilyn, 8
Iwanami Shoten, 64, 183n23

The Japanese Printer, 183
Japaneseness, 28; sense of,
during Tokugawa era, 37
jidai shōsetsu (historical fiction), 94
Jones, Mark, 47, 126n87

Kaizō (Reconstruction), 133
kana: use for readability, 30.
See also *rubi*
Kao Corporation, 181, 185
Kasza, Gregory, 78
Katei no tomo (The Family's
Friend), 47
katei zasshi (family magazine), 11–12,
24–5, 29, 31, 47, 56, 90; broad appeal, 65; conception of a new kind,
52–4, 101–3, 190; defined, 28; eras-
ing difference, 37
Kawahara Nadeshiko, 99
Kawakami Hajime, 105
Kingu (King): advertising for first
issue, 30, 68–9; children's section,
123, 126; delayed release, 52; explanation of title, 86; first issue, 33,
81–97; page length, 82; price, 31, 74;
publicly stated merits, 93, 112, 115;
purchase of copy for articles, 96;
retitling of, 190

Kingu Records, 153–4

Kōdansha, 3; advertising choices of, 68–9; democratic ideals espoused at, 61; demographics of employees in the 1920s, 68; described in *Kingu*, 58–61; dominance of the publishing industry, 61–2; "Kōdansha style," 80; postwar activities, 190–3; slogans, 69; in unofficial service to the state, 66; variety of publications, 62, 67

Kodomo no ie no hikari (Children's Light of the Home), 123–6

kokuhaku kiji (confessional articles), 146

Korean Boom, 197

Kurabu (Club) brand, 181

Kushner, Barak, 109n60, 168n13, 183n23

Kusunoki Masashige, 86

kyōka (moral suasion), 63

Ladies' Home Journal, 24

leisure: as collective and participatory, 7, 27, 129–30, 147, 162; desire for, in rural areas, 142–3, 152

Levine, Lawrence, 40n28

Light of the Home. See *Ie no hikari*

literacy, 21, 43–5, 118; expansion of in rural areas, 45–6

Madison Avenue, 165, 184

magazines: accessibility of, 54, 80, 92–3; American, 28–9, 144, 160–1, 171; audience demographics, 134; categories of, 28; comparative cost of, 29; as conduits, 15, 33, 36, 188; consumption as political, 187; as cultural currency, 140; as cultural development, 34, 37; diverse con-

tent, 95–6; European observers of, 140; as imagined communities, 88; inclusivity of, 77; as individualized experience, 129, 136; as leisure, 27; as meaning makers, 7, 27, 41, 141; as a medium, 5, 27; as mixed visual media, 166; origin of the term, 27; as performative, 139; photography in, 111; pricing of, 74; recent rebirth of, 187; rereading of, 132; as shared experience, 129, 136–8, 160, 189, 199; student readership, 133; subscription comparisons, 71; unsold copies returned to publishers, 74

mail service, 20

manga (comics), 3, 94–5, 194

Marchand, Roland, 167n10, 168n14

mass culture, 6–8, 16, 35–6, 198–9; in the American context, 24; definition, 3–4; as distinct from "high" and "low" culture, 39–40; as eradication of class, 37; inclusionary nature of, 109; masking difference, 168; naturalizing consumerism, 67, 179, 185–6, 189; as paradox of everyday life, 129–30; as perpetuating inequity, 108–9. *See also* magazines

mass mobilization, 109, 188; as compatible with consumerism, 36

mass national audience, 11–12, 23–5, 160, 163, 182, 185, 198–9; after 1960, 178; as erasure of difference, 37, 72; as imagined communities, 38, 77, 189; mechanisms for the creation of, 24–5, 32, 65; political implication of participation in, 139, 188–9; relationship to empire, 16, 39, 79; segmentation of, 197; synchronicity of, 9

massification, 6, 9, 10–12, 36–7, 144, 160, 198–9

matabi mono, 94
Matsusaka, Yoshihisa Tak, 67n50
McClure's, 161
McLuhan, Marshall, 4–5, 9, 11n18
media: creating unattainable ideals, 129, 165; reader's responses to, 127–8
Meiji Taishō showa dai emaki (The Illustrated Meiji Taishō Shōwa), 156–60
militarism, 15, 35, 67, 120, 127, 148, 170n17, 199
movies. *See* film
Myōshun, 194

Nagamine Shigetoshi, 39, 71n59, 132–9
national consumer, 24
nationalism, 15, 130, 148, 168, 199
naturalization, 8, 15, 34, 65, 115, 160, 169, 199; of advertising, 155, 167; defined, 11
newspapers, 23, 26n4, 28, 45–6, 84n14, 107, 127, 135, 146, 183n23; comparative length of, 93; cost of advertising in, 68–9; as a danger, 99; novels serialized in, 45
NHK (National Broadcasting Company), 47
Nobusuke Kishi, 199
Nogi Maresuke, 113
Nōka no tomo (Friend of the Farm Home), 52
Noma Hisashi, 67
Noma Seiji, 58–64; article written for first issue of *Kingu*, 91; attitude about ambition, 32–4, 61, 67; attitude about contemporary music, 153–4; business methods, 59–60; concern for profit, 60, 65–6, 156, 184; death of, 190; editors'

description of, 58–61; as heavily taxed person, 62; lack of disdain for advertising, 167; on magazines as no longer luxury, 91; mission, 33–4, 67, 91; as moral exemplar, 59, 86; opinions of markets, 29–30; preoccupation with youth, 67, 116; previous career as teacher, 62, 86; promoted virtues, 62–3, 66; "top of the bottom" phrase, 64–5; unfailing support of *Kingu*, 184–5
nōmin zasshi ("farmer's magazine"), 191
Nomura Kodō, 94
normalization. *See* naturalization
nōsho (farm manuals), 45

Ohmann, Richard, 7, 35
Oji Paper Company, 81
Okakura Tenshin, 86
Ōkawa Shūmei, 86
Okuhara Kiyoshi, 55, 139
Okuma Shigenobu, 67
ondoku (reading aloud), 26, 138, 147
"one issue per household," 30, 69

Partner, Simon, 13, 135
patriotism, 15, 79, 90, 179
Peace Preservation Law (*Chian iji hō*), 78
pedagogical techniques, 53, 62, 156, 182
postwar rural changes, 190–3
Pratt, Mary Louise, 89n24
print culture: of the classical era, 44; as exclusionary, 47; as mass media, 26; relationship to religious practice, 44; of the Tokugawa era, 44
Printing and Advertising, 183
propaganda, 6, 14, 109, 167, 182;

American, 165; British, 164; compared to advertising, 185
Publishing and Printing, 183

radio, 47–9, 131, 142, 193
rakugo, 94
rallies, 18, 73; announcement of, 148–9; as advertising, 73, 148; details of events, 144, 152; later significance of, 148–50; as spectacle, 131, 147; unrelated to magazines, 160
reader contributions. *See* audience participation
reader demographics, 10, 132. *See also* magazines
reading: groups (*see* fan clubs); magazines, as a leisure activity, 25, 27, 132, 139; social context of, 38, 137, 144
risshin shusse (rising in the world), 32–3, 66–7
rubi, 30, 84, 88, 118
Ruoff, Ken, 169n16, 183, 188n4
rural: areas starved for entertainment, 131, 149; hardships, 54, 142; overemphasis of urban/rural divide, 72

Sadao Araki, 118
Sakata Company, 182
Sangyō Kumiai (Industrial Cooperative): declining membership, 52; founding, 49; membership as advertising advantage, 73; motto, 58; programs, 50, 104–5
Sangyō Kumiai (The Cooperation) publication, 51
Sangyō Kumiaihō (Industrial Cooperative Law), 49
Sankichi fujiko, 126

Sato, Barbara, 49, 146
Satō Takumi, 110, 139
Saturday Evening Post, 24
Sawayanagi Masatarō, 82, 84–5, 97–8
Schudson, Michael, 167–8, 169, 188n5
Seikyōsha, 67
Seitō (Bluestockings), 157
sensō zasshi ("war magazine"), 191
Shimin (The People), 51
Shimura Gentarō, 10, 32, 38, 52, 54–5, 97, 102–3, 148, 155
Shinagawa Yajirō, 105
Shirochun Kurochun (White Mouse, Black Mouse), 126
Shufu no Tomo (Housewife's Friend), 40–1, 69, 103, 127, 134, 146n32; observed by Embree, 46; observed by Smith, 135
Shusse no ishizue (The Cornerstone of Success), 116
Silverberg, Miriam, 12n19, 39, 79, 127
simultaneity: sense of, 38
socialization, 18, 24, 138–9, 185. *See also* naturalization
St. Nicholas, 161
Stanley, Jason, 14, 109, 185
Supreme Command for the Allied Powers (SCAP), 190–2; Land Reform policy, 191; "reverse course," 199
supplements. See *furoku*

table of contents, 99, 173, 177; advertising on, 171
Tachibana Kōzaburō, 105
taishū, 9–10
taishū zasshi (popular magazine), 192
taishūka (massification), 9
Taiyō (The Sun), 47, 64, 80, 132
Tansman, Alan, 32, 36n22

technological advances, 80
Teikoku Kyōikukai (Imperial Education Association), 85
telegraph machines, 20, 127
Thompson, John B.: definition of culture, 6
"top of the bottom," 64–5, 92–3, 163
transportation, 20
transwar, 13–15, 192; continuities, 24, 37, 108–9

Umeyama Ichirō, 104
unified visual experience. *See* magazines: as mixed visual media
Utena, 171, 181

Wada Eisaku, 82
Waga ie (Our House), 69
wakon yōsai (Japanese spirituality, Western technology), 42
Weisenfeld, Gennifer, 170n17

Westney, D. Eleanor, 80n7
Wilson, Sandra, 51n20, 110
Wiswell, Ella, 135, 141
women's magazines, 28, 85n16, 102–3; British, 153; critiques of, 40n13, 106; reader submissions to, 146
Women's World (American publication), 161

Yamada Shunji, 26n4, 146
Yamamoto Taketoshi, 47
Yangita Kunio, 105
Yokoi Tokiyoshi, 105
Yoshikawa Eiji, 94
Young, Louise, 35, 72n60, 127

zaibatsu, 61, 191
zasshi (magazine): first use of the term, 27–8. *See also* magazine
zerrspiegel (fun-house mirror), 168n14

Studies in Book and Print Culture

General Editor: Leslie Howsam

Hazel Bell, *Indexers and Indexes in Fact and Fiction*

Heather Murray, *Come, bright Improvement! The Literary Societies of Nineteenth-Century Ontario*

Joseph A. Dane, *The Myth of Print Culture: Essays on Evidence, Textuality, and Bibliographical Method*

Christopher J. Knight, *Uncommon Readers: Denis Donoghue, Frank Kermode, George Steiner, and the Tradition of the Common Reader*

Eva Hemmungs Wirtén, *No Trespassing: Authorship, Intellectual Property Rights, and the Boundaries of Globalization*

William A. Johnson, *Bookrolls and Scribes in Oxyrhynchus*

Siân Echard and Stephen Partridge, eds, *The Book Unbound: Editing and Reading Medieval Manuscripts and Texts*

Bronwen Wilson, *The World in Venice: Print, the City, and Early Modern Identity*

Peter Stoicheff and Andrew Taylor, eds, *The Future of the Page*

Jennifer Phegley and Janet Badia, eds, *Reading Women: Literary Figures and Cultural Icons from the Victorian Age to the Present*

Elizabeth Sauer, *'Paper-contestations' and Textual Communities in England, 1640–1675*

Nick Mount, *When Canadian Literature Moved to New York*

Jonathan Earl Carlyon, *Andrés González de Barcia and the Creation of the Colonial Spanish American Library*

Leslie Howsam, *Old Books and New Histories: An Orientation to Studies in Book and Print Culture*

Deborah McGrady, *Controlling Readers: Guillaume de Machaut and His Late Medieval Audience*

David Finkelstein, ed., *Print Culture and the Blackwood Tradition*

Bart Beaty, *Unpopular Culture: Transforming the European Comic Book in the 1990s*

Elizabeth Driver, *Culinary Landmarks: A Bibliography of Canadian Cookbooks, 1825–1949*

Benjamin C. Withers, *The Illustrated Old English Hexateuch, Cotton Ms. Claudius B.iv: The Frontier of Seeing and Reading in Anglo-Saxon England*

Mary Ann Gillies, *The Professional Literary Agent in Britain, 1880–1920*

Willa Z. Silverman, *The New Bibliopolis: French Book-Collectors and the Culture of Print, 1880–1914*

Lisa Surwillo, *The Stages of Property: Copyrighting Theatre in Spain*

Dean Irvine, *Editing Modernity: Women and Little-Magazine Cultures in Canada, 1916–1956*

Janet Friskney, *New Canadian Library: The Ross-McClelland Years, 1952–1978*

Janice Cavell, *Tracing the Connected Narrative: Arctic Exploration in British Print Culture, 1818–1860*

Elspeth Jajdelska, *Silent Reading and the Birth of the Narrator*

Martyn Lyons, *Reading Culture and Writing Practices in Nineteenth-Century France*

Robert A. Davidson, *Jazz Age Barcelona*

Gail Edwards and Judith Saltman, *Picturing Canada: A History of Canadian Children's Illustrated Books and Publishing*

Miranda Remnek, ed., *The Space of the Book: Print Culture in the Russian Social Imagination*

Adam Reed, *Literature and Agency in English Fiction Reading: A Study of the Henry Williamson Society*

Bonnie Mak, *How the Page Matters*

Eli MacLaren, *Dominion and Agency: Copyright and the Structuring of the Canadian Book Trade, 1867–1918*

Ruth Panofsky, *The Literary Legacy of the Macmillan Company of Canada: Making Books and Mapping Culture*

Archie L. Dick, *The Hidden History of South Africa's Book and Reading Cultures*

Darcy Cullen, ed., *Editors, Scholars, and the Social Text*

James J. Connolly, Patrick Collier, Frank Felsenstein, Kenneth R. Hall, and Robert Hall, eds, *Print Culture Histories Beyond the Metropolis*

Kristine Kowalchuk, *Preserving on Paper: Seventeenth-Century Englishwomen's Receipt Books*

Ian Hesketh, *Victorian Jesus: J. R. Seeley, Religion, and the Cultural Significance of Anonymity*

Kirsten MacLeod, *American Little Magazines of the Fin de Siècle: Art, Protest, and Cultural Transformation*

Emily Francomano, *The Prison of Love: Romance, Translation and the Book in the Sixteenth Century*

Kirk Melnikoff, *Elizabethan Publishing and the Makings of Literary Culture*

Amy Bliss Marshall, *Magazines and the Making of Mass Culture in Japan*

Lightning Source UK Ltd.
Milton Keynes UK
UKHW010036170419
341161UK00006B/149/P